The SQUASH
COOKBOOK

The SQUASH COOKBOOK

YVONNE YOUNG TARR

VINTAGE BOOKS · A DIVISION OF RANDOM HOUSE · NEW YORK

With a special thank you to Ruth Grossman,
friend and editor

First Vintage Books Edition, June 1978
Copyright © 1978 by Yvonne Young Tarr
All rights reserved under International and Pan-American
Copyright Conventions. Published in the United States by
Random House, Inc., New York, and simultaneously in Canada by
Random House of Canada Limited, Toronto.
Hardcover edition published simultaneously by Random House, Inc.

Library of Congress Cataloging in Publication Data
Tarr, Yvonne Young.
The squash cookbook.
Includes indexes.
1. Cookery (Squash). I. Title.
TX803.S67T37 1978b   641.6'5'62   77-91469
ISBN 0-394-72473-9

Manufactured in the United States of America

In the deep of winter—on a day so cold that tree branches *snap!* like fresh-picked string beans as I brush by them in my walk through the woods—I will suddenly and inexplicably feel a deep hunger to be kneeling in the warm loam of my summer garden. I never can fathom what secret whisper of spring, what early bird song brings forth the feeling, since the lawns and fields and even the frozen bay still sleep, tucked under their snowy security blanket. But what I *can* always predict is that very shortly after this first longing overtakes me, seed catalogs will magically begin to blossom forth in my mailbox. When these arrive, I waste no time lingering over the flowers or berries or fruits, no matter how temptingly they may be depicted. I flip past pictures of corn twice as high as an elephant's eye, of cabbages fatter by far than Paul Bunyan's head. There are only two vegetables that are so prolific, so delicious, so easy to grow and lend themselves to such a tempting variety of recipes that they have become my all-time favorites and demand my immediate attention. As readers of my *Tomato Book* will know (and others will guess) the terrific tomato is one such and the other is by all means . . . squash. When the first tender green days of spring bud forth and warm breezes soften winter frosts, my squash seeds are the first I sow. How can I resist those glossy, succulent zucchini, bumpy golden crook-necks, scallop-edged summer squash, and crisp, meaty, yellow-fleshed winter Acorns, Hubbards and Butternuts? Squash is amazingly obliging and grows equally well in just about every section of the country. As long as you give it the loamy, fertile soil and adequate moisture it demands, you can always count on culinary rewards aplenty. There are dozens of varieties to choose from, all slightly different . . . and all delicious. Quick-growing, marvelously productive summer squash performs with equal facility in either gourmet or farm-favorite recipes, whether prepared alone or in concert with other foods. Besides being highly nutritious, winter squash can substitute for pumpkin, potatoes or other starchy vegetables, and because of their superb storing qualities, make a fine staple for fall and winter meals.

It's a good feeling to know that when you plant squash in your own garden you are perpetuating a tradition that has been going on in this part of the world for centuries. Ancestors of present-day squash varieties were domesticated in Mexico and cooked over primitive fires both as a seed and flesh food as long ago as 5000 B.C. By the time Columbus happened upon them in West Indian gardens on his first voyage, squash was undoubtedly flourishing in Central and North America from coast to coast. Although American Indians surrounded squash fruits with mystic powers and celebrated their remarkable qualities in tribal legend, their high regard did not prevent them from dining on the vegetable, baked, boiled, roasted or dried, as a supplement to their usual diet of game and fish . . . even the seeds were considered a particular delicacy. Our word "squash" is a contraction of the Indian name *askoot asquash* ("eaten green," in Indian parlance) given it by the early colonists, who gratefully warded off starvation during their first tenuous winters on American shores by borrowing Indian techniques for cultivation and storing of the vegetable.

It is particularly difficult to determine where squash begins and other similar vegetables leave off. Squash belongs to the warm-weather-loving Gourd family, a group of tender, vine-bearing annuals that includes both edible and purely ornamental fruits. Besides squash, other edible family members are cucumber, melon and pumpkin (the latter is always classed with squash because its soil requirements and growing habits are so similar). Horticulturally speaking, both are known as cucurbits, a Gourd-family genus whose chief characteristics are hairy vines, oversized leaves, lobed yellow flowers, and large fruits with smooth or furrowed skins. Among cucurbits, names tend to be more than a bit confusing. Size and shape are no guide, either, since crooknecks, straightnecks, marrows and pumpkins are to be found in three of the five cucurbit species that boast squash. Some kinds of squash are bigger than any pumpkin and often more like pumpkin than pumpkin itself . . . what passes for "pumpkin" in commercial pumpkin pie is often some type of squash.

For gardening purposes, therefore, the usual division is between summer and winter varieties. Summer squash (*C. pepo*, var. *melopepo*) includes zucchini, butter-yellow crooknecks and straightnecks, vegetable marrows, and patty pan or scallop squash, called symblings (or cymlings in the South). All have upright, bush-type vines and rapidly developing fruits which should be harvested while small and tender and used immediately. In contrast, the larger winter squash fruits (*C. maxima* and *C. moschata*) develop usually on running vines, take most of a growing season to mature, and keep for months under proper storage. Varieties range from acorn types (often called fall or autumn squash because their keeping qualities are not as good as other winter kinds) through crooknecks to enormous cylindrical field pumpkins, and also include marrows and turban-shaped specimens.

Gardeners today have a wide selection of squash to choose from (for a more detailed description of varieties, see pages 40–53). It's only within the past century or so that named varieties have been developed. All previous types were called, simply, squashes. The first to be named was that mainstay of every nineteenth-century American household, Hubbard, the best-liked and most commonly grown of winter squash even today. Legend has it that the first of these was planted around 1840 in Marblehead, Massachusetts, from seeds that had been shipped from somewhere in tropical America. A Mrs. Elizabeth Hubbard brought it to the attention of her favorite seed merchant, who, in a gallant gesture, named it after her.

Squash has been grown and enjoyed by people all over the world. Africans utilize all parts of the plant, including the leaves and flowers, and Asians dote on the roasted seeds. A relative latecomer to Europe, squash has become a treasured staple of the English diet (often called marrow there). In France, squash are known as *courgettes*, and in Italy as *zucca* (marrow) or *zucchini* (little marrow). The Italians also use the leaves and flowers of the vegetables and it is an Italian varietal that Americans have made into the most popular of their summer squashes.

This book is about squash . . . how to plant, cultivate, harvest, preserve and cook them. The hundreds of recipes presented here are not ordinary, everyday staples with squash arbitrarily added, but special, tested recipes culled from colonial and nineteenth-century cookbooks, farm kitchens, foreign cooks . . . and my own files. Herein, I believe, you will find the most practical as well as some fairly imaginative ways to use your crop to its fullest potential. (Please don't disdain such unusual offerings as Squash Cheesecake or the Candied Zucchini recipes until you have tried them.) This book will, I hope, help you to deal with that feeling of near-panic when you find your harvest inundating your garden, kitchen counters, window sills, refrigerator and storage cellar, and help you to prepare and serve it as well as most efficiently preserve some of that surplus for winter feasting.

PUMPKINS and GOURDS are discussed separately on pages 196–206 and 207–218.

CONTENTS

GROWING

BEGIN WITH SOIL

Few vegetables outrank squash in ease of growing. These long-time favorites in the garden practically raise themselves and are most accommodating producers in just about every part of the country. The difference, however, between squash that flower with abandon, yielding a superabundance of fruits with peak flavor and top quality, and those that merely idle along lies in the preparation of the soil that nurtures them. In successful squash culture, soil is the key.

Soil is much more than a gritty handful of brown dust. Think of it as a gigantic, properly prepared dough composed of a flour of inorganic rocks, sand and silt, mixed through with dead organic matter, vitalized by living organisms (earthworms and insects, hordes of bacteria, yeasts, fungi, algae, and one-celled protozoans) that live in it. This lively interaction of living organisms with both decomposing organic debris and mineral particles abetted by water and air, breaks down and converts nutritive ingredients, speeding the release of the essential soil elements on which plants thrive.

The result of all this activity is humus—a light, spongy, loamy material that improves and enriches soil, helps it maintain its vigor, and anchors soil particles together. Humus aerates and lightens clay soils and binds together sandy ones. A soil containing abundant humus is better able to store nutrients, releasing them to plants upon demand, and is blessed with a greater water-holding capacity, allowing moisture and air to penetrate its surface more deeply and efficiently.

The ideal soil for raising squash is composed of this porous and crumbly loam, well supplied with enough organic matter to keep its microbial and animal inhabitants busy digesting and breaking down the material and relaying the essential nutrients that are the consequence of this breakdown to the waiting seeds and seedlings. No two soils are identical. Some, surfeited with clay, form a bond that is practically impervious to moisture and air. Others have a high sand content, which permits water and air to move through it so freely that nutrients in the soil are leached away. Chances are fairly good that whatever corner of your garden you select for your seedlings will be loamy to some degree, but your role as gardener is to work right along with nature to upgrade or reinvigorate this foundation by digging into it as much organic matter as possible in the form of compost or well-rotted manures. Integrated organic matter loosens and lightens the soil, allowing air and water to penetrate more easily so that roots have a chance to stretch and grow. When organic matter is added, water and nutrients are held and concentrated in upper soil levels where roots have access to them.

12

COMPOSTING

The easiest and cheapest way to build up your soil and/or help it stay that way is to nourish it with compost. Nothing makes squash more obligingly productive than liberal lacings of this natural conditioner applied at regular intervals. If soil is the heart of the garden, compost is the bloodline that supports and sustains vital growth with transfusions of decayed twigs and grasses, nuts and seeds, leaves, feathers, manure and all kinds of healthy natural wastes. A complete fertilizer, compost supplies soil with the life-giving nutrients squash insist on if they are to grow and flourish, and it does this job for a more sustained period of time than do chemical fertilizers.

To build a compost heap is to repeat and accelerate what nature does in converting organic debris into new and revitalized growing materials. Almost any waste material can be used, but there are some important elements you should incorporate right from the start. Primary among these is some form of nitrogen, which plants need in abundance not only because it builds plant proteins and stimulates leaf and stem growth and strong green color, but especially because this valuable nutrient also encourages the proliferation of the soil bacteria that hasten decomposition. Fresh manure is a fine source of nitrogen, but if this is unavailable you may substitute one of the dried, packaged manures or a commercially prepared compost-starter. In addition, you may want to include in your compost heap other nitrogen-producing materials like blood meal, cottonseed or soybean meal, animal hair, feathers, or even activated sewage sludge. Phosphorus and potash are also valuable nutrients, good sources of which can be found in bone meal, rock powders and wood ashes. Healthy green plants, shredded newspapers, vegetable peelings, fruit skins, coffee grounds and moderate amounts of animal fats can all be recycled in the compost heap for their mineral value, as can straw and waste hays if you have access to them.

Pick a well-drained, sheltered site for your compost heap, preferably one within easy reach of a hose and convenient to gardening activities. The heap may be set directly on the ground or below ground level, with or without the benefit of structural support, but probably the most satisfactory method is to drive three or four 6-foot stakes firmly into the earth around the circumference of the area and enclose them with wire mesh. If money is no object, or if your backyard lacks a secluded spot where the heap may be successfully concealed, you might want to investigate the ready-made paneled compost bins, constructed of rugged plastic, which come complete with support posts and are available in two sizes. Garden centers sometimes keep them in stock, or you can order directly from seed houses.

If sod occupies the spot where the heap is to be built, first dig it up and cut it into pieces, then set it back in place, dirt side up. Start off the heap by spreading a 6-inch layer of plant and kitchen wastes directly on the ground. Follow with a 2- to 3-inch layer of some nitrogen-rich material; manure is best, but whatever is available will do. Top this with a 3-inch blanket of garden soil to ensure that bacteria and other soil organisms will rapidly populate your heap, and cover with a light sprinkling of ground limestone. Continue to build the heap in the same manner, layer after layer, using materials at hand. To provide bacteria with more surfaces to work on, break up large waste ingredients—twigs, weeds, and so on—with a power mower or shredder before adding them to the heap. Secure layers of light materials like leaves and hay by covering them with handfuls of soil. As you add each new layer, throw on some rock powder, wood ashes or limestone if you wish, but take care not to combine fertilizer and limestone in the same layer; the limestone will cancel out the fertilizer's effectiveness.

The ideal height for a compost heap is about 5 feet, the size that is most conducive to bacterial activity and its consequent heat build-up. Too shallow—or too high—a heap creates a poor environment for bacteria and may even mean loss of bacterial life. As you add new layers, wet each just enough to moisten it but *do not saturate*; a sodden, waterlogged heap severely limits the air supply available to bacteria. The materials should be only as wet as a wrung-out sponge.

Properly layered and prepared, your heap should heat up to 150 degrees F. by the second day as bacteria set to work oxidizing and reducing ingredients while nature goes about her miraculous transformation. A compost heap that won't heat up indicates a deficiency in nitrogen-producing elements. This is your cue to correct the balance and begin again. Tend the pile by keeping it well aired through frequent forkings, moist during dry spells, and protected with a tarpaulin or piece of heavy plastic during seasons of prolonged rainfall.

The time needed for bacterial conversion of organic wastes into fine, rich-brown compost varies. Oxidation occurs fastest in warm weather. A heap begun one spring should complete its decomposition and be ready to dig under by the following spring. Before using the resulting rich moist humus, you may want to sift it through a screen of ½-inch hardware cloth to separate out any large pieces that need further decomposition. These will make the perfect foundation for your next compost heap.

QUICK COMPOSTING

Compost permitted to ripen and decompose following nature's timetable may take longer than you can afford to wait. If you're in a hurry, try quick composting. This is an accelerated process that reduces waste materials to serviceable compost in a matter of weeks. The trick here is that all the raw materials must be ground or shredded to less than 1 inch. Decomposition in this case is more rapid because bacteria are provided with an infinitely greater number of working surfaces to feed on, which immeasurably speeds oxidation. Quick composting also demands extra attention to details. Adequate moisture is important. The heap must be kept continuously damp but not soggy, and since more air is required, forking over every couple of days is a must.

Air is always vitally important even in conventional composting because the bacteria that reduce the waste materials to nutrient-rich fertilizer flourish and multiply on oxygen. Air circulates between layers of denser wastes and thus discourages anaerobic bacteria, which thrive in the absence of oxygen, from flourishing. But you can compost an airless way, encouraging and using the services of these usually objectionable bacteria. This system involves collecting materials like grass clippings, leaves and other wastes that mat together easily and covering them tightly with black plastic or sealing them in dark clean-up bags. At this point your chores are finished. Leave the materials strictly alone until decomposition is finished and the end product is completely free from odor, then use it like regular compost.

SHEET COMPOSTING

Another fast and efficient way to boost soil fertility and improve its structure is to recycle organic wastes directly in your garden. If you haven't the space or inclination to establish a a compost heap, traditional or otherwise, sheet composting is a highly effective method of improving the physical characteristics of your soil and/or correcting its deficiencies. Particularly good for beginning gardeners or those without sources of compost, this process consists essentially of spreading leaves, grass clippings and other vegetative wastes in a thick layer over the garden bed and then spading it in deeply. During decomposition the buried organic matter performs the same basic function as it would in a compost heap, only it completes its metamorphosis underground. Fall is the perfect season to sheet compost (the waste ingredients will have plenty of time to work their magic), but unless you're using fresh manure, which may burn tender seedlings if applied too close to planting time, this method may be successfully employed up to two months prior to setting in seeds.

GREEN MANURES

Green manures—in reality, green cover crops that are planted in early fall, then plowed under come spring—serve as time-honored and practical alternatives to compost whenever soils are deficient in organic matter. The strong root systems natural to these grasses and legumes effectively loosen heavy soils and bind sandy ones. They have a higher nitrogen content than their dried counterparts and decompose more rapidly, so you can plan on setting out your seedlings within a month of turning the crop under.

Your agricultural agent or extension service is the best source for information about a cover crop that will be suitable to your particular climate and soil. Plant in late August or early September so that growth will be substantial by the time a hard frost brings it to a halt.

SOIL NUTRITION

A plant is a factory that uses raw products—chemical elements drawn from air, water and soil —to manufacture food for its roots and leaves. From the air and water come carbon dioxide, hydrogen and oxygen; from soil, all remaining elements essential to proper growth. Soil is where you as a gardener enter the nutrition picture, for while there's not much you can do about the quality of the air and water available to your plants, there is something you can do to nourish their growing medium. Soil properly conditioned with organic matter is much more receptive to any nutrients you may wish to add to increase fertility or correct a particular deficiency.

Sixteen chemical elements supplied by the combination of air, water and soil are crucial to the healthy life of green plants, but three—nitrogen, phosphorus and potassium—are utilized in greater quantities than any of the others. A deficiency in any one of these will seriously affect both the growth and yield of your crop. To find out if your garden is in short supply, you can ship a soil sample to your county extension service or make an analysis yourself with one of the soil-testing kits currently on the market (see page 18).

Once you have restored your soil to top condition by restructuring and enriching it with organic matter, you can usually count on a good balance of essential nutrients and look forward to healthy, vigorous, productive plants right from the start. Despite your best efforts, however, it is still possible for your plants to display some signs of deficiency in one or another of these major nutrients.

Nitrogen, called the leafmaker, helps plants manufacture the proteins that lead to sturdy green growth of stems and leaves. Stunted growth, lanky, weak stems and pale color that shows up first in the older leaves signal nitrogen-starved plants. Compost, well-rotted or dried manure, blood meal or nitrogen-fixing green manures incorporated into the soil well before planting time should prevent this problem. When it's too late for preplanting measures and your plants display one or all of the characteristics of nitrogen deficiency, you might try an instant remedy that I have used successfully. Simply steep ½ cup of dried manure in a gallon of warm water overnight and apply this liquid diet to the soil around the plants. Whatever you do, don't overreact. Providing additional nitrogen can be a tricky business where squash are concerned. Too much, and growth will run to vines at the expense of fruit setting.

Phosphorus, known as the rootmaker, is not only vital to young growth but also necessary to help plants mature. Phosphorus-poor soils produce plants with poorly developed roots; as a consequence, stem and flower growth is slow and leaves turn dullish, with purple tints. Plants use phosphorus in small amounts, but in order for them to get the little they need, fairly large quantities must be supplied to the soil since this nutrient is particularly sensitive to acid or alkaline soils (see pages 18–19). If the pH level is too high or too low, phosphorus locks up in insoluble form and remains unavailable to plants. A liberal application of either phosphate rock or bone meal is a good countermeasure to correct a phosphorus deficiency, but be sure to check your soil's pH level first.

Last of the big three is *potassium*, or potash, which builds strong stems and contributes to fruit size and yield. The role potassium plays in promoting flowering and ultimately fruit formation is not completely understood, but without it growth is stunted. Suspect a potassium deficiency if the tips and edges of your plants' leaves exhibit yellowing patches. The best way to restore the potassium balance is to apply a thin layer of wood ashes, especially those left over from the burning of hardwoods. Store the ashes in a dry place until needed, then spread in a thin layer over the soil before planting time and spade in well. Since potassium, like phosphorus, tends to lock up and become unavailable to plants in soils that are too acid or too alkaline, it's wisest to check the pH level in your soil before applying. Other organic sources of potassium include granite rock or green manure used as a mulch prior to planting. If you suspect a potassium deficiency this year, it's a good idea to take steps to prevent it from occurring again next year.

ACIDITY OR ALKALINITY

Whenever soil nutrition is out of kilter, the remedy is usually a simple application of the appropriate fertilizer. Usually, but not always. What may change the situation and impair the effectiveness of a reinstated nutrient has to do with soil chemistry—the degree to which a soil is acid or alkaline. Acidity in soil relates to its degree of sourness; alkalinity, to a soil's sweetness. Both are measured on a pH scale which ranges from 0 (most acid) to 14 (most alkaline), with 7.0 regarded as neutral. Improving soil by maintaining the proper pH level needed by vegetables should be a gardener's legitimate concern, but before you start thinking in terms of test tubes and Bunsen burners, let me assure you that neither the reasons for doing so nor the corrective measures involved are terribly complex.

The pH level is important to plant nutrition because your plants will have a hard time utilizing nutrients in a soil that is too acid or too alkaline. Squash, like other vegetables, prefer their growing medium to range on the slightly acid side of neutral—pH 6.0 to pH 6.8. Acids adjust a soil's chemistry, releasing nutrients and making them available to plants. A loamy, friable soil conditioned with rich helpings of compost normally produces its own acids, and since compost is also a complete fertilizer, plants so provisioned should virtually explode with growth. Occasionally, however, even this kind of soil turns uncooperative. If it becomes too acid, all major elements—including nitrogen, phosphorus and potassium—and most of the minor ones will lock up and become unavailable to plants. The same is true in soils that increase in alkalinity.

Chances are that your soil ranges on the acid side of neutral if you live in an area with plentiful rainfall. Wherever a dry climate predominates is alkaline country. The only way to know for sure whether your soil falls within the satisfactory pH range for growing vegetables is to have it tested, particularly when preparing a new garden bed or when growth problems arise in an old one. Your county or state agricultural extension service will analyze your soil's shortcomings and make recommendations for improvement, usually for a small fee, if you ship them a sample securely enclosed in a plastic bag (and envelope). There are also many independent laboratories who perform the same service. Or if you're a do-it-yourselfer, you might investigate the soil-testing kits, complete with recommendations, which are available in practically every price range from garden supply centers or seed houses. Readings will be more accurate if you take the sample during warm weather, rather than in fall or spring.

The traditional method for reducing acidity and raising the pH level in soils is to apply finely ground limestone. Rates of application vary. Generally, more lime is necessary for clay soils than for sandy soils. Moderately alkaline soils (pH 7.5) can usually be lowered to a more neutral pH with substantial amounts of compost dug in thoroughly. Shredded oak leaves, acid peat, leaf mold, wood shavings or sawdust are also effective means of reducing alkalinity.

In regions where rainfall is plentiful, liming acid soils once every three years is good gardening practice, whether or not soil tests are taken. Fall is the ideal time to undertake liming, since the soil sweetener will have plenty of time to work. However, if this task must be put off till spring, apply the lime at least two weeks before adding any fertilizer or the two will interreact instead of reacting with the soil.

SELECTING A SITE

Despite their ease in growing, squash are rather fussy about their living quarters. Like most vegetables, they require their full quota of light and warmth; nothing suits them better than basking in unadulterated sunlight for at least 6—and preferably more—hours daily, although fall and winter varieties do tolerate a little shade. As members of the Gourd family (which also includes melons, cucumbers and pumpkins), squash have such a fondness for light-textured soils richly supplied with well-rotted organic matter that they would probably send down their roots right in the middle of the compost heap if they had their way. Moisture is also essential to the well-being of your squash, but take care since good drainage is a must. Heavy, wet conditions may rot roots or, at the very least, cause bushes or vines to grow slowly. Above all, squash need lots of room—a single winter squash vine, for instance, requires breathing space of up to 20 square feet. If garden space is limited, your best bet is to stick to bush varieties.

Choose a warm, sunny, well-drained site, rich with organic matter and away from competition with roots of shrubs and trees. If possible, dig your garden close to the house so that it can function as an adjunct to the kitchen, with harvesting but a few steps away. A nearby source of water is important—as is good air circulation, although the spot should afford some protection from cold or drying winds, especially when the growing season is short. Treat your plants with the tender loving care they deserve and they will respond with edible gifts through summer and right on into fall.

Kinship aside, there are times when summer and winter squash behave like vastly different vegetables. Summer varieties mature quickly and ripen fruit with uninterrupted, boundless enthusiasm until frost, while the sprawling vines and bushes of winter varieties produce one slow-to-mature crop. For fullest flavor, succulent zucchini, crooknecks and scallop types should be consumed, canned or frozen soon after harvest; their hard-skinned cousins, on the other hand, will keep without significant flavor loss for extended periods under favorable conditions.

Both kinds of squash have one important characteristic in common—they benefit from the same general culture. Starting right with both summer and winter varieties is easy because soil make-up, sowing and cultivation, even insect pests, are identical. All prefer a light, sandy-type loam, heavily provisioned with compost or other well-rotted organic material—a growing medium that holds moisture well, yet is porous enough to allow any excess to drain off. Seeds of either can be planted directly in the garden as soon as the ground warms up and stays warm. As long as you make allowances for the frost-sensitive nature of all squash and plant seeds only when mild-tempered late-spring temperatures stabilize, you can count on summer varieties to begin gracing your table within a matter of weeks. Winter squash varieties require at least 100 consecutive frost-free days to guarantee top production.

Squash have fragile roots and do not take transplanting lightly. There are, however, circumstances under which this is advisable, particularly if the soil defrosts slowly in your area, if your growing season is too short for slow-to-mature winter squash or even if you merely want to hurry nature along a bit. The most obvious method is to start growing indoors (although a hotbed will serve equally well as a temporary nursery) and then transplant to the garden row. Don't undertake either of these measures more than five weeks in advance of transplanting, however, or root and foliage growth will be so luxuriant that switching seedlings to the garden bed may meet with disaster. The trick lies in figuring the average date of the last frost in your area and counting backwards to a month before that. If you launch seedlings too soon, transplants from either house or hotbed may flower prematurely and cause substandard fruit production.

STARTING SEEDS INDOORS

Starting plants from seed indoors is most successful if you keep a few basic rules in mind:

First—give your seeds a disease-free starting medium so they won't be subject to "damping off," a fungus-borne disease common to unsterile soils that rots tender stems at the soil line.

A mixture that works well for squash seedlings combines equal parts of peat moss, vermiculite and sterilized, compost-enriched garden soil. To sterilize the soil, sift it through a fine-mesh screen and spread over the bottom of a shallow pan, sprinkle with enough water to dampen and set in an oven preheated to 160 to 170 degrees F. for 30 minutes on two successive days. For containers, use 3- or 4-inch peat or Fertil pots. These minimize transplanting shock since pot and all are planted. As an alternative, you might try lining salvaged strawberry baskets with sphagnum moss and filling with the same mixture. The aim in either case is sterile soil in a container large enough to guarantee developing roots the growing room they need.

Second—provide both seeds and seedlings with the warmth, moisture and light necessary for good germination and growth. A moist, warm environment speeds sprouting, and sufficient natural or artificial light—or preferably a combination of the two—encourages compact, stocky plants.

Third—allow your seedlings an adjustment period to gradually acclimatize to the conditions they will encounter once they make the transition to the garden. This "hardening off" process consists of exposing indoor-grown seedlings to the outdoors in a fairly sheltered, partially shaded spot for longer periods each day, until they have successfully weathered 24 hours of continuous outdoor exposure. At this point, they can safely be set in the garden.

Before starting the seeds off indoors, dampen the sterile growing materials you've elected to use to the consistency of a wrung-out sponge. Divide this among your containers, make two or three holes to the planting depth specified on the seed packet and set in the seeds, then lightly sprinkle a dusting of planting material back in the holes. Group the containers together on trays, slide them—tray and all—into a plastic bag and twist closed. Sheet plastic is also a great convenience in indoor gardening. It behaves like an improvised terrarium to help maintain the constantly moist condition necessary for speedy germination. Should excess condensation result in soggy soil, simply roll back the plastic (or open the plastic bag if you are using one) to permit a little drying out. Good germination also depends on warm soil temperatures, from 70 to 80 degrees F. Find your seed trays a cozy place in a warm room or arrange them on a radiator set at very low heat, and germination should begin its miraculous process almost at once.

When the first set of leaves appears, shed the plastic wrappings and set the seedlings near a a window or a source of artificial means of lighting where they will receive at least 12 hours of light each day. Even if you have sun, the light available indoors just approaches the intensity required by seedlings, so you should plan on some supplementary, artifical lighting. Fluorescent arrangements or special plant-growing lights are worthwhile investments for more ambitious growers, particularly when head-starting light-hungry squash plants. Since these provide abundant overhead light, they encourage hardy, compact seedlings. A less expensive but worthy substitute is a 75-watt bulb set over seedlings assembled 3 or 4 feet beneath it. Be sure to keep all light bulbs dust-free and the seedlings well aired.

Spray the soil daily to keep it spongy, but if possible avoid getting water on the tender leaves. If the sun makes up part of your lighting arrangement, turn the plants every day so they won't bend in one direction. As soon as the second, or true leaves appear, take your courage in your hands and snip off all but the hardiest and healthiest seedling in each container. Give these remaining plants a boost with half-strength water-soluble fertilizer to keep them growing well. Once warm weather arrives, harden them off by cutting back a bit on moisture and gradually exposing them to the outdoors for longer periods each day; this will accustom plants to the abrupt changes in temperature, sun and wind that they will encounter when they take up permanent residence in your garden.

If your collection of primary garden tools happens to include a working cold frame, you'll find this makes a perfect temporary shelter for hardening off your plants; simply raise its cover during warm days.

STARTING SEEDS IN A HOTBED

A cold frame works on the greenhouse principle. Sunlight streams through the glass or plastic cover and heat is trapped within, creating a tropical mini-climate which is controlled by opening and closing the cover. Your cold frame can double as a hotbed if you add a second source of heat—either by underlaying the soil with a thick blanket of heat-producing fresh manure or with a soil cable—to maintain steady warmth. Since the majority of home gardeners find fresh manure difficult to obtain, the electric soil cable is a more convenient and usually more reliable substitute. Bury the cable according to installation instructions and set your pots or trays of seeds directly in the bed, or spread a 4- to 6-inch layer of starting mixture over the heat source and sow your seeds in this. A thermometer will tell you at a glance when—or if—the cable needs unplugging or the cover must be raised to decrease heat or whether additional insulating materials (blankets and the like) are needed to increase heat. Keep the seedlings amply watered as they grow. Once your seedlings are well established and transplanting time approaches, return the hotbed to its original function—hardening off.

PREPARING GARDEN SOIL

Most gardeners have little choice of soil type. The average backyard garden or country vegetable patch may not be blessed with the light, loamy soil, full of well-rotted organic matter, so perfect for growing squash plants. With proper preparation, however, most soils can come close to this ideal.

The best time to transform your vegetable plot into a rich, silky growing medium is well before actual planting is due to take place. Except in frost-free areas of the country, this means in fall for spring planting. Advance preparation in established gardens has some immediate virtues: post-harvest cleanup undertaken at this time is a good garden housekeeping practice which not only gets rid of weeds and dead plants (both over-winter harborers of insects and diseases) but also provides a fine source of materials for your next year's compost heap. There are also long-term benefits. Digging in mulch materials left over from the just-ended growing season loosens and lightens the soil, and helps it to better hold air and moisture. Spading in additional slow-release organic matter like compost, well-rotted manures, blood meal, activated sludge, bone meal or wood ashes, long before seeds go in, gives the essential nutrients contained in these fertilizers plenty of time to work. Limestone is another slow-acting substance; if a pH test reveals the need for it, the extra months that prior-season liming provides serve to increase its usefulness come planting time.

Advance preparation also pays off when a new garden is on your agenda. First select a well-drained site that will receive maximum sunlight throughout the growing season. Sample shovelfuls of soil from the various garden spots available to you; if one area seems richer and more loosely packed than another, establish your garden there unless you detect a drainage problem. (If the area is abundant with earthworms, so much the better.) A soil test (see page 18) is a good idea if you're in doubt, and the recommendations usually supplied at the same time are very helpful.

Mark off garden boundaries and strip the area of sod, consigning the latter to the compost heap. Squash roots thrive on ample room so dig the marked-off area to a depth of at least 1 foot, and even deeper if you can manage to do so without disturbing the subsoil. Remove stones and debris and break up heavy clods of earth, then spread a thick, even layer of some well-rotted organic matter over the garden bed and spade it well in. Add another layer of organic materials about one week later and baste with subsequent additions as soon as the ground can be worked in spring. Properly prepared soil should remain loose and light without crusting, provide lots of room for root development, and absorb air and water rapidly. The aim is a metamorphosis of what was formerly indifferent dirt into a fertile and nicely textured loam to which your squash plants will respond with healthy, nonstop production.

Squash planted in heavy clay or clay-loam soils tend to grow slowly. If your garden soil falls short of ideal despite your best efforts, one alternative is to dig out, to a depth of 2 feet, wherever each hill of squash or individual squash plant is to be located. Fill in the holes with a rich soil mixture made by combining equal parts of good-quality, loamy topsoil and well-rotted manure. Another popular way to ensure a good harvest when soil proves indifferent or unproductive is to experiment with raised-bed vegetable gardening. Arrange any materials that will serve to brace large amounts of soil—railroad ties, boards, cinder blocks and the like—in a circle, square or rectangle on top of the original garden site. Import enough loamy topsoil to fill the interior of the structure, add some builder's or "sharp" sand and lots of well-rotted manure, and you'll have the perfect garden site in a minimum of time—although not with a minimum of effort and/or expense.

Lay out your garden in rows parallel to the short side of the plot, with more room between rows than between plants (unless the ground slopes, in which case it's best to have rows traverse the slope to minimize erosion during heavy rain). Set one area aside for your squash, avoiding any places where melons or cucumbers were planted the previous year.

Space is always a prime consideration in the vegetable garden, and squash require lots of it. Unless your plot is very large, plan on planting bush-type summer varieties, which give pro-

lific individual yields, and/or bush-type winter varieties like Gold Nugget, Bush Table Queen or Acorn, Emerald, Bush Acorn Table King, Burpee's Butterbush, Little Gem, Bush Buttercup or Sakata F-1 Hybrid—all somewhat less greedy about growing room than vining types.

If you're really eager to harvest vining varieties in a limited growing area, however, there are a couple of planting techniques that will help stretch the space you have available. One method is to train the vines on a fence or trellis, securing them as they grow with heavy cord or stout wire. Another way to double up successfully on space is to revive the American Indian practice of intercropping, in which squash are planted between hills of sweet corn—that other popular garden space-grabber. The stalks eventually grow high enough to dominate the upper, more rarefied regions of the garden, leaving the lower real estate to the horizontally running squash vines. To accomplish this double tenancy, start off first with the corn. Then, when the stalks are 1 foot high, follow up by planting the squash seeds.

The best time for planting squash is when mid-spring arrives and all danger from frost is past. (This usually coincides with apple tree blossoming.) The traditional method of planting squash seeds is in a hill, a term which under ordinary circumstance implies a small, elevated mound but which in gardening parlance refers instead to a group of seeds arranged in a flat, slightly depressed circle. The circle acts as a catch basin where the moisture that vine crops dote on can collect. To plant in a hill, space five or six seeds evenly apart in a 10-inch circle set directly above the area you've prepared. Follow instructions as to planting depth and space requirements as outlined on the seed packet. As a general rule, hills of summer squash and winter bush types should be set 3 to 5 feet apart, while winter vining varieties need from 6 to 8 feet between hills. (I have occasionally fudged on this space requirement with no disastrous results.) Don't be afraid to plant them right next to any Gourd family relatives—they will not cross-pollinate. Once the seedlings reach a height of 4 to 5 inches, fight that parental need to protect and carefully pull out all but the two or three hardiest in each hill. These "orphans" may be planted wherever there is space in the garden. Mulch those that remain in the hill to conserve moisture and keep down weeds (see pages 28–30). Cultivate shallowly only when necessary to protect your plants' extensive root systems.

 Hardened-off seedlings from house or hotbed and nursery-bred seedlings can go into the garden, two or three to each hill, as soon as days are pleasantly warm and night temperatures reach and remain above 55 degrees F. Prepare the undersoil as for seeds and soak the hills well before carefully setting each plant in its scooped-out hole, disturbing the roots as little as possible. Fill in around each seedling with a mixture of organic matter and

soil, tamping the earth down firmly to remove any air pockets, then follow this up with another good soaking. In eight to ten days, give your plants a boost with a mild compost-water solution or some other very diluted water-soluble fertilizer. Be ruthless enough to pinch off any premature flowers or any that appear within a week or two of transplanting to encourage the good root formation so vital to squash production.

Your newly planted squash may be a bit droopy during the first few days in their permanent home. Although recovery is generally rapid, you can usually avoid this setback by choosing a cloudy day to transplant or by providing a little light shade for each plant if the clouds don't cooperate. I find that large baskets with open-slatted sides turned upside down are very effective in shading seedlings from the hot sun and also help to keep the soil moist during this recovery period. As an alternative when baskets are scarce, shield your plants with pieces of pierced cardboard box, anchored with heaped-up soil.

Summer squashes should begin producing within 45 to 55 days after planting as seeds, while fruits from winter varieties will begin to mature toward the season's end. Fruit set, however, is sometimes delayed in either type if rainy conditions persist during flowering. Squash rely on bees to carry their heavy pollen from male to female flowers, but these winged benefactors often respond as we do and tend to linger at home during prolonged spells of wet weather. And don't worry when the first flowers to appear prove almost exclusively male. Squash plants are monoecious—each plant produces both male and female blossoms. Male blossoms predominate in the early growth pattern, but these are soon followed by male and females together and, shortly, fruit set.

Keep summer squash picked to encourage further production. For impeccable quality and flavor, harvest zucchini types and crooknecks when they are 5 to 7 inches long; scallop varieties, when they reach a few inches in diameter. Summer squash are at their most tender and succulent when their skins yield easily to a fingernail's pressure, although even those inadvertently permitted to reach football size can provide you with some delightful dining experiences.

Winter squash take time to mature, but the wait is definitely worth it. If you wish, you may give your plants an added boost by top dressing each with some compost carefully scratched into the soil when the vines begin really to run, but try not to disturb the vines, as this may interrupt the pollination process. Harvest all varieties only when decidedly mature—skins should be hard, with no streaks of green. Before consigning them to root cellar storage (see pages 73–75), all, with the exception of acorn varieties, should be set out in the sun after harvest for a week or ten days, or placed in a warm (80 degrees F.) indoor spot for the same period, to cure and give stem wounds and surface cuts time to heal.

If your ambition runs to record-size squashes—and some winter varieties can grow to immense proportions—keep the vines and all but one or two of the fruits on each plant pinched back. Top dress once or twice during the growing season with light additions of a fertilizer that contains a higher ratio of phosphorus and potassium than it does nitrogen, then sit back and wait for the blue ribbons.

WATERING

Like most vegetables, squash need a moisture supply equivalent to about 1 inch of rain each week throughout their growing season. Normal spring rainfall should furnish this during the early growth stages, but as the season progresses it's a good idea to establish a regular watering routine. Give the soil a thorough soaking on a weekly basis, allowing moisture to penetrate to the level where it will do these deep-rooted vegetables the most good. Avoid shallow watering, which encourages roots to surface in a quest for moisture, and thereby weakens the plant's structure and makes it more vulnerable to high winds or heavy rain. Overhead sprinkling devices have the added benefit of moistening the air as well as the soil during excessively dry hot spells; however, for more efficient use of water wherever the supply is scarce, it's best to use the flat, soaker-type hose. Always water your plants in the morning so that wet foliage can dry by evening.

MULCHING

The best method of keeping your garden soil evenly moist and cool is mulching—an age-old garden technique that retards evaporation and makes watering necessary only during the driest and hottest weather. Mulch is helpful in many ways. It modifies the environment in which plants grow, protects roots from cold, heat or drought, keeps fruit clean and reduces the possibility of soil erosion. By holding down weeds around the hills, it practically eliminates any need for the hoeing that might injure tender roots or vines. For lazy gardeners, those with a minimum of time to spare, mulching makes your garden practically maintenance-free.

Organic mulches—and there are many of these—eventually decompose and enrich the soil with valuable nutrients and improve soil structure at the same time. Any weed-free material, like old straw or hay, autumn leaves, ground bark, buckwheat hulls, cocoa shells, ground-up corncobs, sawdust or fine wood chips, works superbly well. Even grass clippings can go from power bag to garden, but it may prove helpful to first allow them to partially decay and dry in the sun, then spread them out thinly over the garden soil to avoid matting. Peat moss makes an excellent (though expensive) mulch, provided you don't let it dry out too much. Where we live, in eastern Long Island, the salt hay that accumulates near the bay is widely, and successfully, used as a mulch and, because it doesn't decompose rapidly, can be reused year after year. Seaweed is also a popular mulch in coastal areas.

The best time to apply a mulch is when seedlings are up several inches and the sun has thoroughly warmed the soil. Light, bulky materials should blanket the soil to a depth of 6 inches, while denser materials may be layered less thickly—2 to 3 inches is quite sufficient. Mulch immediately after a good soaking rain (or a thorough hosing) to give your garden a head start and keep the soil moist all summer long. Whichever of these organic materials you choose, however, be sure that your plants are well fortified in advance with compost or some form of high-nitrogen fertilizer. Many mulch materials tend to decay with the onset of midsummer heat, triggering soil organisms into feverish activity and often causing them to compete for the nitrogen and phosphorus present in the soil. To avoid a potential nitrogen deficiency in your plants, add some compost, well-rotted manure, blood meal, soybean meal or activated sludge at mulching time, particularly if you're using sawdust, straw, grass clippings or autumn leaves as the soil cover.

The use of trendy black plastic as a mulch has risen dramatically right along with the current boom in vegetable gardening. Perhaps the most complimentary thing one can say about its appearance is that it is neat; nevertheless, its popularity is outdistancing many organic

mulches because of its particular advantages. For one thing, it is easily obtainable, and it permits earlier planting because it absorbs the sun's rays and keeps the soil warm and moist. In addition to retarding evaporation, it diverts the greater part of a heavy rain away from your garden and prevents nutrients from leaching away. Weeds won't grow under it, and it effectively keeps fruit off the ground.

Mulching with black plastic, however, does have some drawbacks. It is lightweight and can easily be whipped away by high winds unless you anchor it securely. And while it is helpful in raising soil temperature during the spring, on hot summer days it makes root-damaging heat soar high. Devotees of black plastic argue that as the plants mature they shade the plastic, and thus less heat is absorbed into the ground, but to be on the safe side it's probably better to remove the plastic when spring yields to summer and replace it with a more traditional mulch. The prime reasons to avoid it, in my opinion, are that it is not organic, it does not decompose and enrich the soil, and it is totally unnecessary since natural mulches work as well.

GROWING SQUASH IN CONTAINERS

Gardenless city-dwellers or those whose gardens are neither large nor loamy enough to accommodate squash need not miss out on the pleasures of a home-grown harvest. A surprising number of these marvelous vegetables take easily to container growing. As long as you can provide your plants with 6 or more hours of sunshine daily, plus the moisture and enriched planting medium they need to germinate and grow, you can sow and reap to your heart's content on patio, porch, sundeck, fire escape, doorstep or rooftop. All it really takes is a penchant for nurturing and a little extra tender loving care.

Summer squash, which begin bearing within an average of 50 days, make perfect candidates for container growing. Try Aristocrat Zucchini, Burpee Hybrid Zucchini, zucchini-type Caserta, Baby Crookneck or Straightneck, Early Golden Summer Crookneck, Early Prolific Straightneck, Early Bush Scallop or St. Pat Scallop—all varieties with bush habits and fruits which are especially delectable when harvested small. Scallopini, a brand new variety and All-America winner, is particularly good for container purposes. Best picked when 2 to 3 inches across, its dark green fluted fruits are similar in flavor to zucchini and may be served raw in salads or fried, steamed or baked. If you're adventurous but must confine your gardening activities exclusively to containers, you might try Gold Nugget, a bush type that does well in a small space. Plan on using an extra-large tub for it, however, and giving it lots of support—its pumpkin-shaped fruits average 1½ to 2 pounds apiece. I won't say it will work for everyone, but I have had luck with it.

Growing vegetables crops in containers is a popular and easy way to beat high supermarket costs. If you do want to grow squash, choose only containers large enough to hold at least 5 gallons of soil. Whether these are ready-made planters like tubs of wood, clay, metal or plastic, or improvised holders like barrels, wooden crates, plastic laundry baskets, large-sized garbage pails or even large wire hanging cylinders lined with sphagnum moss and filled with rich planting mix, your squash will probably be most cooperative. And don't forget, squash can grow down as well as up.

Safeguard any wooden container from wear and tear by finishing it first with a safe wood preservative inside and out. Wood, clay and some ready-made plastic containers usually come equipped with built-in drainage, but you will have to work out some kind of drainage for your improvised plastic containers. Proper drainage calls for lots of small holes drilled in a random pattern around, and at least 2 inches above, the container's bottom. A deep laundry or bushel basket whose open sides will not confine the soil properly may be lined with heavy plastic punched in a dozen or so places for drainage. Gravel, pebbles, clay shards or even a recycled collection of bottle caps should fill the container's bottom right up to the drainage holes.

Any soil formula that duplicates the loamy, organically rich growing conditions that squash revel in makes a suitable planting medium. I prefer to start with a blend of equal parts of garden or commercially purchased topsoil, builder's sand and either compost or leaf mold, then mix in some superphosphate and bone meal. City dwellers who lack ready access to compost or leaf mold may use peat moss as a substitute but they must be sure to add 1½ cups of lime for each bushel of soil to counteract the peat's natural acidity. When weight is a problem, and it is when you're pushing containers around patio or terrace, either perlite or vermiculite will pinch-hit nicely for the sand. Here is a lightweight soil substitute you can prepare yourself: Combine 1 bushel of vermiculite with 1 bushel of peat moss. Add 1½ cups of lime, 1 cup of 5-10-5 fertilizer and ½ cup of superphosphate. Sprinkle water over the mixture from time to time to keep dust at a minimum while you're up to your elbows mixing all ingredients thoroughly.

The natural inclination of all squash vines is to spread, so plan on providing your containerized specimens with sturdy support of some kind. A trellis, or trellis netting suspended between two heavy stakes or poles set in each container, is suitable, but you may also merely position your containers against a sunny wall or fence. Secure the vines to any bracing structure with heavy yarn, cloth strips or nylon stockings. If you intend to allow your squash to become monsters, give the vines some extra support by slipping one of the net bags that onions come in over each growing fruit, then tie or nail the end of the bag to the bracing structure.

Start off your plants by sowing two or three seeds directly in each container when warm weather settles in for an extended stay in your area. Pull out all but the hardiest as soon as the seedlings reach a height of 4 to 5 inches. Keep the soil evenly moist during germination and the early growth stages, then begin a regular routine of daily watering. Plants in containers need to be watered more often than their garden-bed counterparts because the soil dries out both from the surface and from the sides. If necessary, get out the watering can as often as twice daily. Vegetables need lots of water for rapid growth and good production, and sustained or repeated bouts of wilting will do your plants in, in short order. Your containerized vegetables will also wilt less in drying winds if you mist their foliage with water early in the morning so that their leaves can dry out by night.

A good rule is to water whenever the soil feels dry to the touch about ½ inch down from the surface. It's a bit harder to regulate the water supply for squashes growing in plastic containers because air cannot circulate as well as it can in wood or clay. Wood and clay containers "breathe"; consequently, overwatering is less of a hazard. To guard against soggy soil in plastic, make sure that your containers have plenty of drainage holes and are well lined with drainage materials. You'll really appreciate this help when summer rains arrive. Mixing peat into the soil also helps alleviate the drainage problem. To keep the soil cool, mulch the container surface with a layer of finely textured mulch material (see pages 28–30). Mulching is also the perfect way to keep down airborne weeds, which have the habit of turning up in the unlikeliest places.

Your planting mix should provide all the nourishment your plants need for the first three or four weeks of growth, but since containerized squash cannot send roots sprawling in search of nutrients, it's a good idea to begin fertilizing yours regularly at three-week intervals as soon as seedlings reach the two-leaf stage. Use a 5-10-5 or some organic fertilizer, and water thoroughly after each application so that unused portions don't accumulate in the soil.

Squash in containers sometimes suffer from the same diseases and pests as their garden counterparts, especially if other vegetables are growing nearby. For diseases and pest control for your plants, see pages 34–39.

EXTENDING THE GROWING SEASON

Weather is not always as friendly as gardeners might wish: spring may not yield to summer with consummate good grace; damaging pre-autumn frosts can, and often do, arrive unannounced. James Whitcomb Riley's celebrated "punkin" notwithstanding, the whole cucurbit clan is sensitive to cold, and gardeners who want to get a jump on the summer squash-growing season, or ensure their winter squash the 100-odd frost-free days that some varieties need to complete their growing cycle, must exercise a bit of ingenuity.

One way to hurry along production or lengthen a short growing season is to launch the seeds indoors or in a hotbed, then transplant the seedlings to the garden as soon as temperatures permit (see page 26). There are also methods of ignoring the calendar and seeding directly in the garden, provided you offset or modify unfavorable germination conditions by giving your plants, both as seeds and seedlings, some kind of extra help. For one, you can choose a planting area with a southern exposure well protected from the wind; your own backyard has several different climates—some will be better than others at keeping your germinating seeds degrees warmer. For another, you can provide seeds and seedlings with some type of protective covering, then expose them gradually until they are sufficiently hardened to make it on their own.

Good protective covering is any sheltering device you design or resort to. A surprising number of temperature modifications can be effected with inexpensive or recycled plastics, if you also provide good ventilation. You can rig up a mini-greenhouse right over your planting bed, using a cover of polyethylene film stretched tentlike over a rectangular or A-shaped wooden frame. When daytime temperatures are mild, simply lay back the plastic. If temperatures threaten to zoom downward, fill plastic jugs with water and lay them on the soil. These will warm up during the day and throw back heat on a chilly night. Water-filled plastic bags serve the same purpose, although these tend to be fragile. Bushel baskets outfitted with plastic covers work well over single hills on cold nights.

The hotcaps available in garden centers give very good protection to all vine crops during cool weather. The trick is remembering to widen the slits in the caps, or to remove the caps altogether, on warm days. Inexpensive homemade hotcaps of plastic hardware cloth wrapped around and supported by a long pointed stick afford as good, if not better protection and also circumvent the danger of excessive heat build-up which sometimes occurs under the commercial variety. In case frost threatens your still-tender unripe winter squash, just reposition these plastic structures (or blanket the vines lightly with polyethylene film or other lightweight covering, including ordinary blankets). Remove all protection during the day, however, or the consequent heat build-up will do in your squash just as surely as any frost.

POTENTIAL PROBLEMS

Growing squash is one of the most rewarding garden experiences. This is a hardy vegetable, and as long as you follow the basics of squash culture and get your plants off to a good start, they will pretty much take care of themselves while you sip cool drinks on the veranda. There are only a few serious insect pests that afflict vines or fruits, and squash are not particularly subject to disease. Chances are that neither pests nor disease will ever bother your garden. Nevertheless, it can do no harm for you to be aware of a few of the unpleasant happenstances that might afflict your plants and/or fruits.

PREVENTING PROBLEMS

The key to handling potential troubles in the garden is to prevent them from arising in the first place. Resourceful gardeners can take several prior steps to ensure a successful squash crop.

Provide a healthy growing environment from planting to harvest. Good soil management begins with a well-drained, organically rich loam—plants grown in such soils are far less susceptible to the depredations of insects and disease. Also important are both adequate growing space and moisture. Soil that is alternately bone-dry and soggy weakens even healthy plants. Garden housekeeping is also an important part of soil management. By disposing of weeds and diseased plants, both during the growing season and after, and by turning over the soil at fall cleanup, you effectively limit the spread of disease and curb the insect population.

Practice crop rotation. Pests comfortably settled in one locale are usually loath to move. The point of rotation is to starve them out. If possible, switch the squash-growing site each year, from one sunny, well-drained location to another. In any case, don't plant squash in any spot where cucumbers or melons grew the year before.

Encourage natural allies. One way to keep the bug population within manageable limits—and incidentally to keep your garden from serving as a free lunch counter for neighboring wild animals—is to interplant your squash with flowers and other vegetables that act as natural repellents. Nasturtiums grown between squash hills or as border plantings are most adept at stemming invasions of squash bugs, striped cucumber beetles and aphids. But don't be disappointed if these colorful annuals with the peppery leaves do not put on their usual showy bloom in the rich, fertile soil of your squash garden. You might also plant stately gladioli to lure the thrips that may otherwise attack your squash, and marigolds to suppress infestations of soil

34

nematodes. (Their musky scent is also repugnant to many insects.) Other ornamentals that not only lend color and fragrance to the vegetable garden but also make effective pest repellents are calendulas (pot marigolds), coreopsis, cosmos and sunflowers, which the Indians inter-cropped with corn and squash.

The castor-oil plant (*Ricinus*), a quick-growing, tall, showy annual, can do double duty as a pest repellent since it helps to control aphids and discourages the attention of moles and deer. (All parts of the plant are poisonous, however, so do not use if nibbling children are about.) Another effective mole deterrent you may try is the low green foliage of scilla or wood hya-cinths. Planting soybeans around or near the vegetable garden sidetracks ravenous rabbits. Onions, garlic—which contains a potent insect control called allyl—and radishes are other vegetables that can help create a relatively pest-free environment for your squash.

Some insects, of course, are valuable allies to have around. Ladybugs, praying mantises and trichogramma wasps are all natural insect predators who make short shrift of other insects; lacewing larvae, often called aphid lions, love to feast voraciously on aphids. If none of these helpful insects is at work in your garden, you can import some (seed houses supply them), making sure your purchases coincide with the emergence of their natural prey so they won't wander off to feast elsewhere. Naturally, there's no guarantee that these good bugs will take up permanent residence in your garden, but there's no harm in trying.

Track down insect predators yourself. Keep in mind that a few crawling, sucking or chewing insects on your squash plants do not an invasion make. A chewed leaf or two will do no harm. If the creatures are not numerous, you have several options: combat them with the fine spray of your garden hose; douse them with soapy water (at a ratio of 1 tablespoon soap flakes to 1 gallon water); or pick them off by hand and drop them in kerosene or Mr. Clean. Even the most horrendous invasion can be cured this way. Spend an hour a day 5 days in a row with a toothpick in one hand, a cup of some lethal liquid in the other and a great deal of determination, and you generally need not resort to sprays. Chewing insects find gritty substances most unin-viting, so sprinkle the ground around your squash plants with rock powder or wood ashes. Boards or inverted cabbage leaves, set between rows around the vegetable garden at night, make efficient traps. Just turn them over in the morning and kill any night-feeding bugs fool-hardy enough to seek daytime shelter underneath.

In emergencies, there are some very potent insect-repelling mixtures made from common kitchen ingredients that you can whip up at home, without resorting to lethal pesticides. A generous amount of any hot, spicy seasoning—onion, garlic, hot peppers or cayenne—will do. Chop or whirl these in your blender, alone or in combination. Add soap flakes if you wish (it helps the homemade brew cling to leaf surfaces), then steep the mixture in water for a few hours or even overnight, if you have time, and strain. Dilute by a ratio of 1 tablespoon mixture to 2 cups water and pour into a sprayer. When spraying, be sure to cover the underside of the leaves, too. For added protection, distribute the strained pulp around the base of your plants.

Use botanical or biological controls. The above methods are, unfortunately, not foolproof. Insect allies may still depart from companion plantings for the greener pastures of your squash plants, and home-brewed sprays must be repeatedly applied on a routine basis and after heavy rains to carry any impact. In case it comes down to a question of losing your garden to rapacious hordes of insects, here are some sprays and powders you can use.

The most common are pyrethrum and rotenone (used mostly in combination with pyrethrum). Others are ryania and sabadilla, which are not as widely available. All are plant derivatives and spectacularly effective against specific pests. Regard them as a last resort, however, since they may kill off beneficial as well as harmful insects, and when purchased as commercially prepared dusts and sprays may also be dangerous to the health of the gardener.

A good control for caterpillars and grubs is the biological insecticide *Bacillus thuringiensis*, marketed in powder form under trade names like Biotrol, Thuricide and Dipel. Another specific control, the spores of milky spore disease (*Bacillus popilliae*), is a pathogen highly detrimental to the grubs of Japanese beetles. Use all of these according to manufacturer's directions.

Caution: Never use sulfur as an insect control on your squash. Long used as an insecticide or fungicide on many vegetables, it will burn vine crops irreparably and certainly can do the gardener no good either.

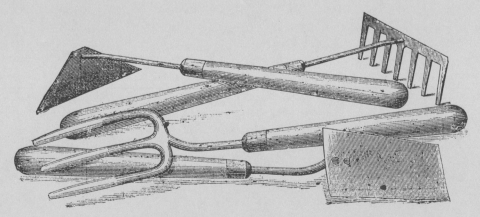

COPING WITH PROBLEMS

Get in the habit of double-checking your squash garden throughout the growing season (not just at feeding and watering times) to spot early signs of trouble. Turn over a few leaves when you're picking vegetables to make sure nothing sinister is lurking underneath. Knowing what kinds of problems to expect gives you time to remedy a situation before it gets too advanced, and may even help you avoid it altogether.

- The tiny, plump-bodied sucking insects that range themselves along the stems, vines and foliage of squash plants are *aphids*, or *plant lice*. There are many different species, all tremendously prolific. They usually shun humus-rich soils; however, if large colonies do show up on your plants, try flooding them with soapy water or spray with a garlic solution. Use pyrethrum or rotenone as a last resort. Aphids' bodies produce a sweet fluid much favored by ants. The grateful ants in turn helpfully move the aphids from one garden spot to another. Covering any holes with bone meal helps get rid of both.

- If your leaves and vines gradually begin to take on a limp, wilted appearance, the reason is sure to be *bacterial wilt*, one of the most serious of cucurbit diseases. Particularly troublesome in the South, it is spread by the *striped cucumber beetle* (see below), which carries the bacteria through the winter in its digestive tract. The best control is to get rid of the beetles, but good housekeeping during fall cleanup also helps. Destroy all affected plants.

- Those large, green or brown caterpillars (larvae change color as they mature) chomping away at the foliage of your squash plants are familiar to gardeners as *corn earworms*, *cotton bollworms* or *tomato fruitworms*. They attack many vegetables, including squash. Pick them off by hand, try a garlic or onion spray or, if the infestation gets out of control, use rotenone.

- The cobwebby patches or powdery-white growths that appear on your summer squashes are both forms of *mildew*, which usually attacks late in the season or during sustained periods of cool, humid weather. Crop rotation is the best practice. Pull out and destroy all affected vines.

- Deformed or puckered foliage, plus mottling of leaves and fruits, is the mark of the *mosaic virus*. Aphids and striped cucumber beetles help spread the disease, but tobacco is also a culprit. Prevention is the best cure. Keep the garden free of the weeds that play host to these insects, and if you smoke or use tobacco in any form always wash your hands and tools well in soapy water, or dip your hands in milk, before doing any gardening chores. A plant spray made with skim milk and water is also effective.

- Slender, yellowish green worms with a row of black spots on their backs are *pickleworms*, a particular nuisance to squashes grown in Southern gardens. Their attacks usually come late in the season, so one way to thwart them is to plant early. Other effective ways to control an infestation are to hand-pick them or to dust the plants with rotenone or sabadilla.

- Brown, slightly concave spots showing up on your summer squash? The cause is a fungus-borne disease known as *scab*. Pull out and destroy all affected plants. The best antidote is crop rotation each year.

- Some soft-bodied, light-shy creatures you may never see at all can be responsible for squash damage. *Snails* and *slugs* (not insects at all but properly mollusks) hide by day and creep forth to feast at night. Place inverted cabbage leaves or boards around the garden to trap them, then drop them in kerosene. If the thought of touching these creatures is repulsive to you, spray them with salty water or set out shallow pans or cans set flush with the ground and fill with beer. If you're lucky, the slugs, attracted by the smell, will crawl in, get soused and drown. Since snails and slugs abhor gritty substances, other controls are scattering wood ashes or sand over the soil or mulching with salt hay.

- The tiny winged insects eagerly devouring your newly developed squash blossoms are *12-spotted cucumber beetles*, easily identifiable by their yellowish-green backs with 12 black spots. You can foil these mainly Southern pests by enclosing your young plants in cheesecloth or muslin frames, by handpicking the beetles themselves or by trapping them under wooden boards. They will also succumb to dustings of pyrethrum or rotenone.

- Clusters of oval-shaped brown eggs found attached to the foliage of young plants just as the vines are beginning to run means that another generation of *squash bugs* will be at work as soon as the eggs hatch, sucking plant juices and turning leaves black and crisp. Pick off and crush the eggs, or spray them with sabadilla, ryania or a strong garlic preparation, before the red-headed nymphs emerge. Adult squash bugs, recognizable by their ¾-inch flat rust-brown bodies, are harder to control; hand-picking helps, but don't be surprised by their disagreeable odor—squash bugs are relatives of the true "stink bug." Fall cleanup is also an effective control, since adults winter in garden debris.

- When holes begin to show up in the stems of your plants near the base of each runner, the culprit is that most serious of squash pests, the *squash vine borer*. This inch-long white grub with a dark head evidently finds all cucurbits delicious but is especially partial to squash. Only Butternut is immune. The traditional technique for repulsing an infestation is to cut into the stem with a knife at all points of damage and kill the grub hidden there. Follow up by heaping moist soil around the wounds. A newer and more unconventional control is to take advantage of the habits of this particular insect. Grubs are larvae laid in the young plants by female moths which instinctively guide themselves to their targets by means of shadows cast by the stems. Studies have shown that aluminum foil strips arranged around the base of each plant will reflect only the sun, thereby confusing the moth and reducing its damage.

- If the leaves and stems of your plants begin disappearing, blame the *striped cucumber beetle*, a black-and-yellow-striped creature about ¼ inch long. This winged predator is triply detrimental—as a larva it demolishes plant roots and as an adult it not only feeds voraciously aboveground but also serves as a host for bacterial wilt (see above). Control by hand-picking the adults or by trapping them under boards. Other effective deterrents are enclos-in the young plants in cheesecloth or muslin frames or intercropping squash hills with radishes. Dust with pyrethrum or rotenone as a last resort.

- Whitened leaf surfaces and brown-flecked leaf edges are sure signs that minuscule yellowish-brown insects with fringed wings have been sucking juices from your plants. *Thrips* are partial to—and destructive of—many vegetables, including squash. Rotenone, pyrethrum or ryania are effective controls.

- If all that remains of your once-thriving squash plants are 1-inch stubs cut off at ground level, chances are that *wild animals* are afoot. Wire fencing sunk 10 to 12 inches into the ground will foil most of them, but for instant measures against rabbits, shrews, woodchucks and deer, try hanging bags of blood meal nearby. If this doesn't repel them, spray the plants with watered-down Epsom salts or a garlic or onion brew, or dust the ground with limestone, wood ashes or cayenne pepper. (For companion plants that curb animal pests, see page 35).

One trait that sets squash apart from other home-garden favorites is their incredible diversity of colors, sizes and shapes. Varieties range in size from petite Scallopini, barely as big as the palm of your hand, to giant Hungarian Mammoth, which can (and often do) weigh in at upwards of 100 to 150 pounds. Summer squash in general tend to be smaller than their winter cousins and taste best when harvested young, but don't worry if you inadvertently grow a yardlong specimen; these are also delicious when properly prepared.

Squash come in a fantastic array of shapes. Aside from those which still emulate the pumpkin characteristics of their ancestors, the most common shape is oblong, either crooknecked or straightnecked, but squash may resemble acorns, drums or bananas; some are squat and turban- or heart-shaped, others develop into bell shapes (with or without scalloped edges) or remain flat and scalloped. Still others grow swollen bodies on short necks or heavy bulbous ends on long, thick necks.

Fruit skins may be smooth, furrowed, warty or ridged, and colors run the gamut from brilliant to subdued. Greens predominate—among the summer squashes in particular—from the palest and most subtle tints to the deepest hues, but many green squashes, summer and winter types both, are lavishly variegated with overtones of yellow, silver or black. Squashes also come in white, white tinged with the palest of greens, cream color, buff and tan—and even pink or blue. For dramatic contrast, there are bold oranges, striking yellows and vivid red-golds.

What separates summer and winter squash into two distinct groups is the use made of their respective fruits. Rapid-growing summer squash are exceptionally moist and at their tender best when harvested young and used shortly thereafter. Their leisurely one-crop winter relatives, on the other hand, require a full season to develop the hard skins and firm, meaty, yellow-orange flesh that make them adapt beautifully to long storage for fall and winter use.

Within the summer and winter groups themselves there are further divisions. Summer squashes, all nontrailing bush types, subdivide into zucchini, yellow butter straightnecks and crooknecks, oblong marrow squashes and the smooth-skinned patty pan or scalloped-edge types. Winter squashes fall into three classes: Acorn or Danish types, which grow on either bush or vine; *maxima* kinds, which include the small-fruited, bush-type Gold Nugget as well as such medium to large vining squashes as Buttercup, Hubbard and Banana; and Butternut types, characterized by small fruits on large vines.

Available squash varieties also change from year to year as seedsmen develop new cultivars or improve old ones. To help you find your way through this maze of varieties, I have listed them along with their general characteristics. The list is meant to be merely a guide—not an unqualified endorsement. Most are varieties you will find in catalogs, seed racks or as seedlings in your friendly neighborhood garden center. Particular varieties are carried only by specific seed houses. Sources of seeds are listed after each variety, and their addresses can be found on page 54.

Picking the right squash for your garden need not be a problem. Where space is limited, plant bush types. Zucchini hybrids are heavy bearers and give tremendous dividends for the space invested. Gold Nugget and the bush Acorns are winter varieties that won't gobble up your real estate. If you're looking for the best returns from winter squash, try Blue Hubbard, heaviest of all in production by weight. If you're planning to can, freeze or go in for root storage, select varieties adapted for these purposes.

Space is an important consideration in any garden, but if possible, do try to plant one or two of the vining winter squashes. These are every bit as easy to raise as summer varieties and far more delicious than those available in most supermarkets. The bad press winter squash sometimes receives is largely due to premature harvesting. Unripe winter squash do have a somewhat disagreeable flavor, but when allowed to mature completely winter squash is not only delectable but one of the most nutritious foods that will ever grace your dining table.

Knowing how much of any variety to plant depends not only on your family's size but on how much preserving you intend to do. Six summer squash plants, kept picked to produce at maximum volume, should provide you with approximately 50 pounds of fruit over a summer. A hill of winter squashes (three plants) varies in total poundage from one variety to another, but the average is 30 pounds per season. Three medium summer squashes, one 6-inch Acorn squash or half an 8-inch Butternut will all give you enough squash for four ½-cup servings.

Note: The number of days designated for each variety on the list refers to the approximate time from planting seeds to first harvest.

SUMMER SQUASH VARIETIES

ZUCCHINI VARIETIES

VARIETY	DESCRIPTION
Hybrid Senator Zucchini (41–45 days)	Early and prolific, with heavy-bearing vines. Yellowish-green fruits are excellent for canning. (Asgrow-Mandeville)
Zucchini Select (47 days)	Extra length and dark green skin flecked with light green are distinguishing features of this early hybrid. Good tolerance to mildew. (Stokes)
Ambassador Hybrid (48 days)	Smooth, dark green fruits of high quality and flavor are plentiful on this productive bush. Open-growing habit makes harvesting easy. (Earl May, Nichols, Park, Vesey)
Aristocrat Hybrid (48 days)	An All-America winner and exceedingly prolific. Smooth, dark green fruits grow upright, won't become football-size overnight, either. (Burpee, Hart, Jackson & Perkins, Earl May, Nichols, Northrup-King, Park)
Black Jack Zucchini (48 days)	A black-green hybrid, darkest available. Smooth-skinned, uniform fruits are easy to pick. (Burgess, Stokes)
Seneca Gourmet (46 days)	A dark green zucchini type, early and prolific. (Olds)
Diplomat Zucchini (48 days)	Dark, waxy green fruits with long stems on compact, open bushes. (Stokes)
Zucchini Elite (48 days)	Early, vigorous and very prolific hybrid. Slim, tapered fruits are glossy green with flecks of light green. For peak flavor, harvest at 6 to 8 inches. (Harris)
Eldorado (49 days)	A yellow hybrid, really a golden version of Elite. Uniform, glossy fruits are smooth and slightly tapered. Vigorous and easy to pick. (Harris)
President Hybrid (49 days)	Fruits from highly productive vines are long, slim and dark green. For all culinary uses. (Park)
Burpee Hybrid Zucchini (50 days)	Very popular. Medium-size bushes are heavy-yielding and vigorous. Pick when 6 to 8 inches long for best flavor and texture. (Burpee)
Caserta (50 days)	Productive bush whose flavorful fruits should be used when small and immature. Perfect for container growing. (DeGiorgi, Olds, Roswell)
Clarita (50 days)	A gray-green type that produces an excess of female flowers and, consequently, a superabundance of 6-to-7-inch fruits. Excellent for salads. (Glecklers, Nichols, Park)

VARIETY	DESCRIPTION
Greyzini (50 days)	Silver-gray markings make the fruits of this hybrid especially distinctive. Very productive and suitable for growing in all parts of the country. (Farmer, Field, Gurney, Earl May, Jackson & Perkins, Olds, Shumway, Stokes)
Park's Dark Green Zucchini (50 days)	Dark green, slightly mottled fruits with a delightfully distinctive flavor. (Park)
Zucchini Black Italian (50 days)	Another black-green variety, this time with creamy white interiors. (Asgrow-Mandeville)
Abondance (52 days)	A French hybrid with bright green skin and slightly tapered stem ends. Best when medium-size. (Le Jardin du Gourmet)
Blackini (52 days)	A dark green hybrid, fine-textured and richly flavored. Pick when 6 to 8 inches long. (Gurney)
Verte des Zenattas (52 days)	This French squash, or *courge*, is a bush type whose dark green, cylindrical fruits are most tender as *courgettes*, or small-size. (Le Jardin du Gourmet)

VARIETY	DESCRIPTION
Black Zucchini (53 days)	Slightly ridged, cylindrical fruits have dark green skins, greenish-white flesh. (DeGiorgi, Field, Hart, Johnny's Selected Seeds, Northrup-King)
Gray Zucchini (53 days)	Medium green fruits are mottled with gray and swell slightly at blossom ends. Good keeping quality after picking. (Johnny's Selected Seeds)
Burpee's Golden Zucchini (54 days)	Slender, golden-skinned fruits with distinctive, delicious zucchini flavor. (A Burpee exclusive)
Chefini Hybrid (55 days)	This vigorous hybrid is an especially heavy yielder. Fruits are best if picked when 6 to 8 inches long. (Farmer, Glecklers, Gurney, Olds, Park)
Burpee's Fordhook Zucchini (57 days)	An All-America winner. Straight or slightly curved fruits are blackish-green with creamy white interiors. Allow to grow to 8 to 12 inches long for best results. (Burpee)
Cereberus (55 days)	Long, thin, dark green fruit with a nice firm texture. (Nichols)
White French Bush (55 days)	A new variety from France with a nice mild flavor. Firm-fleshed meat contains very few seeds. (Nichols)

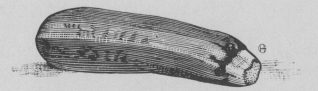

BUTTER-YELLOW VARIETIES

VARIETY	DESCRIPTION	VARIETY	DESCRIPTION
Hybrid Goldneck (45 to 50 days)	Early-maturing and exceptionally vigorous. Compact, bushy plants are ideal for small gardens. Golden fruits are delicious from 4 to 5 inches on up. (Burgess, Field, Gleckers, Jackson & Perkins, Nichols, Park, Reuter, Shumway)	Hybrid Baby Crookneck (51 days)	Small (6-inch) butter-yellow fruits with gently curving necks. Good for container growing. (Park, Stokes)
		Hybrid Baby Straight-neck (51 days)	A straightnecked, very vigorous version of Hybrid Baby Crookneck. (Stokes)
Saticoy F-1 Hybrid (45 days)	A vigorous and early producer and compact bush type. Fruits are golden yellow, with smooth skins and curved necks. (Hart)	Seneca Butterbar Hybrid (51 days)	Open-growing habit of this early-maturing variety makes its smooth-skinned, cylindrical, yellow fruits easy to pick. (Burpee, Park)
Early Prolific Straightneck (50 days)	An All-America winner. Lots of creamy yellow fruits that can be used as soon as they're 4 to 6 inches long, yet remain delicious up to a foot in size. (Burgess, Burpee, DeGiorgi, Field, Gurney, Hart, Northrup-King, Olds, Reuter, Roswell)	Early Golden Summer Crookneck (53 days)	The flavor and texture of its meaty fruits make this crookneck a favorite. Tastiest when small, it eventually resembles a winter variety in looks and size if allowed to grow larger. (Burpee, DeGiorgi, Gurney, Hart, Earl May, Northrup-King, Olds, Park, Reuter)
Goldbar (50 days)	A straightnecked butter-yellow hybrid that bears extremely early on vigorous bushes. (Hart, Earl May, Reuter, Vesey)		
Golden Girl (50 days)	Resembles Seneca Prolific, but is hardier, matures earlier and has a glossier color. This hybrid produces slim, uniform fruits all summer long. (Harris)		
Goldzini (50 days)	Length makes the fruits of this deep yellow hybrid particularly distinctive. (Gurney, Stokes)		

VARIETY	DESCRIPTION
Seneca Prolific Hybrid (51 days)	A long-time favorite among yellow summer squash, tender and delicious. Keep picked for summer-long production. (Harris, Northrup-King)
Giant Summer Crookneck (55 days)	Curved-neck, finely warted yellow fruits will grow to large size and still keep their fine flavor. (Roswell, Shumway)

VARIETY	DESCRIPTION
Giant Summer Straightneck (55 days)	A popular, straightnecked version of Giant Summer Crookneck. (Shumway)
Yellow Crookneck (62 days)	A late yielder, but its firm texture and buttery flavor when cooked make this variety superior in quality to many hybrids. (Johnny's Selected Seeds)

SCALLOP OR PATTY PAN VARIETIES

VARIETY	DESCRIPTION
Patty Green Tint Hybrid (50 days)	Early, vigorous and long-bearing. White fruits tinged faintly with green grow on open bushes, making harvesting easy. (Field, Park)
St. Pat Scallop (50 days)	An early, vigorous hybrid and All-America winner. Light green, glossy fruits are bell-shaped with scalloped edges. Especially delicious when picked very small. (Burpee, Farmer, Gurney, Stokes)
Scallopini (50 days)	The newest hybrid summer squash, a scallop type with zucchini's dark green skin. Best when 2 to 3 inches across, delicious raw or cooked. An All-America winner for 1977. (Burgess, Burpee, Farmer, Field, Hart, Jackson & Perkins, Earl May, Nichols, Olds, Park, Reuter, Stokes)

VARIETY	DESCRIPTION
Early White Bush (White Patty Pan) (50–54 days)	Flat, scallop-edged fruits begin as pale green, then change to white as they ripen. Flesh is milk-white and delicious. (Burpee, DeGiorgi, Hart, Nichols, Reuter, Roswell, Shumway)
Hybrid Patty Pan (Early Bush Scallop) (50–54 days)	A green-tinted scallop type on small, compact bushes. Pick when 3 to 4 inches across, use for canning or freezing. (Burgess, Gurney, Harris, Jackson & Perkins, Olds, Park)

VARIETY	DESCRIPTION
Bennings Greentint (56 days)	Fruits are white scallop type fringed with pale yellow-green. Use when small for best quality and flavor. (Johnny's Selected Seeds, Northrup-King)
Golden Custard (65 days)	A very productive, bush scallop type that grows to large size, yet is excellent for cooking while still green and immature. Mature fruits are yellow-skinned and excellent for pies. (Shumway)

MARROW VARIETIES

VARIETY	DESCRIPTION
Cocozelle (60 days)	This Italian marrow lacks zucchini's fame·but is equal in looks and flavor. Dark green skin with light green stripes encloses firm, buttery-tasting, greenish-white flesh. Fruits are best when 6 to 8 inches long. Not as prolific as zucchini but will bear well if kept picked. Give it lots of space—vines are quite luxuriant. (Burpee, DeGiorgi, Hart, Johnny's Selected Seeds, Nichols, Northrup-King, Shumway, Stokes)
Vegetable Marrow Bush (70 days)	A great favorite in England. Harvest when marrows are 8 inches long and snow-white in color. (Stokes)

VARIETY	DESCRIPTION
Cucuzzi Caravazzi	Also known as Italian Edible Gourd, this extra-long, light green squash often exceeds 4 feet in length. Pick when small and fuzzy-skinned, then steam or fry. Does best with trellis support. (Burgess, Hart, Northrup-King)

ACORN VARIETIES

VARIETY	DESCRIPTION
UConn (70 days)	Acorn-type fruits are grayish-green, with pointed ends. Dwarf-size bushes are ideal for small gardens and highly productive, too — 8 or 9 fruits per bush. An All-America winner. (Shumway)
Bush Acorn Table King (75 days)	An All-America winner. Each compact, bushlike plant bears 4 to 6 fruits averaging 1½ pounds apiece, with thick, golden flesh and small seed cavity. (Burpee, Farmer, Gurney, Hart, Harris, Jackson & Perkins, Earl May, Northrup-King, Olds, Park, Stokes, Vesey)

VARIETY	DESCRIPTION
Table Ace (78 days)	An early bush acorn and heavy producer. Black-green, attractively ridged exteriors enclose smooth, high-quality flesh. Semi-bush habit, but compact. (Field, Harris, Jackson & Perkins)
Bush Table Queen or Acorn (80 to 90 days)	Hard, acorn-shaped, 5-to-6-inch fruits with high-quality, sweet flesh with nutty flavor. Semi-bush habits and a good keeper. (Burgess, Burpee, DeGiorgi, Farmer, Field, Gurney, Harris, Hart, Johnny's, Kelly, Earl May, Nichols, Northrup-King, Olds, Roswell, Shumway, Stokes)
Ebony Acorn (80 days)	An improved Table Queen type and very vigorous. Dark green skin with pale orange flesh of delectable flavor. Perfect for baking in the shell. (Gurney, Jackson & Perkins, Olds)
Royal Acorn (82 days)	A larger version of Table Queen. Dull green skins turn dull orange during storage, with sweet, fine-flavored flesh. A good keeper. (Burpee, Le Jardin du Gourmet, Stokes)
Mammoth Table Queen (85 days)	Another large version of Table Queen. Dark green fruits measure 8 inches in length, with a diameter of 6 inches. (DeGiorgi)

MAXIMA VARIETIES

VARIETY	DESCRIPTION
Little Gem (70 days)	A small Hubbard type with golden skin and flesh. Productive vines yield an abundance of 3-to-4-pound fruits with yamlike flavor. Highly suitable for small gardens. (Glecklers, Vesey)
Bush Buttercup (75 days)	A small (3 to 4 pounds each) bush variety that's popular with gardeners whose space is limited. Each plant yields about 5 fruits with superior flavor. (Vesey)
Kindred (80 days)	An orange-skinned version of Buttercup. Slightly smaller, too, and needs less garden space. 8-inch fruits average 3½ pounds apiece. (Farmer, Gurney, Hart, Northrup-King, Olds, Park, Stokes)
Tetsukabuto F-1 Hybrid (80 days)	Extremely popular in Japan, this winter squash hybrid bears almost spherical, glossy green fruits with a yamlike flavor. (Glecklers)
Emerald (85 days)	A slightly smaller, bush version of vining Buttercup. Yields same high-quality fruit in less space. An excellent keeper. (Farmer, Harris)
Home Delite (85 days)	A Japanese variety similar to Buttercup, but its fewer side shoots enable it to set more fruit. (Sakata)
Perfection (85 days)	Buttercup without the turban. Dark green, drum-shaped fruits are equally sweet. Ideal for canning—there's no waste. (Stokes)

Buttercup (90 to 105 days)	Dark green fruits with gray spots and silvery stripes bear prominent "buttons," resembling turbans, on their blossom ends. Thick, orange flesh with rich, sweet flavor makes this a *very* popular variety. (Burgess, Burpee, DeGiorgi, Farmer, Field, Gurney, Harris, Hart, Jackson & Perkins, Johnny's Selected Seeds, Earl May, Northrup-King, Olds, Shumway, Stokes, Vesey)
Faribo Hybrid "R" (90 days)	Fiery orange-skinned fruits weigh in at 4 to 5 pounds. Fine-flavored, bright orange flesh. Extra-hard rind makes this variety tops for winter keeping. (Farmer)
Golden Hubbard (90 days)	Slightly warted rind of this Hubbard type ripens to a rich orange-red. Fruits average 8 to 10 pounds, with deep orange flesh. A good keeper. (Kelly, Nichols, Olds, Stokes)

VARIETY	DESCRIPTION
Mooregold (90 days)	Developed by the University of Wisconsin, the vigorous vines of this new *maxima* variety produce lots of squat, bright orange fruits of high quality, weighing 4 to 5 pounds each. (Olds)
Baby Blue (95 days)	A short-vined cross between Blue Hubbard and a bush Buttercup strain. Early-maturing fruits resemble miniature Hubbards, average 5 pounds. High-quality and a good keeper. (Farmer, Johnny's Selected Seeds)
Gold Nugget (95 days)	Gardeners with limited space will appreciate this All-America winner. A bush type that's not only a heavy bearer but an excellent keeper. (Burgess, Burpee, Farmer, Gurney, Harris, Hart, Northrup-King, Olds, Park, Stokes, Vesey)
Sakata F-1 Hybrid (95 days)	Ideal for gardeners with limited space. A heavy yielder, producing lots of 5-to-6-pound fruits consecutively on short vines. Flavor is much like sweet potatoes. A good keeper. (Nichols, Sakata)
Baby Hubbard (100 days)	Also called Kitchenette. A small Hubbard for small families. Slightly warted, dark green skin with sweet, orange-yellow flesh. (Gurney, Shumway, Stokes)
Golden Delicious (100 days)	Sweet, golden flesh, fine for canning or freezing or for baby food— unusually high in vitamin C. (Gurney, Harris, Stokes)

VARIETY	DESCRIPTION
Golden Turban (100 days)	A cross between Buttercup and a Turkish variety. Turban-shaped fruits are bright orange. Flesh is dry and delectable. (Farmer)
Hyuga Early Black (100 days)	A Chinese variety whose origins date back to antiquity. Its exterior is dark, ribbed and warty-skinned, its flesh dry, sweet and full-flavored. (Nichols, Sakata)
Kikuza (100 days)	A rare winter squash with origins in South China. Tops for eating quality, its 4-to-4½ -pound fruits yield flesh that is firm, fine-textured and sweet. (Nichols, Sakata)
Turk's Turban Ornamental Squash (100 days)	Purely decorative, richly colored variety. Comes in various shades of bright orange-red, with prominent "buttons," 8 to 10 inches in size. (Burgess, Burpee, DeGiorgi, Harris)

COPYRIGHT 1889
BY J.J.H.GREGORY.

VARIETY	DESCRIPTION
Blue Banana (105 to 115 days)	Really gray-blue or green in color with irregular stripes, this banana-shaped variety grows to 2 feet in length and 6 inches in diameter, and is especially resistant to insect pests and diseases. Sweet, solid flesh is fine for pies or baking. (DeGiorgi, Field, Roswell)
Pink Banana (105 to 115 days)	Identical to Blue Banana in shape, quality and resistance to insect pests and diseases, but skin tones are orange-yellow. (Burgess, DeGiorgi, Gurney, Northrup-King)
"Big Red" (110 days)	A county fair candidate. Monstrous fruits grow up to 4 feet long, often exceed 100 pounds. Good eating quality, too. (Nichols)
Guatemalan Blue (110 days)	This sweet-flavored, fiber-free squash is a type that was grown and savored by South American Indians 1,000 years before Columbus. Abundant fruits grow 3 feet long and up to 8 inches in diameter. Seeds are tasty, too. A good keeper, it also freezes well. (Nichols)
New England Blue Hubbard (110 days)	A select strain of Blue Hubbard that's one-third bigger than its namesake. Extra-large fruits are good keepers. (Johnny's Selected Seeds, Stokes)

Vegetable Spaghetti (100 days)	This novelty squash makes a great low-calorie substitute for spaghetti. Simply boil oblong fruit for 20 minutes, cut open and remove seeds, then serve plain with salt and pepper or top with spaghetti sauce. A good keeper, too. (Burgess, Burpee, Field, Gurney, Johnny's Selected Seeds, Earl May, Nichols, Northrup-King, Park, Sakata, Shumway, Stokes)
Green Delicious (102 days)	Heart-shaped, medium-size fruits are green with fine-grained orange flesh. Tops for freezing. (Hart, Stokes)
Sweet Meat (103 days)	An old-time favorite and still high in popularity. Slate-gray fruits average 10 to 15 pounds, with extra-thick, golden-yellow flesh. An excellent keeper. (Burgess, Harris, Nichols, Northrup-King)

VARIETY	DESCRIPTION
Hubbard Improved Green (120 days)	Another Hubbard variety, this time with slightly warted, dark green exterior and thick, dry and sweet yellow flesh. Excellent keeper. (Farmer, Northrup-King, Stokes)
Hungarian Mammoth (120 days)	This is the biggest of them all, larger than any pumpkin—100 to 150 pounds each. Oval-shaped squash with skin tones ranging from golden through green to gray-blue. Great for canning or freezing, tops for county fairs. (Gurney, Stokes)
Mexican Banana (120 days)	An R. H. Shumway exclusive. Long, cylindrical fruits are gray-blue, with sweet and delicious yellow flesh of high quality. (Shumway)

Umatilla Marblehead (110 days)	An old-time Oregon favorite— prolific vines produce quantities of large, thick golden squash weighing up to 40 pounds. Flesh is almost fiber-free; seeds are delicious when roasted. (Nichols)
Warted Hubbard (110 days)	Dark green, warted skin encloses yellow flesh of extreme tenderness. An excellent winter keeper. (Gurney, Stokes, Vesey)
Chicago Warted Hubbard (110 days)	Heavily warted fruits are dark green and average 14 pounds. Fine-grained, dry, sweet flesh. (DeGiorgi, Farmer, Earl May, Shumway)
True Hubbard (115 days)	An all-purpose squash that merits its popularity. Yellow-orange flesh is perfect for pies and other culinary delights. Fruits weigh in at 12 pounds apiece. (Burgess, Burpee, Field, Hart, Olds, Roswell)
Blue Hubbard (120 days)	Larger than True Hubbard. Blue-gray, ridged fruits weigh 15 pounds apiece, have fine-grained, sweet yellow-orange interiors. Good for freezing and root cellar storage. (Burpee, DeGiorgi, Farmer, Gurney, Hart, Le Jardin du Gourmet, Park; Harris has own special strain)

BUTTERNUT VARIETIES

VARIETY	DESCRIPTION
Burpee's Butterbush (75 days)	Brand-new for 1978, this is a small edition of Butternut, just right for small gardens and the perfect size for two servings. Compact plants produce 4 to 5 fruits apiece, each weighing 1½ to 1¾ pounds. A good keeper. (Burpee)
Baby Butternut (80 days)	An extra-early, smaller Butternut. Fruits are 6 to 7 inches long, with tasty, sweet flesh and small seed cavities. Tops for all culinary purposes. (Farmer)
Hercules (82 days)	Larger and thicker than Butternut, the fine-textured, orange flesh of this variety is dry and flavorful. A good keeper. (DeGiorgi, Farmer, Earl May, Olds, Roswell)
Waltham Butternut (85 days)	An improved and plumper strain of Butternut and an All-America winner. Straightnecked fruits reach 7 to 9 inches at maturity, have rich-flavored flesh and small seed cavities. An excellent keeper. (Burpee, Farmer, Field, Gurney, Harris, Hart, Jackson & Perkins, Johnny's Selected Seeds, Earl May, Olds, Park, Shumway, Stokes)
Ponca (85 days)	A new, smaller-size version of Butternut; earlier, too. Fruits are 6 to 8 inches long, creamy tan with small seed cavities. Flesh is richly colored and delicious. (Harris)
Butternut (85 days)	Dry, sweet orange flesh has delectable, nutty flavor. Buff-colored, smooth-skinned fruits average 6 to 8 inches long, 4 to 5 inches across at base when mature. Also delicious in smaller, immature stage. Resistant to squash vine borer. (Burgess, Burpee, DeGiorgi, Gurney, Kelly, Le Jardin du Gourmet, Northrup-King, Park, Stokes)
Delicata or Sweet Potato (100 days)	Small, oblong fruits are cream-colored, with dark stripes, and 6 to 8 inches long. A good keeper. (Johnny's Selected Seeds, Stokes)
Eat-All (105 days)	A highly nutritious New Hampshire sweet potato squash, with tasty, flavorful flesh and hull-less, edible seeds. (Farmer)

🖝 SOURCES FOR SQUASH, PUMPKIN AND GOURD SEEDS 🖝

Not all seed houses carry every variety of squash, pumpkin and gourd and many varieties described in this book are not available at garden centers. Stocks occasionally change, too—older varieties are dropped in favor of newer, more vigorous ones; popular kinds sell out quickly.

Alongside each description (pages 43-53, 200-203, 212 and 218) are the names of the seed houses offering that variety. Their addresses are listed here for your convenience in ordering.

W. Atlee Burpee Company, Warminster, Pennsylvania 18974

Burgess Seed and Plant Company, P.O. Box 3001, Galesburg, Michigan 49053

DeGiorgi Company, Inc., Council Bluffs, Iowa 51501 (50¢ for catalog)

Farmer Seed and Nursery Company, Faribault, Minnesota 55021

Henry Field Seed and Nursery Company, 407 Sycamore Street, Shenandoah, Iowa 51602

Glecklers Seedsmen, Metamora, Ohio 43540 ($1.00 for seed list)

Gurney Seed and Nursery Company, Yankton, South Dakota 57078

Joseph Harris Company, Inc., Moreton Farm, Rochester, New York 14624

Chas. C. Hart Seed Company, Wethersfield, Connecticut 06109

Jackson & Perkins Company, Medford, Oregon 97501

Johnny's Selected Seeds, Albion, Maine 09410 (50¢ for catalog)

Kelly Brothers Nurseries, Inc., Dansville, New York 14437

Kitazawa Seed Company, 356 West Taylor Street, San Jose, California 95110

Le Jardin du Gourmet, West Danville, Vermont 05873 (25¢ for catalog)

Earl May Seed and Nursery Company, Shenandoah, Iowa 51603

Nichols Garden Nursery, 1190 North Pacific Highway, Albany, Oregon 97321 (24¢ for catalog)

L. L. Olds Seed Company, P.O. Box 7790, Madison, Wisconsin 53707

George W. Park Seed Company, Inc., P.O. Box 31, Greenwood, South Carolina 29647

Reuter Seed Company, Inc., New Orleans, Louisiana 70179

Roswell Seed Company, Inc., 115-117 South Main, Roswell, New Mexico 88201

Sakata Seed America, Inc., 120 Montgomery Street, San Francisco, California 94104

R. H. Shumway Seedsman, Rockford, Illinois 61101

Stokes Seeds, 2485 Stokes Building, Buffalo, New York 14240

Tsang and Ma International, 1556 Laurel Street, San Carlos, California 94070

Vesey's Seeds Ltd., York, Prince Edward Island, Canada

Note: Northrup-King Seeds and Asgrow-Mandeville, Inc., do not publish catalogs. The seeds they offer are widely available in garden centers, supermarkets and other retail outlets.

NUTRIENTS IN FRESH SUMMER AND WINTER SQUASH BY POUND

	Yellow Crooknecks and Straightnecks	Scallop Varieties	Zucchini and Cocozelle	Acorn	Butternut	Hubbard
Food Energy (calories)	89	93	73	152	171	117
Protein (grams)	5.3	4.0	5.2	5.2	4.4	4.2
Carbohydrate (grams)	19.1	22.7	15.5	38.6	44.4	28.1
Calcium (milligrams)	124	124	121	107	102	57
Phosphorus (milligrams)	129	129	125	79	184	93
Iron (milligrams)	1.8	1.8	1.7	3.1	2.5	1.8
Potassium (milligrams)	898	898	870	1,324	1,546	650
Vitamin A Value (international units)	2,040	840	1,380*	4,140**	18,100**	12,870**
Thiamine (milligrams)	.24	.24	.23	.16	.14	.13
Riboflavin (milligrams)	.38	.38	.37	.38	.35	.33
Niacin (milligrams)	4.6	4.6	4.4	2.0	1.8	1.7
Ascorbic Acid (milligrams)	111	82	82	49	29	32

*Applies to squash including skin; flesh has no appreciable vitamin A value.

**Value for freshly harvested squash; the carotenoid content increases during storage, with the amount of increase varying according to variety and conditions of storage.

After all your preparation (the digging, the raking, the composting), after the weeks of careful nurturing (the planting, the weeding, the mulching), your garden is suddenly, magically alive with nature's bounty. Splendid, glossy summer squash begin arriving "not single spies, but in battalions," even before the summer really gets under way. All season long, your gathering baskets overflow, your refrigerator swells with tender green and yellow fruit, your kitchen counter groans with the weight of a copious harvest. Soon, as summer winds down, rows of ripening winter squashes, their flamboyant or subtly hued shells hardening in the retreating sun, await your attention.

What to do with all this bounty—prepare it for the freezer, home-can it, dispatch it to the root cellar? Any one of these procedures will efficiently preserve summer's surplus for your winter pleasure. This section is devoted to preserving, to help you make the most satisfying use of an abundant harvest. And no matter which method or methods you choose, you'll have the comfort of knowing that the squashes you've grown and preserved will arrive at your dinner table naturally delicious, uncontaminated by deadly sprays, and vastly superior to the local supermarket product.

FREEZING SQUASH

Nothing beats the freezing process for ease and speed in preserving the garden-fresh, just-picked quality of home-grown produce. From vine, bush or stalk to freezer, each step is simple and virtually foolproof. Pick tender young vegetables in prime condition, prepare and briefly parboil them, wrap in suitable packaging and deposit in the freezer for their long winter's rest.

Like that other star of the vegetable world, the tomato, summer squash is succulent and plumped with moisture at its fresh-picked best. This plus, unfortunately, is reduced to something of a minus when it comes to freezing; flavor and nutrition remain intact, but texture is apt to be a bit soggy. Nevertheless, frozen summer squash performs beautifully when partnered with other vegetables or used as a delicate addition to winter casseroles and soups.

Summer squash is most delicious when cooked as a purée before freezing (see page 62). Puréeing is also a superb way to preserve your surplus winter squash when a root cellar is out of the question. In preparing any purées destined for the freezer, it's wise to omit pungent flavorings—cloves, garlic and onions, for instance—or even milder ones like salt, cinnamon or herbs. The stronger ingredients tend to produce bitter and unpleasant off-flavors during freezer storage, while blander seasonings frequently disappear completely. Add these flavorings instead during final, post-freezer cooking.

The ultimate success of your frozen squash is also determined by the kind of freezer protection you choose for it. Nearly any container will serve, whether purchased new or salvaged and recycled, as long as it is strong and tight enough to insulate the food against moisture loss and excess exposure to air during storage. Dehydration and oxidation can have disastrous effects on both the flavor and nutrition of frozen foods.

Most familiar and convenient containers are the sturdy plastic variety, with tight-fitting, snap-on lids (the straight-sided, rectangular or square types take up much less space than round ones); with any of these, however, ½ inch of headspace should be left between the top of the food and the container lid to allow for expansion while freezing. Plastic-lined paper boxes, with room allotted for headspace, are also practical, as are heavy-duty plastic bags. The latter can easily be made airtight. Simply place a straw in the bag with the vegetables, twist the top of the bag around the protruding straw and suck out as much air as possible, then withdraw the straw and seal the bag. This pulls the bag tightly against its contents and prevents the formation of ice crystals.

59

The food industry has been endlessly ingenious in dreaming up new packaging methods. Recycling these salvaged items for use in the freezer is not only ecology-wise but economical. Just make sure that whatever you use is moisture-proof, vapor-proof and as airtight as possible, and that you leave the proper amount of headspace between the food and the top of the container.

Waxed or plastic-coated milk or juice cartons, or those deep aluminum dishes of every conceivable size, can serve double duty as recycled containers for either squash slices or purées. Wash and rinse these thoroughly, dry well and store until needed. To use for freezer storage, add the prepared squash, leaving ½ inch of headspace. Slip the containers into heavy plastic bags or wrap in freezer paper, seal tightly and freeze.

The reusable plastic containers that ice cream, dairy and delicatessen foods are packed in work as well as those purchased especially for freezing. Allow ½ inch of headspace when filling and seal the lid tightly before freezing. If you suspect that the container is not airtight, give it added protection with a layer of aluminum foil or freezer plastic wrap under the lid.

Tin cans of any size with plastic lids are equally serviceable, but because these tend to rust when wet, line them with plastic bags prior to filling and leave ½ inch of headspace. Crisscross the lid top with freezer tape to ensure airtight protection.

Wide-necked peanut butter or mayonnaise jars are more suitable for freezer use than jars with shoulders, since their frozen contents slip out more easily. Be warned, however; glass has its drawbacks—fragile to begin with, it becomes more so when frozen. Careful handling is a must! If you do decide to use glass for your purées (although I don't recommend it), leave a minimum of 1½ inches headspace between the jar top and its contents. Liquids expand when frozen, and a jar may burst if headspace is insufficient.

Tray freezing is a superb technique for readying sliced summer squash or winter squash pieces for freezer storage: wrapping is minimal and pieces don't stick together, which makes them easier to remove individually after they're frozen. To tray-freeze, merely arrange the blanched and chilled squash slices or pieces in a single layer on a baking tray, unwrapped and without touching one another. Set the tray in the freezer just long enough to solidly freeze the

 squash, then pop the pieces into heavy plastic bags and seal and store in the freezer, ready for use in any amount you desire.

The most efficient way to store your frozen squash is in portions large enough to serve your family. Pint packages will feed four nicely, quart-size containers will hold enough for six or eight. Always label containers according to contents, quantity and date frozen, and use the oldest packages first.

THE FREEZING PROCEDURE

Remember that peak flavor and appearance of any frozen vegetable depend additionally on how fast it makes the trip from your garden row to your freezer shelf. Properly stored in plastic bags, newly harvested summer squash will keep up to one week in the refrigerator without significant loss of quality, flavor or nutrition, but don't keep the crop you plan to freeze waiting that long. Select only young, tender green or yellow specimens 5 or 6 inches long for this purpose, freeze them the same day they're picked and, if possible, within the same hour.

This race against time is immeasurably eased if all your supplies are lined up and on hand as your harvest is brought in. Aside from a number of containers, the most important item you'll need will be a large kettle for blanching, or briefly cooking, the squash. Blanching is vital to the freezing process because nature, in her grand design, has providentially built into all vegetables and fruits enzymes which ensure that produce on the vine will ripen and mature on schedule. Even after harvest, this enzyme action stubbornly persists—from ripe to riper to overripe— right on into your refrigerator or freezer, accompanied by unpleasant changes in the vegetable's color, taste and texture. Blanching brings this enzyme action to a halt but allows the vegetables to retain their color and flavor throughout freezing.

The ideal kettle for blanching is one with an 8- or 10-quart capacity, a tight-fitting lid and, if you're using the Steaming Method (see page 62), a rack high enough to keep the vegetables well above the water line. The kettle should preferably be constructed of stainless steel or unchipped enamel, although aluminum will also do nicely. (Don't use copper or cast iron.) A wire basket or colander with handles—or, in a pinch, a large piece of cheesecloth—completes the equipment list.

BLANCHING SUMMER SQUASH: Blanching is partial cooking of produce by boiling or steaming for a short, specified length of time.

The Boiling Method: Bring 4 or more quarts of water to a vigorous boil. Meanwhile, wash the small, perfect vegetables you have chosen and cut them into slices of equal size. Fill a large, clean container or your scoured, well-rinsed and stoppered sink with ice and water. Arrange about 1 pound of squash slices in your basket, colander or cheesecloth bag. (Overloading at this point may arrest boiling action and result in unevenly blanched slices.) Lower the vegetable slices into the boiling water and cover the kettle tightly; then, counting from the exact moment your vegetables were submerged, allow them to remain in their boiling water bath for 3 minutes, no longer. A minute too long at this point can mean the difference between a firm or soggy finished product. (If you happen to live in an area that's 5,000 feet or more above sea level, however, it *is* necessary to add 1 more minute to the total boiling time.)

Immediately lift the basket and plunge the vegetables into the waiting ice water to prevent further cooking. Chill the slices for a period of at least 6 minutes, or (as a rule of thumb) for twice as long as they were blanched. Drain thoroughly, place in appropriate-sized containers, label with date and contents, and freeze.

The Steaming Method: Bring 2 inches of water to a rapid boil in a kettle equipped with a rack high enough to keep the vegetables well above the water line. Lower your basket with its pound of sliced squash onto the rack. Cover the kettle tightly and allow to steam for 4 minutes (add 1 extra minute if you live 5,000 feet or more above sea level). Chill in ice water for twice as long as the vegetables were blanched. Drain, package and freeze.

To prepare frozen summer squash slices for table, place the partially defrosted block in a saucepan, with or without a bit of water, and simmer gently over low heat. The moment the slices are tender, stop cooking, toss with butter and season to taste with salt and pepper, and serve immediately. The result will be a softer vegetable than when fresh-cooked, so you may prefer to prepare with other vegetables.

FREEZING PURÉED SUMMER SQUASH: Puréed summer squash is easy to prepare for the freezer and adapts perfectly for winter use. Simply wash and chop tender unpeeled squash and simmer in a stainless-steel or enamel saucepan over low heat, stirring frequently, until soft. Cool quickly by setting the saucepan in ice water, then purée in a blender or food processor. Pour into suitable containers, leaving ½ inch headspace, seal and freeze.

FREEZING WINTER SQUASH: Since winter squash ranks among those few vegetables that increase rather than lose in quality after picking, a root cellar is, not surprisingly, the most economical and practical storage place. But if you lack the convenience of a root cellar, most winter squash varieties will also take beautifully to freezing. Butternut types are best for this purpose, although Acorn Table King, Bush Table Queen, Guatemalan Blue and Blue Hubbard perform equally well. Frozen winter squash purée can go forth alone as a vegetable, star as the main ingredient in soups and other recipes, or pinch-hit for pumpkin in pies.

FREEZING PURÉED WINTER SQUASH: Select mature, vine-ripened specimens with hard rinds cured by a full week in the sun. Quarter them and scrape out and discard all the seeds and stringy parts, then peel the quarters and cut into large dice. Place in a heavy saucepan with 1 cup of water, cover and cook over low heat for 25 minutes, or until the pieces are soft enough to pierce easily with a fork. Drain off water and chill pieces quickly. Purée in a food processor or blender and pour into serving-size containers; seal, label and freeze.

Squash purée is also easily prepared in the oven. Preheat the oven to 350 degrees F. Cut the squash in half and scrape out and discard the seeds and stringy pulp. Arrange the cleaned halves in a large roasting pan and add hot water to a depth of ½ inch. Bake for 1½ to 2 hours, or until the pulp is tender. Scrape out and purée the pulp, pour into containers and freeze.

To reheat squash purée, turn the partially defrosted block into a heavy saucepan, with or without a bit of butter and/or water. Cover and cook gently over low heat, stirring frequently, until the purée is piping hot. Stir in additional butter if desired and season to taste with salt and a pinch of ground nutmeg or cloves before serving.

FREEZING WINTER SQUASH PIECES: Winter squash may also be frozen as pieces, used as is in recipes or puréed after reheating. To prepare, halve, quarter and clean the squash, then peel and cut into 1-inch cubes or slices. Blanch for 3 minutes (4 minutes if you live 5,000 feet or more above sea level) as directed for summer squash (see page 61), chill, drain and freeze.

CANNING SQUASH

To the uninitiated, canning summer's abundance for winter's feasting may seem a troublesome, mysterious, risky business. True, canning does demand meticulous care. There are time-consuming tasks to perform and prescribed equipment to use and properly maintain. Still, once the initial cleaning, cutting up and preprocessing of foods is behind you, canning is only slightly more arduous than is the blanching involved in preparing foods for freezing, and as a way of preserving the quality and flavor of your fresh-picked produce it is both economical and perfectly practical. In fact, few food processes give more satisfaction for the time invested. A walk through the storage cellar with its shelves of jewel-clear jars of fruits and vegetables has warmed many a winter heart yearning for spring.

Despite its formidable reputation, canning is really easily mastered. The process relies for its effectiveness on the correct combination of heat and time, plus scrupulous attention to directions. There can be no shortcuts in canning. Processing food in standard canning jars at the required heat for the designated length of time has two essential purposes: it destroys the various yeasts, molds, bacteria, spores and other spoilage microorganisms present on food, and simultaneously drives air out of the jars to seal them tightly against the entrance of other spoilage organisms at a later date.

What makes otherwise courageous people uneasy about the canning process is the fact that improperly canned produce is not only dangerous but occasionally even lethal when eaten. Most notorious and deadly of all the spoilage agents that may appear in canned food is *Clostridium botulinum*, which causes the deadly food poisoning known as botulism. This bacterium, virtually undetectable by sight or smell, not only proliferates in low-acid food where careless processing has created conditions favorable to its growth, but actually thrives in the absence of air. To be on the safe side when canning, follow all processing instructions to the letter, especially those that relate to method, heat and required time. When using any home-canned food, always check first for telltale signs of spoilage—puffed or bulging jar lids, leaks, jars that spurt when the lid is lifted, mold or unpleasant odors. If any of these are present, discard the food at once! Take no chances even if the jar's contents appear wholesome—*always bring every home-canned product to a boil and continue to boil, covered, for 15 minutes*. If you observe any signs of spoilage or foaming during boiling, or detect any sour or "off" odors, get rid of the food immediately by disposal where neither people nor animals can come in contact with it.

PROCESSING EQUIPMENT

CANNERS: Forget any reports you may hear to the contrary. The only infallibly safe ways to can fresh produce at home are in either the Boiling Water Bath Canner or the Steam-Pressure Canner. These are similar processes; the difference between them is that in the boiling water bath, foods are processed at 212 degrees F., while under steam pressure the same job is accomplished at the much higher temperature of 240 degrees F.

What determines the type of processing necessary for each food is the amount of acid that the food contains. Acidity in food acts as a natural preservative and inhibits the growth of the virulent bacterium *C. botulinum*. A few foods—fruits, some varieties of tomatoes, pickled vegetables—are highly acid and may safely be processed at the relatively low temperatures reached in a boiling water bath canner. However, all other foods—summer and winter squash among them—are either low in acid or have none at all, and are therefore highly susceptible to every kind of spoilage agent, especially botulism. Only a steam-pressure canner, with its ability to reach and maintain temperatures well above the boiling point of water, can generate enough heat to kill off all of the dangerous organisms found in low-acid foods such as squash, and it is this canner we will for the most part concern ourselves with here.

The *boiling water bath canner* is used to process squash only when the vegetable is combined with vinegar and made into pickles. The standard model is a large, very deep kettle equipped with a cover and removable rack; the latter is specially designed to keep the jars from touching one another or the bottom or sides of the canner. You may duplicate this canner with any oversized metal cooking pot you happen to own, as long as it meets three requirements: it must have a tight-fitting cover, have room for a rack to hold the jars steady, and be deep enough to allow at least 2 inches of water to circulate briskly above the jar tops without the water overflowing. A steam-pressure canner (see below) also will double nicely as a water bath canner if it meets these requirements. To adapt one for water bath processing, just place the cover on top without fastening and leave the petcock open for steam to escape.

The standard *steam-pressure canner* is usually made of cast aluminum and comes equipped with a shallow, removable rack and a sturdy, tight-fitting cover that fastens down with clamps. Built into the cover are a pressure gauge to indicate pressure poundage inside the canner, a petcock which, when closed, enables pressure to mount, and a safety valve to allow steam to escape should pressure get too high.

The covers of some steam-pressure canners feature a one-piece combination pressure gauge and safety valve which is completely automatic—all you have to do is select the pressure.

This weighted-gauge pressure control is precision-made and needs only to be kept clean. However, if your steam-pressure canner comes equipped with the more familiar dial-type pressure gauge, this should be checked every year against a master gauge before canning begins to make absolutely certain that your canned foods will be safe. Either return the gauge to the canner manufacturer or the dealer who sold it to you for checking, or ask your county extension office to provide this service. Any gauge that is off by 5 pounds should be replaced. If your gauge is inaccurate by less than 5 pounds, follow the Pressure Compensation Chart on page 71.

JARS AND LIDS: Second in importance only to processing food at the right temperature for the designated length of time is using good-quality standard canning jars made by major manufacturers. Recycled mayonnaise, peanut butter or pickle jars, or even the old-style canning jars you may have inherited, are simply not sturdy enough to withstand the intense heat generated by steam-pressure processing temperatures.

Standard canning jars come in various shapes and sizes. Most are wide-mouthed with either straight or sloping shoulders and range in size from ½ pints to 1 quart, and each comes equipped with its own lid. Pints and quarts are the most practical sizes. The most popular type of lid is the two-part flat metal lid with metal screw band which is self-sealing by vacuum. Other types include the porcelain-lined zinc cap with shoulder rubber ring and the all-in-one metal lid.

Choose the jar type and size that fits your family's needs, figuring that one ½-cup portion will serve one person. Carefully read and follow manufacturer's directions for handling and sealing the jars—each *must* have the proper vacuum seal to guarantee safety.

THE CANNING PROCEDURE

Best results in canning depend on getting your harvest from garden to jars to canner as quickly as possible. All equipment—canner, jars, lids and so on—should be on hand well before canning day, and each item should be clean and in good working condition. To ensure the accuracy of the dial gauge on your steam-pressure canner, have it checked well in advance by the manufacturer, your dealer or county extension service agent, then clean it by drawing a string through the petcock and safety valve opening. If yours is a weighted gauge, clean it according to manufacturer's directions. Discard any jars with chips or cracks and purchase new jars or new lids, or both—some lids need brand-new seals or rings each time you use the canning process.

Once canning day arrives, wash your jars, lids and screwbands in hot soapy water, and rinse and dry them well. Wash and rinse both canner and cover (don't submerge the cover if you're using a steam-pressure canner), and dry both pieces thoroughly.

Harvest the squash you intend to process as soon as these preliminary preparations are finished. Choose only perfect, blemish-free specimens—6-to-8-inch-long yellow or green summer squash that are tender enough to yield easily to the fingernail, or vine-ripened, fully mature winter squash whose tough skins can withstand a fingernail's pressure. Wash the vegetables thoroughly in several changes of water, lifting them out of the water each time rather than letting the water drain over them, so that all dirt and dirt-borne bacteria are left behind. Finish by rinsing and draining produce thoroughly.

RAW PACK AND HOT PACK: There are two methods of filling canning jars prior to processing. One is the *raw* (or cold) *pack* method, in which fruits and vegetables are first cleaned, peeled if necessary, left whole, sliced or cut up. Next they are packed into clean, hot jars, with the recommended amount of headspace, and covered with boiling water, juice or syrup, or hot pickling liquid.

In the *hot pack* method, the food is prepared for processing as in raw pack, but there is one intermediate step. Just before being packed into clean, hot jars, the fruits or vegetables are heated or precooked. The vitamin-rich cooking liquid is then poured over them (leaving the recommended amount of headspace).

USING THE BOILING WATER BATH CANNER: Because squash is a low-acid food, both summer and winter varieties *must* be processed in a steam-pressure canner—with one exception: whenever squash is to be combined with vinegar and made into pickles, it may safely be processed in the boiling water bath.

To use the water bath canner, fill the hot, clean jars as directed in the pickling recipe, leaving the recommended headspace. Run a knife or spatula around the inside of each jar to eliminate any air bubbles, then wipe its neck and top and fit the lid according to manufacturer's directions.

Fill the canner about ⅔ full of hot water, adjust the jar lids if necessary and arrange the jars upright on the rack. The water should reach a level at least an inch or two higher than the jar tops. Add more hot water if necessary, but avoid pouring it directly on top of the jars. Cover the canner and bring the water to a boil.

Count processing time from the minute the water begins to boil briskly and steadily, and process for the *entire recommended time*. Don't court disaster by cutting corners at this point —bacteria can only be killed by applying boiling temperatures for a specific time period. Process for the time directed in the individual recipe, adding boiling water as needed to keep the jars covered. If you live in an area that's 1,000 or more feet above sea level, additional processing will be required. Consult the altitude chart on page 71 to calculate how much.

As soon as processing time is up, immediately remove the jars from their boiling water bath, completing the seals if necessary according to manufacturer's directions. Set them several inches apart on a rack or folded towel, uncovered and away from any draft, to cool evenly for at least 12 hours.

USING THE STEAM-PRESSURE CANNER: Summer and winter squash, like all low-acid vegetables, are especially vulnerable to those pathogenic bacteria that are resistant even to boiling temperatures. Steam-pressure canning, therefore, is the only recommended method.

Manufacturers usually include specific instructions for using new canners, but if you have lost or misplaced yours, here are some general rules for any steam-pressure canner.

1. Pour several inches of boiling water into the bottom of the canner.
2. Arrange your filled and sealed jars (see below) in the canner rack. Be sure that steam can circulate freely. If your canner allows room for two jar layers, stagger the second layer so that jars do not touch.
3. Fasten the cover securely so that steam escapes only through the petcock or weighted gauge opening.

4. Set the canner over medium-high heat until steam pours steadily from the vent for 10 minutes and drives all air out of the canner. Then close the petcock or put on the weighted gauge.
5. Thorough processing demands that pressure rise to 10 pounds. As soon as pressure reaches this figure (or the figure given in the Pressure Compensation Chart, page 71), start counting processing time and maintain the pressure at 10 pounds for the entire time specified. Keep the pressure from rising or falling by regulating the heat under the canner. *Never open the petcock to lower the pressure*, and be sure that there are no drafts blowing on the canner.
6. As soon as processing time is up, carefully remove the canner from the heat.
7. Allow the canner to cool slowly. Never try to hurry cooling along by dousing the canner with water or refrigerating it. When the inside pressure registers zero, wait 10 minutes, then slowly open the petcock or take off the weighted gauge. Unfasten the far side of the cover first, tilting it up so that steam escapes away from you. As you lift each jar from the canner, set it upright several inches from its neighbor on a rack or folded towel to cool undisturbed for at least 12 hours. Never place any hot jars on a cold surface or in a draft.
8. Because it takes more than 10 pounds of pressure to reach 240 degrees F. at altitudes 2,000 feet or more above sea level, you'll need to increase the processing pressure if you live in these higher elevations. At an altitude of 2,000 feet, process your canned squash for the times given at 11 pounds pressure. At 4,000 feet, use 12 pounds pressure; at 6,000 feet, 13 pounds pressure; at 8,000 feet, 14 pounds pressure; at 10,000 feet, 15 pounds pressure. If your steam-pressure canner is equipped with a weighted gauge, it may need to be corrected for altitude by the manufacturer.

To prepare summer squash for steam-pressure processing, first wash and trim your vegetables, then cut into ½-inch slices without peeling them. If some slices are larger than others, halve or quarter these to make pieces of uniform size. You may figure that roughly 2 to 4 pounds of fresh summer squash will equal 1 quart canned.

For *raw pack*, pack the pieces tightly into clean, hot jars, filling them to within 1 inch of the top. Add ½ teaspoon noniodized salt to each pint jar, 1 teaspoon to quarts. Cover the tops of the squash pieces with boiling water, leaving ½ inch of headspace. Wipe the jar necks and tops and set on and adjust the jar lids. Process in the pressure canner at 10 pounds pressure (240 degrees F.)—pints for 25 minutes, quarts for 30 minutes. Remove jars and complete seals if necessary.

For *hot pack*, prepare the squash as for raw pack and place in a saucepan. Add boiling water to cover, then bring to a boil again. Drain immediately, reserving the cooking liquid, and pack the squash pieces loosely into hot, clean jars, leaving ½ inch headspace. Add ½ teaspoon noniodized salt to pints, 1 teaspoon to quarts. Cover with the hot cooking liquid to within ½ inch of the top, then wipe the jar necks and tops and adjust the lids. Process in the pressure canner at 10 pounds pressure (240 degrees F.)—30 minutes for pint jars, 40 minutes for quarts. As soon as you remove the jars from the canner, complete the seals if necessary.

Summer squash also combines tastily with other vegetables—tomatoes and peppers, for example. Prepare these combinations as for hot pack and process in the steam-pressure canner for the time period and at the pressure recommended for the single ingredient in the dish that requires the longest cooking time and the highest pressure.

Winter squash may be prepared for steam-pressure processing either as cubes or purée, both by the hot pack method only. To ready for canning, thoroughly wash the vegetable, then cut into quarters and scrape out and discard all the seeds and stringy parts. Peel the quarters and cut into 1-inch cubes. One and a half to 3 pounds of winter squash will yield 1 quart canned squash.

If canned as cubes, place the squash pieces in a saucepan with water to cover and bring to a boil; drain, reserving the cooking liquid, and pack into hot, clean jars to within ½ inch of the top. Add ½ teaspoon noniodized salt to pints, 1 teaspoon to quarts. Cover the cubes with the hot cooking liquid, leaving ½ inch headspace. Wipe the necks and tops of the jars and adjust the lids. Process in the pressure canner at 10 pounds pressure (240 degrees F.)—55 minutes for pints, 90 minutes for quarts. Complete seals if necessary immediately after removing the jars from the canner.

To can winter squash pieces as purée, prepare as above but place in a saucepan with 1 cup water and steam until tender. Purée quickly in a food processor or blender, or put through a food mill. Return the purée to the saucepan and simmer gently over low heat until heated through, stirring frequently to keep the squash from sticking. Pack into hot, clean jars without adding any salt or liquid, wipe the necks and tops of the jars and adjust the lids. Process at 10 pounds pressure (240 degrees F.)—pint jars for 65 minutes, quarts for 80 minutes. Complete the seals if necessary as soon as the jars are removed from the canner.

CHECKING AND STORING YOUR CANNED SQUASH

The ultimate test in the canning process comes when you check the seals on the cooled jars. If processing has gone according to plan, the air inside the jars has been forced out and the partial vacuum that forms inside each jar as it cools creates a perfect seal. To ensure that flat metal lids are absolutely airtight, press each lid's center; if the lid is down and resists the pressure of your finger, the jar is properly sealed. Other types of lids can be checked by turning the jars partly over in your hand and inspecting for seepage. If you suspect a faulty seal or find a leaky jar, eat the squash immediately or treat the jar's contents as though it were fresh and repack and process all over again.

The screw bands that come with the special two-piece seals may be removed if you wish and the jars stored without them, but wait until the jars and their contents have cooled completely. A lid will provide a tight seal by itself, and you eliminate the possibility that the band may rust and prove balky when it's time to open the jar. Keep the screw bands handy for the next time you process by washing them carefully and storing in a dry place.

A dry, dark storage spot, one where the temperature will remain cool and constant, is the best place to store your canned foods. Dampness may corrode metal lids, while fluctuating temperatures may spoil the jar's contents or make the food less palatable. Label each jar according to contents and processing date. If you've canned more than one batch in one day, add the lot number, too. Use up the jars of food with the earliest canning dates first, and always check for signs of spoilage before opening. Carefully dispose of any jar that displays one or more of the danger signals listed on page 64.

CANNING SQUASH PRESSURE COMPENSATION CHART

If the gauge reads high:
1 pound high, process at 11 pounds
2 pounds high, process at 12 pounds
3 pounds high, process at 13 pounds
4 pounds high, process at 14 pounds

If the gauge reads low:
1 pound low, process at 9 pounds
2 pounds low, process at 8 pounds
3 pounds low, process at 7 pounds
4 pounds low, process at 6 pounds

BOILING WATER BATH HIGH-ALTITUDE CHART
Additional Processing Times

Altitude	Less than 20 Minutes	More than 20 Minutes
1,000 feet	1 minute	2 minutes
2,000 feet	2 minutes	4 minutes
3,000 feet	3 minutes	6 minutes
4,000 feet	4 minutes	8 minutes
5,000 feet	5 minutes	10 minutes
6,000 feet	6 minutes	12 minutes
7,000 feet	7 minutes	14 minutes
8,000 feet	8 minutes	16 minutes
9,000 feet	9 minutes	18 minutes
10,000 feet	10 minutes	20 minutes

ROOT CELLAR STORAGE

A root cellar is, classically, a space dug under a house or outbuilding in which durable root produce can be stored until consumed—sometime after its natural harvest and prior to its going soft and horrible. Root cellars smell wonderfully earthy, have an even moist/dry atmosphere somewhat reminiscent of the Mammoth Cave, and make the owner feel secure against the oncoming winter and in touch with his or her roots (both lineage and legume).

Time was when a root cellar was a fixture in every home and the only sure way to prolong summer's garden bounty. Today, freezing and canning have supplanted root cellar storage in popularity, but as an economical, convenient and functional extension of gardening this method has never outlived its usefulness and still has several remarkably obvious advantages.

Given the right conditions, vegetables in root cellar residence can be preserved well beyond their normal harvest and retain their fresh-picked taste and appearance with little or no nutrition loss. A root cellar harbors bushels of produce inexpensively (a feature which gives this method a decided plus over freezer storage), safely (root cellar vegetables signal their dissatisfaction with their storage environment obviously and instantly) and easily (the only work involved is to pack your harvest and transport it from garden row to storage shelf).

In the old days, the root cellar—a cool, moist lean-to shed or an excavated cellar with stone walls and earthen floors—was a traditional feature of most country homes. Nowadays, poured concrete basements, central heating, ping-pong tables and workshops have preempted the root cellar, but although commercial cold-storage techniques, freezing and the like have turned the root cellar from a necessity to something of a luxury, it is still surprisingly convenient, practical and economical to boot.

You can improvise a more than adequate root cellar in any excavated area where cool temperatures, good ventilation and proper humidity can be uniformly maintained. Ideally, your root cellar should consist of a dirt floor, two windows for cross-ventilation and a series of wooden shelves. You can approximate these conditions by partitioning off a northern (preferably northeastern) corner of your basement, provided it has at least one window. A slatted wooden floor set several inches above your concrete floor makes a perfectly adequate substitute for the classic packed-earth floor, but you can also construct a floor of sorts with planks set on bricks or concrete blocks, and use these same materials to improvise shelves. The precise method or materials you use aren't terribly important, so long as you keep the air circu-

lating around your stored vegetables (produce will mildew if it's set on concrete floors or placed against concrete walls).

Isolate your root cellar from the rest of the basement with two interior walls (preferably 2-by-4 studding and insulation board—perhaps Celotex), which will shield your root cellar from the drying effect of furnace heat. To complete the job, hang a door of the same materials and edge it with felt weather-stripping for a tight fit. If there are any overhead heating ducts, be sure to insulate these as well. Next, set up your storage shelves, hang up a thermometer, open the window and you're in business.

All of nature's bounty, unfortunately, does not take kindly to root cellar storage. Summer squash, for one, remains faithful to its name and maintains its star quality only when consumed summer-fresh from the vine, or when frozen or canned. Winter squash, on the other hand, makes an ideal candidate for the root cellar. Not only do most varieties keep unusually well, but their vitamin A content actually increases during storage.

Winter squash tends to be a bit fussy about its storage environment, preferring to spend the fall and winter in a climate that averages 55 degrees F., so outdoor root cellars or pits won't do. The best way to ensure a steady supply of fresh, whole or raw winter squash is to settle your crop as long-term tenants in a basement root cellar where the proper temperature, good ventilation and fairly dry humidity can be uniformly maintained.

Good choices for winter keeping are the turban-shaped Buttercup; Emerald; Bush Acorn Table King; both Bush Table Queen and Ebony Acorn, an improved Table Queen type; any of the Hubbards, especially True Hubbard, which if properly stored, will keep till spring; Waltham Butternut; Gold Nugget; Sweet Meat; and Vegetable Spaghetti. Select only sound, vine-ripened, mature specimens, free from any defects or bruises, for your root cellar. Size is usually a good indication of maturity, but until their rinds turn hard and tough and their leaves brown, winter squash are best left on their vines.

Winter squash are frost-sensitive and should be gathered before the first frost, yet unless they are allowed to mature and harden they fail to keep well. Should an early frost threaten before your crop is ready, cover the rows at night with heavy plastic tenting or light blankets, removing these during the day. Leave 2 to 3 inches of stem when you harvest, and handle carefully, please—despite their tough-guy appearance, winter squash do bruise easily, and one bruise can rot a squash quickly, even in root cellar storage.

Except for Acorn varieties, all winter squash should be allowed to cure in the sun for a week while the stem wounds heal, before being introduced to their winter quarters. If damp or cold conditions prevail during this period, a warm (80 degrees F.) room indoors will serve equally well as a curing spot.

After curing, your squash will feel perfectly comfortable on your root cellar's higher shelves, where the climate tends to be milder and drier. Shred clean paper or arrange salt hay over the shelves and store the squash side by side, without touching, until needed.

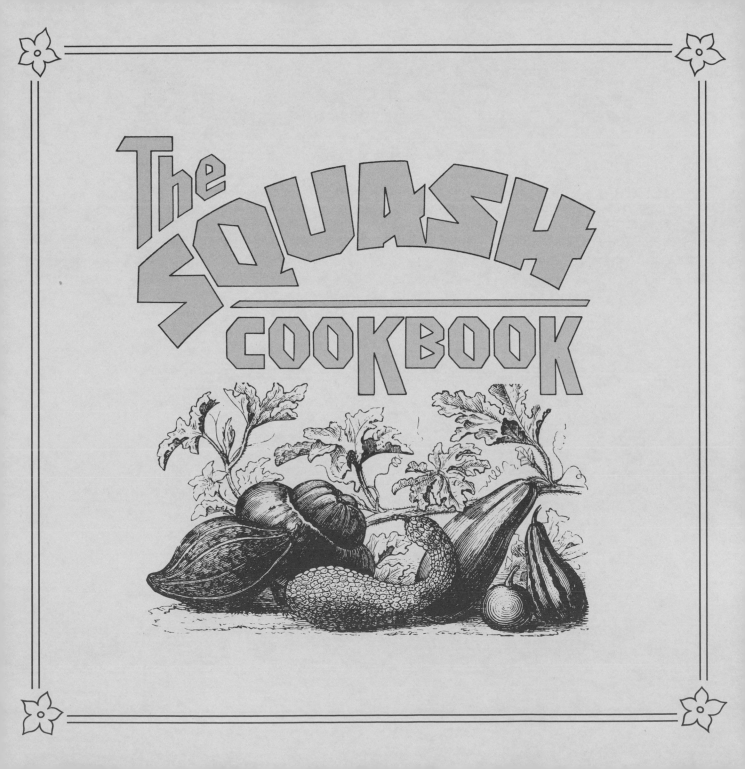

The SQUASH COOKBOOK

SUMMER SQUASH

Whether you are cooking zucchini, crooknecks or straightnecks, scallop types or marrows, preparation of young summer squash is remarkably easy. First, thoroughly scrub each vegetable under running water until the skin feels clean, then cut off and discard the stem end and scrape off the other end. Most vegetables are now ready to be used in any recipe. Only when the skin is unusually tough or the surface feels especially gritty after a good rinsing is it necessary to peel. If you wish, or if your recipe calls for it, you may seed yellow summer squash or zucchini by inserting a vegetable parer carefully into each end and hollowing out the center. This method also works well when preparing a whole summer squash for stuffing.

Depending on the recipe, you may grate or slice the squash, cut it into pieces of various shapes but uniform sizes or leave them whole. All summer squash are full of moisture, some of which must be removed, or the vegetable will swim in its juices and not cook properly. Although other methods may be used, generally the best way to remove moisture is to sprinkle the cut vegetable with salt, let it stand while the salt draws out the juices, and then squeeze between two flat plates, in a ricer or a towel. The reserved juices may be saved and used in soups or sauces.

Of the almost endless ways to cook summer squash, the easiest are the following:

To steam: Arrange the slices, pieces or whole vegetables in a strainer or on a rack over ½ inch of boiling water, cover and steam until barely tender. Drain well, then toss with melted butter or your favorite sauce, and season with finely chopped herbs (in whatever combination pleases you), salt and freshly ground black pepper.

To sauté; Cook in butter over medium-high heat, stirring frequently until barely tender. Season with minced herbs, salt, and freshly ground black pepper.

To parboil: Cook in boiling water to cover until slightly underdone. Drain and freshen in cold water. Drain well.

WINTER SQUASH

The usual method of preparing any variety of winter squash for cooking is to scrub the exterior well, then cut the vegetable in half and scoop out all seeds and stringy fibers. Leave the skin on or remove it before cooking as your recipe dictates or as you prefer. If the squash is

78

small, it may be cooked without cutting, but extra-large squash will need to be cut into pieces of more manageable size if they are to be boiled or steamed. Large squash may be baked without cutting into smaller pieces, but baking time is shorter if these, too, are cut into pieces.

Should your kitchen equipment include a microwave oven, you'll find that a large winter squash will be infinitely easier to cut up or to peel if you puncture the whole vegetable all over and microwave-cook it for 30 seconds or so, turning it several times.

To bake squash halves: Preheat oven to 350 degrees F. Arrange the cleaned, unpeeled vegetables in an appropriately sized pan or casserole. Add boiling water to a depth of ½ inch and bake until the pulp is tender. The halves may be filled with fruit juice, ground-meat combinations or a mixture of hot water or juice, brown sugar and butter. *To steam:* Arrange prepared slices or pieces in a strainer or on a rack over 1 inch of boiling water, cover and steam until barely tender.

Cooked mashed winter squash also makes a superb substitute for mashed potatoes. Season the well-drained pulp with salt and pepper, mash thoroughly or purée in a food processor or blender, then add a pat or two of butter and as much milk or cream as is necessary to bring the vegetable to the consistency you prefer. Judicious use of brown sugar and nutmeg will enhance the flavor.

DRYING WINTER SQUASH

Cut squash into ¼-inch-thick slices, string on twine and hang up to dry in a clean, well-ventilated place. Cover lightly with cheesecloth if there are insects about. To prepare, soak overnight, drain and cook as little as possible.

PREPARING THE SQUASH BLOSSOMS

Those lovely yellow-orange blossoms that appear early on in the life cycle of your squash or pumpkins can provide a delightful bonus for the gardener-cook. When properly prepared and cooked, they are delicious as well as decorative. Each squash and pumpkin plant produces both male and female flowers. Male blossoms predominate at first; then male and female flowers bloom together. Because of their disconcerting tendency to drop off, the earliest male flowers often make novice squash gardeners feel that their plants may never settle down and set fruit. Once this growth pattern is recognized, however, the male blossoms can be turned into delectable stuffed or fried tidbits.

Male blossoms are easy to distinguish . . . they are the ones without the slight bulge or swelling on the long tubular flower base immediately below the petals. Unless you don't mind limiting fruit production, choose male flowers only. Harvest early in the morning, before the sun has forced blossoms to close, or when the vines are shaded. Cut carefully, leaving 1 inch of stem. To keep just-picked blossoms fresh until preparation time, set them in a bowl of water, loosely covered with plastic wrap and refrigerate.

To use, rinse the blossoms under running water, then gently blot dry on paper towels. Remove the stem and stamen from each flower. If your recipe calls for frying the blossoms, carefully cut the base of each and flatten the whole flower before dipping it in batter. To stuff whole blossoms, open the petals and spoon in only enough filling to enable you to close them again, then twist the ends. Squash-blossom fritters may also be prepared with chopped flowers.

VEGETABLE SPAGHETTI · SPAGHETTI SQUASH

Most assuredly the *in* vegetable these last few seasons has been that dazzler of the squash family, the smooth, lemon-blond beauty Vegetable Spaghetti. If avid interest is any indication, this new-squash-in-town will soon be nurtured in as many gardens across the country as its superstar sister, petite zucchini. Curiosity about this mysterious newcomer seemed to reach a fever pitch during last year's harvesting season, when I received a multitude of requests for recipes and Spaghetti Squash Lore buzzed incessantly at lazy late-summer cocktail parties. Hence this special note devoted to one lone variety.

True to the confusing habits of Gourd family members, this unique squash really belongs among the *C. pepo*, but because it has only one crop, it is usually listed along with its winter squash cousins. As is true with so many of those singled out for success, this star on the rise has a particularly interesting history. Although its immediate forebears were European, the squash as it now appears in our gardens comes to us from the exotic Orient. Around the turn of the century, T. Sakata and Co. of Japan began to experiment with an irregularly shaped, light green squash with dark green spots that was known as Spaghetti Squash and was originally cultivated in Italy and Spain. As I gather, some seventy years of trial and error, persistence and perhaps just a dash of good fortune have crystallized into a winning variety which is slightly smaller than the original but which produces more female flowers (and therefore a greater abundance of fruits), matures earlier and is easier to grow. A genuine triumph and one that is sure to bring pride, not to mention ample remuneration, to the company since according to Jun Obara, vice-president of Sakata Seed America, Inc., it is the Sakata strain that all seed companies presently offer.

This novelty squash is best boiled or baked whole. The fruits can reach 8 to 10 inches in diameter, so be sure to have a large pot on hand. Vegetable Spaghetti is a dieter's delight . . . it slightly resembles spaghetti but is minus a good many of the calories. Boil or bake the whole unpeeled squash for 20 to 30 minutes or until tender (extra-large specimens cook faster when pierced at one end). Cut the squash in half and remove the seeds. The inside pulp should separate easily from the skin. Shred with two forks into strands or chop as desired. Season to taste with salt and pepper, then toss with olive oil or melted butter and serve sprinkled with grated cheese, anchovies or pesto. The squash may also be baked in a microwave oven but must be pierced over the whole surface and turned frequently during baking. If you are in a special hurry, you may cut the squash into 1-inch-wide wedges, remove and discard the seeds, and boil or steam until the vegetable is tender. Discard the skin. Serve as above.

This unique squash may be substituted for other varieties in the following recipes, simply by using the cooked, peeled, seeded and shredded or chopped spaghetti squash instead of the variety indicated in the recipe. The results are different—but equally (if not more) delicious.

Fillet of Fish with Zucchini Lorraine
Squash and Chicken with Two Cheeses
Grossmutter's Chicken-Squash Biscuit Pie
Zucchini and Chicken with Sour Cream Sauce
Summer Squash Frittata
Summer Garden Quiche
Zucchini Cheese Pudding
Tomato-Zucchini Omelet Domini
Potato-Squash Cheese Omelet
Eggs Baked in Zucchini
Squash Flower Fritters
Parmesan-Zucchini Pancakes
Lamb-Zucchini Pancakes
Farm-Style Potato-Squash Pancakes

Valley-of-God's-Pleasure Squash Pie
Summer Squash Soufflé Contessa di Pompeii
Sister Endicott's Scalloped Squash
Sour Cream–Squash Pancakes
Summer Squash in Egg Cream Sauce
Sherried Creamed Winter Squash
Rumanian Winter Squash
Summer Squash Salad Mimosa
Summer Squash Slaw
Vegetable Patch Relish
Winter Squash–Green Tomato Relish
Summer Squash–Corn Relish
Zucchini-Cucumber Conserve

NOTES

- All summer squash are presumed to be tender specimens—washed, trimmed and left unpeeled unless otherwise indicated. However, if your garden produces specimens with unusually tough skins or seeds, by all means peel and seed them before using them in recipes.
- All black pepper is freshly ground unless otherwise stated.
- Herbs fresh from your garden add an extra dimension, a more subtle flavor to your squash cookery than their dried counterparts. If fresh herbs are not available, you may substitute ¾ teaspoon dried for each tablespoon garden-picked. Drying concentrates the natural oils of herbs, making small amounts much more powerful. Crush or chop fresh herbs to extract maximum flavor. Dried herbs yield their concentrated fragrance more easily when soaked in oil or vinegar shortly before using.
- All vegetables and fruits should be well washed.
- All recipes that call for mayonnaise will be greatly enhanced if prepared with your own made-at-home mayonnaise.
- Squash sizes are as follows:

Summer Squash
Very small—4″ long x 1″ diameter
Small—6″ long x 1½″ diameter
Medium—8″ long x 2″ diameter
Large—10″ long x 3″ diameter
Very large or oversize—10″ or longer

Winter Squash
Winter squash vary so in size—from petite Acorns to giant Hubbards—that it was necessary to choose one variety to serve as a standard. Therefore, 1 medium winter squash equals the quantity of flesh produced by one 8″ Butternut.

CHEESE-FILLED ZUCCHINI
YIELD: ENOUGH TO SERVE 6

When zucchini are very small—a mere 3 to 4 inches and barely thicker through than your thumb—there is no finer treat to be found in the vegetable world. These young squash gracefully transform a variety of dishes to which their older, and larger, relatives dare not aspire.

6 Very small zucchini, halved lengthwise
12 Ounces cream cheese, softened
2 Tablespoons butter
1 Tablespoon each sour cream and
   mayonnaise
Paprika, curry powder or minced herbs
Minced chives

Directions: Plunge zucchini halves into boiling salted water. Immediately remove pot from stove and let stand 8 minutes. Drain, then freshen in cold running water. Drain well and place cut side down on paper towels. With a small spoon carefully scoop out the centers to form small zucchini "boats" with ⅓-inch thick walls. Blot the cut sides with paper towels and place upside down to drain.

Blend the cream cheese, butter, sour cream and mayonnaise. If the filling is too moist to hold its shape when forced through a pastry tube nozzle, blend in a little more cream cheese. Force the filling through a fluted nozzle of a pastry tube into cavities of the zucchini "boats." Chill. Before serving, cut the boats in half lengthwise to form a slender, cheese-filled zucchini "finger." To serve plain, sprinkle with paprika, curry powder, minced fresh herbs or chives; or try one of the following tasty combinations. Use your imagination to create your own *spécialités de la maison.*

EGG AND ANCHOVY

Flavor the cream cheese filling with 2 teaspoons anchovy paste. Garnish with sieved egg yolk.

BLUE CHEESE AND PECAN

Flavor the cream cheese with 3 tablespoons softened blue cheese. Garnish with finely chopped pecans.

SHRIMP AND DILL

Decorate each "finger" with 3 or 4 tiny cooked shrimp. Garnish with minced dill.

EGG AND OLIVE

Decorate each zucchini "finger" with 3 thin slices pimiento-stuffed olive. Garnish with sieved egg yolk.

PIMIENTO AND CAPER

Decorate each zucchini "finger" with thin pimiento strips alternated with capers. Garnish with minced chives.

SUMMER SQUASH APPETIZER
YIELD: ENOUGH TO SERVE 6

2 Medium-size or 1 oversize summer squash, peeled
and cut in ½-inch cubes (discard seeds)
3 Strips country-cured bacon, diced
2 Medium-size onions, peeled and chopped
3 Ribs celery, trimmed and chopped
3 Tablespoons each honey and catsup
1½ Teaspoons lemon juice
⅓ Teaspoon salt
⅛ Teaspoon ground cinnamon
Generous pinch each ground cloves and marjoram

Directions: Parboil the squash cubes in water to
cover for 3 minutes, then drain well. Sauté the
bacon, onions and celery over medium heat for 5
minutes. Add the squash and remaining ingredients
and cook, stirring continuously, for 5 minutes more
or until the mixture is fairly thick. Serve cold or at
room temperature on crackers or toast points.

ZESTY SUMMER SQUASH DIP
YIELD: ABOUT 1½ CUPS

This refreshing dip plays it straight as a partner for
fresh vegetables at cocktail time, doubles as a topping for cottage cheese or boiled potatoes, or even
serves as a cold soup when thinned with cream.

1 Medium-size summer squash
¼ Cup mild vinegar
⅓ Teaspoon salt
1 Medium-size onion, peeled and grated
¾ Cup sour cream
Tabasco sauce to taste

Directions: Finely grate the squash into a large
shallow bowl. Stir in 3 tablespoons vinegar and
the salt. Fit a small plate over the squash and
weight down with a heavy pot or jar. Let stand for
1 hour, then pour off the accumulated liquid. Repeat this process of weighting and draining until
most of the liquid has drained from the vegetable.
Finally, remove the weight and the plate and stir
the onion, sour cream, Tabasco and the remaining
1 tablespoon of the vinegar into the squash. Cover
and refrigerate the dip until needed.

CANAPÉS LIMOGES

1 Medium-size summer squash, peeled and
very thinly sliced
2 Anchovy fillets, minced
6 Tablespoons sweet butter, softened
Toast rounds (about 1½ inches in diameter)
Cooked, chopped tongue
Mayonnaise
Melted butter
Grated Swiss cheese
Capers

Directions: Salt squash slices and drain on paper
towels. Cut into rounds to fit toast. Mash the
anchovy fillets with the softened butter until well
blended; spread in a thin layer over toast rounds.
Combine cooked, chopped tongue with enough
mayonnaise to bind and spread mixture over toast
rounds. Dip squash rounds in melted butter; set
over tongue mixture. Sprinkle each round with
grated cheese and a caper. Broil until cheese bubbles and lightly browns. Serve hot.

COLD CRAB MEAT AND ZUCCHINI HORS D'OEUVRES
YIELD: ENOUGH TO SERVE 6

12 Very small zucchini*
1 Tablespoon butter
1 Cup crab meat, flaked and picked over
½ Rib celery, trimmed and minced
1 Tablespoon each minced fresh chives and tarragon
⅓ Cup mayonnaise
2 Tablespoons capers

Directions: Cut the zucchini in half lengthwise and remove a little of the pulp in a V down the center of each. Finely chop the removed zucchini pulp and sauté in the butter. Drop the zucchini shells in boiling salted water and parboil 1½ minutes. Do not overcook! Drain the shells and chill well.

Pound the crab meat and cooked zucchini together, and stir in the celery, chives, tarragon and just enough mayonnaise to make a thick mixture. Chill well. Fill the zucchini shells with the crab meat, and top with a thin ribbon of mayonnaise and a caper or two. Serve cold.

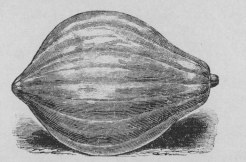

*If very small zucchini are difficult to obtain, substitute small plum tomatoes or cherry tomatoes for 6 of the squash.

ZUCCHINI CIRCLES WITH HORSERADISH CREAM FILLING
YIELD: ENOUGH TO SERVE 6

Here are just a few suggestions for filling these tasty zucchini snacks . . .

6 Small zucchini
2 8-ounce packages cream cheese
2 Tablespoons prepared horseradish
½ Cup chopped pecans
1 Tablespoon minced chives

Directions: Hollow out the centers of the squash with a melon ball cutter, and blanch the squash shells with hot salted water for 8 minutes. Freshen with cold water, drain well and chill. Thoroughly mix the cream cheese, horseradish, pecans and chives. Dry the squash cavities with paper towels, but do not cut the squash. Stuff with the cream cheese mixture and chill well. Cut into ¼-inch slices. Serve cold with a small piping of mayonnaise in the center if desired.

ZUCCHINI CIRCLES WITH CURRIED CRAB FILLING

Follow directions for Zucchini Circles with Horseradish Cream Filling, but substitute 4 ounces flaked crab meat for 4 ounces of the cream cheese and 2 teaspoons curry powder for the horseradish.

ZUCCHINI CIRCLES WITH CAPERED HAM FILLING

Follow directions for Zucchini Circles with Horseradish Cream Filling, but substitute 4 ounces minced cooked ham for 4 ounces of the cream cheese and 2 tablespoons minced capers for the horseradish.

PARMESAN-ZUCCHINI PANCAKES
YIELD: 12 PANCAKES

3 Medium-size zucchini
2 Eggs
3 or 4 Tablespoons all-purpose
    flour
2 Tablespoons grated Parmesan
    cheese
1 Teaspoon chopped fresh chives
¼ Teaspoon minced fresh parsley
1 Small clove garlic, peeled and
    crushed

Directions: Wash and trim zucchini, then finely grate. Drain thoroughly before combining with the eggs, 3 tablespoons of the flour, the cheese, herbs and garlic. If the mixture seems too moist, add the additional tablespoon of flour.

Drop the batter by tablespoons onto a lightly oiled griddle or skillet, and cook until golden brown on both sides, turning once. Serve hot or cold with 1 cup cold sour cream or yogurt mixed with 2 peeled and crushed cloves of garlic.

LAMB-ZUCCHINI PANCAKES
YIELD: ABOUT 24 TINY PANCAKES

Follow directions for Parmesan-Zucchini Pancakes but substitute for the cheese 3 tablespoons *very* finely ground fresh lamb. Drop the batter by *teaspoons* onto a *well*-oiled griddle or skillet, and fry to a golden brown on both sides, turning once. Serve as above.

CURRIED SUMMER SQUASH AND ONION TART
YIELD: ENOUGH TO SERVE 6

2 Small summer squash
3 Medium-size onions, peeled and thinly sliced
3 Tablespoons butter
1 Cup sour cream
2 Eggs
¼ Teaspoon curry powder
⅛ Teaspoon salt
½ Recipe Double-Crust Pie Pastry (see page 193)
2 Strips country-cured bacon, finely chopped

Directions: Preheat oven to 350 degrees F.

Thinly slice the squash and sauté, with the onion, in the butter until the squash is barely tender. Beat together the sour cream, eggs, curry powder and salt, and mix with the vegetable slices. Line a 9-inch pie plate with pie crust, fill with the vegetable mixture and top with minced bacon. Bake about 45 minutes or until filling is firm and bacon is brown. Serve warm, not hot.

SUMMER SQUASH AND ONION TART
YIELD: ENOUGH TO SERVE 4 TO 6

½ Recipe Double-Crust Pie Pastry (see page 193)
2 Small summer squash, sliced
4 Tablespoons butter
7 Small white onions, peeled and sliced
6 Scallions, each with 3 inches green top, sliced
3 Eggs, lightly beaten
1 Cup sour cream

Generous pinch each salt, pepper, nutmeg and thyme
½ Teaspoon curry powder
2 Slices country-cured bacon, minced

Directions: Preheat oven to 400 degrees F.

Sauté the squash slices in 2 tablespoons butter until they are barely tender. Remove with a slotted spoon and place on paper towels to drain. Sauté the onions and scallions in the remaining butter until they are soft. Line a 9-inch pie plate with pastry and crimp the edges. Beat together the eggs, cream and seasonings. Arrange the squash and onion slices over the pastry, and pour the egg mixture over all. Top with bacon and bake for 35 minutes or until the center is firm. Serve warm.

ZUCCHINI TARTLETS
YIELD: 6 TARTLETS

---

3 Shallots, peeled and minced
1 Very small zucchini, minced
3 Tablespoons lightly salted butter
1½ Cups Swiss cheese, cut into ¼-inch dice
½ Recipe Double-Crust Pie Pastry (see page 193)
6 Egg yolks
2 Cups heavy cream
  Pinch each salt and nutmeg
6 Teaspoons sweet butter

Directions: Preheat oven to 350 degrees F.

Sauté the shallots and zucchini in 2 tablespoons of the salted butter until lightly browned. Cool. Line 6 individual tartlet pans with pie dough rolled very thin and brush with butter. Beat together the egg yolks, cream, salt and nutmeg. Sprinkle the zucchini mixture and the Swiss cheese over the bottoms of the tarts, and pour the custard over both. Place 1 teaspoon sweet butter in the center of each tartlet and bake 25 to 30 minutes or until the custard is firm. Serve immediately.

TOMATO-AND-ZUCCHINI-STUFFED EGGS
YIELD: ENOUGH TO SERVE 6

---

12 Hard-cooked eggs
1½ Cups finely chopped zucchini
2 Large ripe tomatoes, peeled, seeded and finely chopped
2½ Tablespoons butter
2 Teaspoons minced fresh dill
2 Teaspoons sour cream
2 Teaspoons mayonnaise
  Salt to taste

Directions: Cut eggs in half lengthwise. Separate yolks from whites. Mash yolks and set aside.

Sauté the zucchini and tomatoes in butter until thick and moisture free. Cool to room temperature. Stir in mashed egg yolks and dill. Add enough mayonnaise and sour cream to flavor but not to thin the mixture, which should be stiff enough to hold its shape. Salt to taste. Spoon the mixture into the egg-white halves, chill and serve.

COLD ZUCCHINI AND TOMATO HORS D'OEUVRE
YIELD: ENOUGH TO SERVE 6

2½ Pounds small zucchini, peeled
1½ Pounds medium-size ripe tomatoes, peeled and
    seeded
3 Large garlic cloves, peeled and minced
3½ Tablespoons olive oil
2 Tablespoons lemon juice
1 Tablespoon each minced fresh tarragon and chervil
    Salt and black pepper
1 Large lemon, with skin and seeds removed
    (be certain to cut away all the bitter white
    underskin)
1 Tablespoon minced fresh thyme leaves

Directions: Cut zucchini into ½-inch slices and
tomatoes into coarse dice. Sauté vegetables and
garlic in olive oil for 1 minute. Add lemon juice,
tarragon, chervil, and salt and pepper to taste. Bring
to boil, then lower the heat and simmer, uncovered,
until zucchini are tender and most of the juices
have evaporated. Chop lemon, stir into the vegetable mixture, and chill well. Sprinkle with thyme
leaves before serving cold.

SQUASH WITH MISO
YIELD: ENOUGH TO SERVE 6

3 Tablespoons almond kernel oil
1 Large summer or winter squash, peeled, seeded and
    cut in ¾-inch cubes
2 Tablespoons each granulated sugar and red miso*
1 Tablespoon vinegar
4 Tablespoons water
8 Scallions, each with 3 inches green top, minced

Directions: Parboil winter squash cubes 8 minutes.
Dry well.

Using a Teflon skillet, heat the oil over high
flame and stir in the squash cubes; lower the heat
to medium and cook for 5 minutes, stirring occasionally. Mix the sugar, miso and vinegar with the
water and pour over the squash. Cook over low
heat, stirring continuously, for 3 or 4 minutes. Add
the scallions and stir for 1 minute more, or until
the mixture is fairly thick. Serve hot or cold as an
hors d'oeuvre.

*A soybean paste available at health food stores or Oriental
groceries.

MARINATED MUSHROOMS AND SUMMER SQUASH
YIELD: ABOUT 4 CUPS

2 Pounds fresh mushrooms, thinly sliced
3 Small summer squash, thinly sliced
½ Cup olive oil
   Juice of 1 lemon
2 Medium-size onions, peeled and thinly sliced
2 Cloves garlic, peeled and minced
3 Bay leaves
½ Teaspoon each black pepper, marjoram and thyme
3 Cups canned Italian plum tomatoes in tomato sauce
1 Cup red wine vinegar
1 Teaspoon granulated sugar
   Dash hot pepper sauce
   Salt
2 Tablespoons each minced chives and parsley

Directions: Sauté together the mushrooms and squash, half of each at one time, in the oil until lightly browned. As each batch is finished, remove with a slotted spoon and place in a large bowl. Sprinkle the mixture with the lemon juice and set aside. Add the onions and garlic to the oil in the skillet and cook until the onions are translucent. Stir in the bay leaves, pepper, marjoram and thyme, then cook for 1 minute more. Drain and chop the tomatoes, reserving the sauce. Add the tomatoes to the onion mixture, along with ¾ cup of the reserved tomato sauce, vinegar, sugar and hot pepper sauce. Bring the mixture to a boil, then lower the heat and simmer for 20 minutes.

Pour the tomato mixture over the reserved mushrooms and squash and season to taste with salt. Cool to room temperature, cover and refrigerate for at least 12 hours. Bring to room temperature before serving with rye or pumpernickel squares, buttered and sprinkled with chives and parsley.

DRIED BEANS AND SUMMER SQUASH IN GARLIC OIL CARQUEIRANNE
YIELD: ENOUGH TO SERVE 6

¾ Cup each small dried white kidney beans and dried green flageolets (or 1 20-ounce can each)
   Salt
3 Small zucchini or yellow summer squash, thinly sliced
2 Cloves garlic, crushed
   Black pepper
⅓ Cup olive oil
   Pimiento
⅓ Cup minced fresh parsley

Directions: In separate saucepans, soak each variety of dried beans for 1 to 2 hours in enough water to cover the beans by 1 inch. Add 1 tablespoon salt to each pan of beans and simmer until tender, then drain well and set aside to cool. (If using canned beans, place in a strainer and rinse thoroughly under running cold water, then drain well.)

Combine the beans and squash slices in a serving dish. Crush the garlic with a generous pinch of salt, add black pepper to taste and blend with the olive oil. Pour the dressing over the beans and squash; allow to marinate in a cool place for at least 1 hour. Serve garnished with thin strips of pimiento and a sprinkling of parsley.

SUMMER SQUASH SOUP SMYRNA
YIELD: ENOUGH TO SERVE 6 TO 8

2 Medium-size summer squash
3 Cups plain yogurt
4 Tablespoons each lemon juice and vinegar
3 Tablespoons olive oil
1½ Tablespoons curry powder
3 Cups tomato juice
  Salt and black pepper
6 Tablespoons minced fresh parsley

Directions: Seed and chop the squash. Simmer until tender in enough water to barely cover. Drain well, then purée. In a large bowl, beat the yogurt until smooth, then mix in the lemon juice, vinegar, olive oil and curry; stir in the squash and tomato juice. Season the soup to taste with salt and pepper, and refrigerate, covered, for 4 hours. Serve cold, garnished with minced parsley.

MOTHER'S YELLOW SQUASH SOUP
YIELD: ENOUGH TO SERVE 6

5 Small yellow squash, cut in 1-inch pieces
1 Cup fresh or frozen peas
1 Clove garlic, peeled and minced
¼ Teaspoon salt
⅛ Teaspoon each oregano and chervil
5½ Cups chicken broth
1 Cup sour cream
2 Teaspoons minced fresh dill

Directions: Place the squash, peas, garlic, salt, oregano and chervil in a large soup kettle. Add the broth and cook, covered, over medium heat for 30 minutes, or until the vegetables are very soft. Purée the soup in a food processor or blender, or force through a fine sieve. Cool to room temperature, then stir in the sour cream until smooth and well blended. Chill thoroughly before serving cold, garnished with dill.

MARY BRECKENDORF'S CREAM OF ZUCCHINI SOUP
YIELD: ENOUGH TO SERVE 6 TO 8

5 Tablespoons butter
2 Medium-size zucchini, coarsely chopped
2 Medium-size carrots, scraped and sliced
2 Medium-size onions, peeled and thinly sliced
1 Teaspoon salt
½ Cup water
4 Tablespoons all-purpose flour
  A pinch each nutmeg and black pepper
5 Cups cold milk
⅔ Cup heavy cream
1 Teaspoon minced chives

Directions: Melt 3 tablespoons butter in a large skillet; add the vegetables, ½ teaspoon salt and the water. Cover the skillet and simmer for 25 minutes, stirring occasionally.

Melt the remaining butter in a heavy saucepan, add the flour, ½ teaspoon salt, the pepper and nutmeg, and stir until smooth. Add the cold milk, all at one time, and bring to a boil over medium heat, stirring constantly. Lower the heat, cover the sauce and simmer for 5 minutes.

Reserve and coarsely chop ¼ cup cooked carrots. Purée the remaining cooked vegetables and stir into the white sauce. Simmer over *very* low heat for 30 minutes.

Just prior to serving, heat the soup and stir in as much heavy cream as necessary to bring the soup to the consistency you prefer. Garnish with reserved carrots and chives. Serve hot.

COLD CREAMED ZUCCHINI SOUP WITH GARDEN VEGETABLES
YIELD: ENOUGH TO SERVE 6 TO 8

1 Recipe Mary Breckendorf's Cream of Zucchini
   Soup (see page 90)
2 Large tomatoes, peeled, seeded and
   coarsely chopped
4 Scallions, each with 3-inch green top,
   coarsely chopped

Directions: Chill the soup. At serving time, stir the well-drained tomatoes and the scallions into the soup. Garnish with carrots and chives. Serve cold.

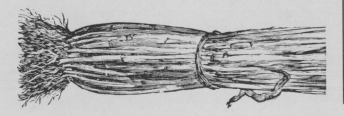

COLD CREAMED ZUCCHINI SOUP WITH HARD-COOKED EGGS AND SHRIMP
YIELD: ENOUGH TO SERVE 6 TO 8

1 Recipe Mary Breckendorf's Cream of Zucchini Soup
   (see page 90)
3 Hard-cooked eggs, shelled and coarsely chopped
20 Cooked shrimp, shelled, cleaned and coarsely chopped

Directions: Reserve ¼ cup cooked shrimp. Stir the remaining shrimp, the eggs and all of the carrots into the soup. Chill the soup and serve cold, garnished with chives and the reserved shrimp.

WINTER SQUASH BISQUE

Prepare one recipe Mary Breckendorf's Cream of Zucchini Soup (see page 90), but substitute 2 small or 1 medium-size acorn squash for the zucchini. Serve hot or cold.

CHILLED ZUCCHINI AND ALMOND SOUP NIVERNAIS
YIELD: ENOUGH TO SERVE 6

1 Large onion, peeled and sliced
3 Small zucchini, thinly sliced
2 Cups blanched almonds, grated or finely chopped
4 Cups chicken broth
   Salt and white pepper to taste
⅛ Teaspoon each nutmeg and cayenne pepper
2 Cups light cream
1 Cup whipped cream
2 Tablespoons minced chives

Directions: Simmer onion and zucchini until tender in chicken broth to barely cover. Purée. In a large saucepan simmer the purée, almonds, remaining chicken broth and spices for 10 minutes. Stir in the light cream and simmer 3 minutes without boiling. Refrigerate several hours or overnight. To serve, top each plate of soup with a dollop of whipped cream and garnish with 1 teaspoon chives.

QUICK SWEET WINTER SQUASH SOUP
YIELD: ENOUGH TO SERVE 6

3½ Cups Best Winter Squash Purée
    (see page 142)
4½ Cups light cream
  5 Tablespoons honey
  2 Tablespoons butter
  3 Tablespoons light brown sugar
  1 Teaspoon salt
  ¼ Teaspoon each ground cinnamon,
      mace and nutmeg
  1 Orange, juice and zest*
    Whipped cream
    (optional)

Directions: Combine the squash purée, 2 cups of the cream, the honey and butter, and cook over low heat, stirring continuously, until warm.

Mix together the spices and sugar; add to the squash mixture and simmer gently without allowing to boil.

Grate the orange zest and squeeze and strain the juice, then add both a bit at a time to the hot soup,

*The thin outer skin of the fruit, with none of the bitter white underskin included.

blending well. Allow the soup to simmer for 10 minutes, then remove from heat and cool to room temperature.

Stir in the remaining cream and chill well. Serve cold, with dollops of whipped cream if desired.

MINESTRA DI PASTA E ZUCCHINI
YIELD: ENOUGH TO SERVE 6

½ Pound smoked ham, finely
    chopped
  1 Large onion, peeled and coarsely
    chopped
  2 Large cloves garlic, peeled
    and minced
  2 Tablespoons butter
  2 Tablespoons tomato paste
  8 Cups water
1½ Cups of your favorite pasta
  5 Small zucchini, cut in
    ¼-inch slices
  ¼ Cup grated Parmesan cheese
  4 Scallions, each with 3 inches green
    top, chopped

Directions: In a heavy soup kettle sauté half the ham, the onion and the garlic in the butter until the vegetables are wilted. Stir in the tomato paste and the water, and bring to a boil. Add the pasta, lower the heat and cook until the pasta is nearly tender. Add the zucchini and cook a minute or two (the slices should still have a bit of "crunch"). Ladle the hot soup into a tureen; garnish with the remaining chopped ham, the Parmesan cheese and the chopped scallions.

SCOTS SQUASH AND HAM SOUP THICKENED WITH OATMEAL
YIELD: ENOUGH TO SERVE 6 TO 8

To transform this into a quick soup, simply substitute boiling beef stock for the ham bone and water, omit the 2-hour cooking time and begin instructions at paragraph two.

1 Meaty ham bone
8 Cups water
3 Cloves garlic, peeled and crushed
2 Medium-size summer squash, coarsely chopped
3 Tablespoons butter
8 Tablespoons quick-cooking rolled oats
  Salt and black pepper to taste

Directions: Place the hambone and water in a soup kettle and bring to a boil. Skim off the froth, lower heat, cover and simmer for 2 hours. Remove the hambone and chop the meat.

Sauté the garlic and squash in the butter for 5 minutes. Stir the vegetables into the boiling stock. Cover and boil for 15 minutes. Add the oats and ham, and boil for 10 minutes more. Adjust seasoning and serve hot.

SQUASH SOUP WITH YOGURT AND MINT DARDANELLES
YIELD: ENOUGH TO SERVE 6

5 Small yellow summer squash or zucchini, thinly sliced
2 Tablespoons butter
6 Scallions, each with 3 inches green top, finely chopped
8 Cups chicken broth
1½ Teaspoons vegetable salt seasoning
⅛ Teaspoon ground nutmeg
6 Tablespoons plain yogurt
2 Tablespoons minced fresh mint leaves

Directions: Sauté the squash in the butter for 2 minutes, stirring occasionally. Add the scallions, broth and spices, and simmer until squash slices are barely tender—about 5 to 10 minutes. Serve hot, topped with yogurt and mint.

ZUCCHINI SOUP REGINA
YIELD: ENOUGH TO SERVE 6

1 Small chicken, cut in pieces
4½ Cups water
3½ Cups beef broth
3 Very small zucchini, thinly sliced
1 Cup blanched almonds
3 Slices bread, trimmed
1 Hard-cooked egg, shelled and quartered
  Garlic Croutons (see page 193)
  Grated Parmesan cheese

Directions: Cover the chicken with the water, and cook over low heat until tender. Mix 3½ cups of the chicken stock with the beef broth, and add the zucchini slices. Reserve chicken meat and remaining chicken stock.

In a food processor or blender whirl the almonds, boned chicken meat, bread, egg and ½ cup reserved chicken stock until ingredients are minced and well mixed. Place the meat mixture in the bottom of a soup tureen. Bring the broth and zucchini to a boil; ladle the steaming soup into the tureen and top with croutons. Serve immediately with grated cheese.

PINEAPPLE–WINTER SQUASH SOUP
YIELD: ENOUGH TO SERVE 6 TO 8

1 Large onion, peeled and chopped
2 Tablespoons minced fresh parsley
6 Tablespoons butter
3 Cups Best Winter Squash Purée (see page 142)
3 Cups canned, crushed pineapple with juice
⅛ Teaspoon each allspice, cinnamon and nutmeg
1 Cup chicken broth
4 Tablespoons cornstarch
2 Cups milk
2 Cups heavy cream
 Salt

Directions: Sauté the onions and parsley in the butter until the onions turn golden and transparent. Stir in the squash purée, pineapple and spices; simmer for 15 minutes, stirring occasionally, then add the chicken broth and simmer the mixture, covered, for 30 minutes.

Blend the cornstarch into the milk, stirring until smooth. Mix 1 cup of the hot squash mixture into the cornstarch-milk mixture and stir into the rest of the soup. Cook over medium heat, stirring continuously, until the soup comes to a boil, then lower the heat and stir in the cream to the consistency you prefer. Season to taste with salt and serve hot, topping each serving with a dollop of whipped cream. Delicious cold, too.

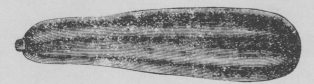

GARDEN FAVORITE SUMMER SQUASH AND LETTUCE SOUP
YIELD: ENOUGH TO SERVE 6 TO 8

1½ Cups grated summer squash
1½ Cups shredded iceberg lettuce
 3 Tablespoons butter
 8 Cups chicken broth
 6 Egg yolks, lightly beaten in
   a large bowl
½ Cup sunflower kernels
 3 Scallions, each with 3 inches green top, cut
   in ¼-inch pieces
 1 Cup sour cream (optional)

Directions: Sauté the squash and lettuce in the butter for 6 minutes, stirring constantly. Bring the broth to a boil, stir in the vegetables and boil 5 minutes. Stir the hot soup into the egg yolks and serve immediately, topped with sunflower kernels, scallions and a dollop of sour cream.

YEMENITE SOUP
YIELD: ENOUGH TO SERVE 6 TO 8

1½ Pounds boneless veal, cut in 1-inch cubes
8 Cups water
6 Small onions, peeled and cut in quarters
2 Medium-size tomatoes, peeled, seeded and cut in quarters
1 Cup minced fresh spinach
1 Clove garlic, peeled and minced
½ Teaspoon each salt and black pepper
1½ Teaspoons each ground coriander, cumin, fenugreek and turmeric
3 Medium-size zucchini, cut in quarters
1 Medium-size carrot, scraped and cut in 1-inch pieces
2 Medium-size potatoes, peeled and cut in eighths
⅓ Cup uncooked rice

Directions: In a large soup kettle, cover the veal with the water and bring to a boil; lower the heat, partially cover the kettle and simmer for 30 minutes. Skim off any foam. Add the onions, tomatoes, spinach, garlic and seasonings, then cover again and simmer for 20 minutes.

Add the remaining ingredients and allow the soup to simmer for 25 minutes more, or until the vegetables and rice are tender. Serve at once.

OLD COUNTRY TOMATO-ZUCCHINI SOUP
YIELD: ENOUGH TO SERVE 8

2 Medium-size onions, peeled and chopped
2 Ribs celery, chopped
⅓ Pound country-cured bacon, chopped
3 Tablespoons olive oil
1 Cup uncooked rice
5 Ripe tomatoes, peeled, seeded and finely chopped
½ Teaspoon granulated sugar
6½ Cups beef broth or bouillon
5 Small zucchini, thinly sliced
3 Tablespoons minced fresh chives
Salt and black pepper
1½ Cups grated Parmesan cheese

Directions: Sauté the onions, celery and bacon in olive oil until the onions are golden. Add rice and sauté for 3 minutes, stirring once or twice. Stir in tomatoes, sugar and broth. Cook over medium heat until the rice is barely tender. Stir in the zucchini and chives. Cover and cook the soup for 5 minutes, then remove from heat and let stand for 5 minutes more. The zucchini should still have a bit of "crunch." Season to taste with salt and pepper before ladling into soup bowls and serving with grated cheese on the side.

VEGETARIAN BOUILLABAISSE
YIELD: ENOUGH TO SERVE 4

2 Tablespoons vegetable oil
1 Large onion, peeled and coarsely
   chopped
2 Small zucchini, cut in ¼-inch slices
2 Large potatoes, peeled and thickly sliced
3½ Cups boiling water
1 Cup shelled peas
1 Teaspoon minced fresh thyme
  Generous pinch saffron
  Salt
2 1-inch strips orange zest*
4 Eggs
  Garlic Croutons
   (see page 193)

Directions: Heat the oil in a large, deep skillet and sauté the squash and onion until the onion is transparent. Add the potato slices and cook 2 minutes on each side. Do not let them brown. Pour the boiling water over the cooked vegetables; stir in the peas, thyme, saffron, salt to taste and orange zest. Cover the skillet and cook over medium heat until the potatoes are barely tender.

Push the vegetables aside and crack 1 egg into the broth. Repeat with the remaining eggs, making room for each by pushing the vegetables aside. Cover and cook only long enough for the eggs to poach as you like them. To serve, place one egg in each soup bowl, ladle soup and vegetables over each and top with croutons.

*The thin outer skin of the fruit, with none of the bitter white underskin included.

POOR MAN'S GARDEN CHOWDER
YIELD: ENOUGH TO SERVE 6 TO 8

6 Strips country-cured bacon
2 Medium-size onions, peeled and sliced
6 Frankfurters, sliced
2 Medium-size summer squash, peeled and
   cut into ½-inch dice
1 Large potato, peeled and sliced
1 Cup corn, cut from the cob
  Salt
½ Teaspoon black pepper
¾ Teaspoon caraway seeds
2 Teaspoons minced fresh thyme
1 Teaspoon minced fresh basil
5 Cups beef broth
1 Cup dry white wine
  Milk

Directions: Crisply brown the bacon in a deep, heavy kettle and set it aside. Sauté the onions and franks in the bacon fat until the onions are golden. Stir in the squash, sauté 5 minutes and then add the potatoes, corn, salt to taste, pepper, caraway seeds, thyme, basil and beef broth. Bring to a boil, cover and simmer for 30 minutes or until the potatoes are tender. Stir in the wine and enough milk to bring the soup to the consistency you prefer. Heat but do not boil. Serve immediately, sprinkled with the reserved chopped bacon.

COUNTRY-STYLE VEGETABLE SOUP
YIELD: ENOUGH TO SERVE 6 TO 8

6 Tablespoons butter
3 Medium-size carrots, scraped and chopped
1 Leek, coarsely chopped
1 Rib celery, chopped
1 Medium-size onion, peeled and coarsely chopped
1 Clove garlic, peeled and minced
4 Medium-size tomatoes, peeled, seeded and chopped
1 Tablespoon minced fresh parsley
¼ Pound salt pork, finely chopped
1 Large potato, peeled and diced
¾ Cup dried lentils
6½ Cups beef broth or bouillon
Salt and black pepper
2 Small yellow summer squash, coarsely chopped
2 Small zucchini, coarsely chopped
1 Cup shelled green peas
½ Cup pastina
Croutons (see page 193)

Directions: In a deep soup kettle heat the butter and sauté the carrots, leeks, celery, onions and garlic until the onions turn golden. Add the tomatoes, parsley and salt pork; cook for 5 minutes, stirring occasionally. Stir in the potatoes and lentils.

Cover the kettle and simmer the vegetables over very low heat for 20 minutes, stirring occasionally. Add the broth, season to taste with salt and pepper, and bring the soup to a boil. Lower the heat, re-cover the kettle and allow the soup to simmer for 1½ hours, stirring from time to time; add hot water as necessary if the soup becomes too thick.

Add the yellow squash, zucchini, peas and pastina, and cook 30 minutes more. Serve piping hot, garnished with croutons.

IL MINESTRONE DI BEATRICE
YIELD: ENOUGH TO SERVE 6 TO 8

½ Cup butter
3 Medium-size carrots, peeled and finely chopped
1 Leek, trimmed and finely chopped
2 Ribs celery, trimmed and finely chopped
1 Medium-size onion, peeled and finely chopped
2 Cloves garlic, peeled and minced
1 Thin slice lard, finely chopped
3 Large tomatoes, peeled, seeded and sliced
2 Tablespoons minced fresh Italian parsley
4 Small zucchini, cut in ¼-inch dice
2 Large potatoes, peeled and cut in ½-inch dice
½ Pound fresh white beans or 1 small can white beans
½ Pound fresh green peas, shelled
½ Cup dried lentils
8 Cups water
2 Beef bouillon cubes
¼ Teaspoon fennel seeds
Salt and black pepper
8 Croutons (see page 193)
Grated Parmesan cheese

Directions: In a large soup kettle heat the butter and gently sauté the carrots, leeks, celery, onions and garlic until the onions turn golden. Add the lard, sliced tomatoes and parsley, and cook for 5 minutes, stirring once or twice. Add the zucchini, potatoes, beans, peas, lentils and 1 cup water to the vegetables in the kettle, then cover and cook over very low heat for 20 minutes, stirring occasionally.

Add the remaining 7 cups water, bouillon cubes, fennel seeds, and salt and pepper to taste; bring the soup to a boil and allow to boil for 5 minutes, then lower the heat, cover the kettle and simmer the soup for 2 hours, stirring occasionally. If too much water evaporates during the cooking, a bit more may be added. Serve the soup piping hot, garnished with croutons and accompanied by a bowl of grated Parmesan.

MARY ELLA'S DILLED TOMATO-SQUASH SOUP
YIELD: ENOUGH TO SERVE 6

---

1 Oversize summer squash, peeled and cut in 1-inch cubes

3 Tablespoons each butter and vegetable oil

6 Medium-size ripe tomatoes, peeled, seeded and chopped

2 Medium-size onions, peeled and finely chopped

1½ Cloves garlic, peeled and minced

2 Bay leaves, crumbled
Pinch marjoram

8 Cups beef broth or bouillon

⅓ Cup uncooked rice
Salt and black pepper

½ Pound finely ground veal

⅛ Teaspoon each nutmeg and oregano
Flour
Garlic Croutons (see page 193)

2 Tablespoons minced fresh dill

Directions: Sauté squash pieces in butter and oil, covered, for 30 minutes or until lightly browned, stirring frequently. Add tomatoes. Reserve 2 teaspoons chopped onions, then add remaining onions to the squash-tomato mixture, along with the garlic, bay leaves and marjoram. Cook over low heat for 15 minutes, stirring occasionally. Add broth and rice, and season to taste with salt and pepper. Simmer soup, covered, for 40 minutes, then bring to a boil.

Mix together the veal, reserved onions, nutmeg, oregano, and salt and pepper to taste. Shape into ½-inch balls, roll in flour and cook in the boiling soup for 15 minutes. Serve hot, garnished with croutons and dill.

CREAM OF SQUASH SOUP

An elegant but easy cream soup may be quickly prepared by combining either Summer Squash Purée (see page 133) or Best Winter Squash Purée (see page 142) with light cream. Simply dilute the purée with enough cream to bring the mixture to the consistency you prefer. Season to taste with nutmeg, thyme, salt and white pepper. Serve hot or cold, garnished with minced fresh herbs.

EVE'S SUMMER SQUASH AND SHRIMP IN CREAM
YIELD: ENOUGH TO SERVE 6

1½ Pounds shrimp, shelled and deveined
 3 Tablespoons butter
 1 Small onion, peeled and finely chopped
 3 Small summer squash (zucchini, yellow summer, patty pan, etc.) sliced
 1 Cup shelled small peas
 2 Teaspoons minced fresh marjoram
18 Black olives, pitted and sliced
1½ Cups heavy cream
 3 Tablespoons buttered bread crumbs

Directions: In a large skillet sauté the shrimp in the butter until bright pink on all sides. Add the onion, squash, peas and marjoram, and cook over low heat for 4 minutes, stirring occasionally. Stir in the olives and cream, and simmer until the peas are tender. Spoon into a shallow gratin dish, sprinkle with the bread crumbs and place under the broiler until lightly browned. Serve immediately.

ZUCCHINI BOATS WITH CRAB MEAT MORNAY
YIELD: ENOUGH TO SERVE 6

 3 Medium-size zucchini, split lengthwise
 3 Shallots, peeled and finely chopped
 1 Pound cooked crab meat, flaked and picked over
 2 Tablespoons butter
1⅓ Cups Mornay Sauce (see page 189)
 ½ Teaspoon Dijon-type mustard
 2 Tablespoons whipped cream
 ¼ Cup grated Parmesan cheese

Directions: Scoop out the centers of the zucchini to form 6 boat-shaped shells with walls ½ inch thick. Finely chop the scooped-out zucchini pulp. Drop the zucchini shells into boiling salted water and parboil 5 to 8 minutes or until barely tender. Do not overcook! Drain the shells.

Sauté the shallots and chopped zucchini in the butter for 3 minutes, add the crab meat and stir over low heat for 5 minutes more. Set aside ¼ cup Mornay Sauce and stir the remainder, along with the mustard, into the crab meat. Spoon the crab meat into the shells and arrange the boats in an ovenproof serving dish. Fold the reserved Mornay Sauce and the whipped cream together, and spread the mixture over the crab meat. Sprinkle with Parmesan and brown under the broiler. Serve immediately.

SPAGHETTI WITH ZUCCHINI AND OYSTER SAUCE
YIELD: ENOUGH TO SERVE 6

1 Pound thin spaghetti
4 Very small zucchini, sliced
3 Shallots, peeled and minced
1 Tablespoon minced fresh thyme
3 Tablespoons butter
2 Dozen shucked small oysters,
    with their juices
1 Cup white wine
1 Cup heavy cream
2 Tablespoons minced parsley

Directions: Boil the spaghetti in salted water until tender but still firm. Drain well and keep warm. Sauté the zucchini, shallots and thyme in the butter until the squash slices are not quite tender. Remove the vegetables with a slotted spoon and set aside. Simmer the wine for several minutes, add the oyster juices and simmer several minutes more. Mix in cream and simmer, stirring occasionally, until the sauce thickens. Add the oysters and vegetables, and cook until the edges of the oysters curl. Spoon the sauce over the spaghetti and serve immediately, sprinkled with parsley.

TRUITE FARCIE EN CROÛTE
YIELD: ENOUGH TO SERVE 6

6 Shallots, peeled and minced
2 Small zucchini, minced
1 Tablespoon minced fresh dill
3 Tablespoons butter
1 Cup boned, flaked flounder
2 Tablespoons heavy cream
    Salt and black pepper to taste
6 Medium trout, cleaned and with backbones removed
    Double recipe Double-Crust Pie Pastry (see page 193)
1 Egg yolk
    Milk or cream

Directions: Sauté the shallots, zucchini and dill in the hot butter until the squash is tender. Stir in the flounder, heavy cream and salt and pepper, and cook 1 minute longer. Divide the stuffing equally to fill the trout.

Preheat oven to 425 degrees F.

Roll out the pastry and cut it into 6 pieces, each large enough to envelop 1 fish. Place 1 fish on each piece of dough, shape the dough around the fish (molding it to shape) and place the pastry-wrapped fish on a baking sheet. Cut any remaining dough into small crescents shaped to resemble scales, moisten lightly and arrange attractively over the tail of each fish. Mix the egg yolk with a bit of milk or cream, and brush the glaze over the tops of all the dough-wrapped fish. Bake for 15 minutes, then lower the heat to 350 degrees F. and bake 15 to 20 minutes longer, or until the crust is crisp and browned. Serve immediately.

TROUT AND ZUCCHINI IN HERBED WINE SAUCE TANTE CHRISTINE
YIELD: ENOUGH TO SERVE 6

3 Shallots, peeled and
   chopped
1 Large clove garlic, peeled and
   minced
2 Teaspoons each fresh marjoram, sage,
   thyme and rosemary, minced
3 Teaspoons fresh fennel
8 Tablespoons (1 stick) butter
6 Small zucchini, cut in ¼-inch slices
6 Trout, cleaned
   Salt
1 Cup dry white wine
1 Teaspoon beurre manié
¾ Cup heavy cream
¼ Teaspoon lemon juice
   Salt and black pepper

Directions: Place the shallots, garlic, herbs and half the butter in a large skillet. Stir in the zucchini slices and sauté over low heat until the vegetable is barely tender (about 3 minutes). Using a slotted spoon, remove the zucchini slices to a serving platter and keep them warm. Melt the remainder of the butter in the skillet, arrange the trout in the pan, pour over the wine, cover and simmer the fish for 4 to 5 minutes or until tender. Carefully transfer the fish to the serving platter and arrange attractively over the zucchini slices.

Strain the sauce into a small saucepan, reduce to ⅔ cup and thicken slightly with beurre manié.

Add the cream and stir the sauce over low heat for 5 minutes (do not let boil). Season to taste with salt and pepper and stir in a few drops of lemon juice.* Pour the sauce over the fish and vegetable. Serve immediately, garnished with chopped fresh fennel.

COUNTRY GARDEN FISH STEW
YIELD: ENOUGH TO SERVE 6

2 Tablespoons each butter and olive oil
2 Large onions, peeled and coarsely chopped
3 Large garlic cloves, peeled and crushed
1 Bay leaf
3 Small summer squash, sliced (or 1 medium-size
   winter squash, peeled, seeded and cut into
   ⅓-inch cubes)
1 Large tomato, peeled, seeded and
   chopped
1 Large potato, peeled and cubed
½ Cup dry white wine
2 Tablespoons minced fresh parsley
1 Tablespoon minced fresh marjoram
2 Whole cloves
   White pepper
5½ Cups water
   Salt
1½ Pounds swordfish, boned and
   cut in cubes
   Croutons (see page 193)
   Grated Parmesan cheese

*If liquid accumulates on the platter, blot it up with paper towels before adding the sauce.

Directions: Heat the butter and olive oil together in a deep skillet and sauté the onions, garlic and bay leaf until the onions are golden. Stir in the squash, tomatoes, potatoes, wine, 1 tablespoon parsley, marjoram, cloves and white pepper to taste, then add the water and salt to taste and bring the mixture to a boil.

Lower the heat and simmer for 20 minutes, or until the cubed squash and potatoes are tender. Add the fish and continue to cook over low heat for 6 to 7 minutes, or until the fish flakes when tested with a fork. Garnish with croutons and the remaining parsley; serve at once, with cheese on the side.

FILLET OF FISH WITH ZUCCHINI LORRAINE
YIELD: ENOUGH TO SERVE 6

6 Fish fillets (sole or flounder are best)
6 Very small zucchini, thinly sliced
Butter
1¾ Cups cream
2 Teaspoons flour kneaded with 2 teaspoons butter
2 Large egg yolks, lightly beaten
2 Shallots, peeled and minced
1 Teaspoon each minced tarragon, chervil and parsley
1 Teaspoon lemon zest*
1 Teaspoon Dijon-type mustard
1 Large lemon

Directions: Prepare the fillets "as you like them"— either sautéed in butter or poached in white wine. Place fillets on a platter and keep them warm. Sauté the zucchini slices in 2 tablespoons butter until barely tender and arrange over the fillets. Keep warm. Heat the cream slightly, blend in the flour and butter, add the shallots, herbs, lemon zest and mustard, and stir over low heat until the sauce is thick. Beat in the egg yolks and stir over very low heat until the sauce is thick, but do not let it boil or it will curdle. Stir in the juice from the lemon, spoon the sauce over the hot fish and vegetables, and serve immediately.

*The thin outer skin of the fruit, with none of the bitter white underskin included.

SQUASH AND CHICKEN WITH TWO CHEESES
YIELD: ENOUGH TO SERVE 6

This dish has a marvelous garden-fresh taste as is, but it may also be enhanced with fresh herbs such as thyme, sage, marjoram or rosemary.

2 3-Pound chickens, cut in quarters
  Water
3 Tablespoons butter
2 Onions, peeled and sliced
2 Medium-size zucchini or other summer squash
4 Slices fresh white bread, with crusts removed
1 Cup heavy cream
1 Egg
5 Tablespoons Parmesan cheese
  Salt and black pepper
¼ Pound Cheddar cheese, cut in ¼-inch dice

Directions: Remove skin from the chickens. Place chicken pieces in a large pot with water to cover, and cook over heat until tender, about 35 minutes.

Meanwhile, prepare the squash. Peel if skins are tough and cut into ½-inch slices. Sauté squash and onion slices in butter 10 minutes, stirring frequently. Cover pan and cook over low heat until vegetables are tender.

Cut the bread into ½-inch cubes; add cream, egg and Parmesan, and mix to a paste.

Preheat oven to 375 degrees F.

Spread vegetables in a shallow ovenproof dish and top with chicken pieces. Sprinkle with salt and pepper to taste. Spread the bread paste evenly over all, dot with Cheddar and bake 20–25 minutes or until golden brown.

If you're in a hurry, place dish on middle oven shelf and broil 10–15 minutes or until nicely browned.

GROSSMUTTER'S CHICKEN-SQUASH BISCUIT PIE
YIELD: ENOUGH TO SERVE 6

3 2½–3 Pound chickens, cut into serving pieces
3 Cups water
3 Tablespoons butter
3 Cups diced winter or summer squash (peeled and seeded if necessary)
2 Tablespoons all-purpose flour
1 Cup cold heavy cream
1 Teaspoon minced fresh thyme
1 Tablespoon minced chives
½ Teaspoon salt
⅛ Teaspoon white pepper
½ Recipe Winter Squash Biscuits (see page 161)

Directions: Bring the chicken pieces and the water to a boil in a large heavy kettle. Partially cover the pot, lower the heat and simmer for 30 to 40 minutes, turning once and skimming any scum which rises to the surface.

Melt 2 tablespoons of the butter in a medium-size skillet and sauté the summer squash for 5 minutes or winter squash for 15 minutes, stirring frequently. Use a slotted spoon to remove and set aside the squash pieces. Melt the remaining butter in the skillet, blend in the flour until smooth, add the cream all at once and bring to a boil, stirring constantly.

Preheat oven to 425 degrees F.

Pull the cooked chicken from the bones in large pieces and set it aside. Stir 1 cup of the cooking liquid into the cream sauce and cook over medium heat until boiling. Mix in the chicken, squash and seasonings, and place in an ovenproof dish. Top with rounds of biscuit dough and bake for 15 minutes or until the biscuits are lightly browned.

FARM-FRIED PIES WITH SQUASH FILLING
YIELD: ENOUGH TO SERVE 6

1 Large winter or summer squash, seeded, peeled and chopped
1 Medium-size onion, peeled and chopped
4 Strips country-cured bacon, minced (or 4 tablespoons butter or oil)
¼ Cup Basic White Sauce (see page 189)
2 Tablespoons pine nuts
Double recipe Double-Crust Pie Pastry (see page 193)
Vegetable oil for frying

Directions: Sauté the squash and onion with the bacon (or in the butter) until tender, then remove from the heat and stir in the white sauce and pine nuts. Set aside.

Roll out the pastry to medium thickness and cut into 6-inch squares. Place 2 to 3 tablespoons of the squash mixture on one side of each square; moisten the edges of the crust and fold the other side over to form a triangle, pressing the edges together with a fork. Fry in 1½ inches hot oil until brown on one side, turn and brown the other side. Drain briefly on paper towels and serve immediately.

CREAMED NOODLES AND ZUCCHINI TRIESTE
YIELD: ENOUGH TO SERVE 6

¾ Pound fine noodles
  Water
4 Small zucchini, cut into ¼-inch slices
2 Large onions, peeled and coarsely chopped
3 Tablespoons butter
1½ Cups cooked and boned chicken meat, diced
1 Ounce foie gras, diced
2 Cups Curry Sauce (see page 190)
¼ Cup grated Parmesan cheese

Directions: Cook the noodles in boiling salted water. Drain well. Sauté the zucchini and the onions in the butter until the squash slices are barely tender.

Preheat oven to 400 degrees F.

Spread ⅓ of the noodles in the bottom of a well-buttered baking dish. Cover with ⅓ of the zucchini slices and onion, ¾ cup chicken meat and ½ ounce fois gras, and top with ⅔ cup curry sauce. Add another layer of noodles, cover with the remaining zucchini and onions, the remaining chicken and fois gras, and ⅔ cup curry sauce. Arrange over this the remaining noodles and curry sauce, sprinkle with the cheese, dot with butter and brown lightly. Serve hot.

CHICKEN BEYNAC WITH APPLE BRANDY SAUCE
YIELD: ENOUGH TO SERVE 4

1 Small chicken, quartered
3 Tablespoons butter
4 Very small zucchini or yellow summer squash, sliced
2 Shallots, peeled and chopped
1 Ounce apple brandy
1 Cup each white wine and heavy cream
  Generous pinch each salt, white pepper, nutmeg and thyme
  Garlic Croutons (see page 193)

Directions: Brown the chicken pieces in 2 tablespoons butter, turning them frequently until they are nicely done. Arrange the chicken on a heatproof platter and keep warm. Sauté the squash and shallots in the remaining tablespoon butter until the slices are barely tender. Arrange the squash around the chicken. Flame the brandy in the pan, add the wine and cook 2 minutes. Add the cream and seasonings, and simmer several moments more or until the sauce has thickened somewhat. Garnish the platter with the croutons, pour the hot sauce over all and serve hot.

CHICKEN, ZUCCHINI AND MEATBALL PIE
YIELD: ENOUGH TO SERVE 4

1 3-Pound chicken (or 2 cups leftover chicken)
5 Tablespoons butter
2 Small zucchini, cut into ¼-inch slices
½ Cup lean ground chuck
½ Cup mashed potatoes
1 Chicken liver, minced
1 Teaspoon minced fresh thyme
1 Egg yolk
1 Tablespoon vegetable oil
1 Tablespoon all-purpose flour
  Water or chicken broth
  Salt and black pepper
  Double-Crust Pie Pastry (see page 193)
1 Tablespoon minced chives

Directions: Sauté the chicken pieces in 3 tablespoons of the butter until lightly browned on all sides, then cover and cook over very low heat for 15 minutes. Set aside the chicken and pan juices.

Mix the ground meat, potato, liver, thyme, salt and pepper to taste and egg yolk, and shape into walnut-sized meatballs. Heat 1 tablespoon each butter and oil in the skillet, and brown the meatballs on all sides in the hot fat. Remove with a slotted spoon and set aside. Sauté the zucchini slices until barely tender, stirring occasionally. Do not overcook. Remove the vegetable slices with a slotted spoon and set them aside also.

Melt the remaining tablespoon butter in the skillet, add the flour and blend until smooth. Combine the reserved pan juices with enough water or chicken broth to make ¾ cup. Stir the liquid into the flour mixture and continue stirring until the gravy is thick and smooth. Season to taste with salt and pepper. Cool to room temperature.

Preheat oven to 425 degrees F.

Roll out the pie dough and line a 7½-inch glass pie plate with one crust. Pull the chicken from the bones and cut it into bite-size pieces. Spoon the chicken, meatballs and squash into the pastry shell, pour the cooled gravy over all and sprinkle with chives. Top with second crust, moisten the bottom edge and flute the crusts together. Cut a dime-size hole in the center of the top crust to allow steam to escape.

Bake for 15 minutes, then lower the heat to 375 degrees F. and bake for 30 minutes longer, or until the crust is well-done and nicely browned. Serve immediately.

CHICKEN AND SQUASH IN EGG SAUCE
YIELD: ENOUGH TO SERVE 6

Leftover ham and turkey are also delicious served in this manner.

3 Small zucchini, cut in ½-inch dice
5 Scallions, each with 3 inches of green top,
   finely chopped
2 Teaspoons minced fresh thyme leaves
5 Tablespoons butter
2 Tablespoons all-purpose flour
2 Cups cold light cream
3 Hard-cooked eggs
1 Tablespoon brandy
¾ Teaspoon salt
   Pinch of mace
4 Cups chopped cooked chicken
6 Slices toast, buttered and
   trimmed
   Freshly ground black pepper

Directions: In a skillet sauté the zucchini, scallions and thyme in 3 tablespoons butter until the squash is barely tender. Spoon the vegetables into a dish and set aside. Melt 2 tablespoons butter in the skillet, stir in the flour until smooth and add the cream all at once. Bring the sauce to a boil over low heat, stirring constantly. Finely chop the egg whites and add them, with the brandy, salt, mace, chicken and zucchini, to the sauce. Press the egg yolks through a sieve, mix with 1 cup of the sauce and stir into the remaining sauce. Reheat and serve over toast points with a sprinkle of freshly ground black pepper.

ZUCCHINI AND CHICKEN WITH SOUR CREAM SAUCE
YIELD: ENOUGH TO SERVE 6

This caraway-flavored sour cream sauce brings out the best in both the chicken and the squash.

2 Three-pound chickens, skinned and cut into serving pieces
6 Tablespoons butter
3 Small zucchini, cut into ¼-inch slices
3½ Tablespoons all-purpose flour
3 Cups sour cream
1 Tablespoon caraway seeds
¼ Cup minced chives
 Salt and black pepper

Directions: Preheat oven to 325 degrees F.

Melt 3 tablespoons of the butter in a skillet, brown the chicken pieces on all sides and set them aside. Sauté the squash slices in 3 minutes, stirring constantly. Use a slotted spoon to transfer them to a baking dish or casserole. Melt the remaining butter in the pan, stir in the flour and blend until smooth. Add the sour cream and simmer for 3 or 4 minutes, stirring constantly. Stir in the caraway seeds, 3 tablespoons of chives and salt and pepper to taste.

Arrange the chicken pieces over the squash, spoon the sauce over all and bake 40 minutes. Serve immediately, sprinkled with the remaining tablespoon of chives.

SOUTHERN-FRIED CHICKEN WITH SOUTHERN-FRIED SQUASH
YIELD: ENOUGH TO SERVE 6 TO 8

2 Three-pound chickens, quartered
2 Cups all-purpose flour
½ Teaspoon each sage, thyme and marjoram
5½ Cups cracker crumbs (approximately)
3 Eggs
½ Cup milk
 Vegetable oil
3 Medium-size summer or winter squash, peeled, seeded and cut into strips
 Salt and black pepper

Directions: Rinse and thoroughly dry the chicken pieces. Mix the flour with the herbs and mound on a paper plate. Make another mound of cracker crumbs. Beat the eggs with the milk. Heat 1 inch oil in a large skillet.

First dredge the chicken pieces in the flour (shake off any excess), then dip them in the egg mixture and finish by rolling each in cracker crumbs. Fry the pieces to golden brown on both sides, turning once.

Preheat oven to 325 degrees F.

Transfer each piece to a shallow ovenproof dish, taking care not to break the crusts. Bake for 20 to 30 minutes or until chicken is cooked through.

Parboil winter squash 3 minutes. Dry on paper towels. Dip the squash sticks first in flour, then in egg and finally in cracker crumbs. Fry to golden brown on all sides. Keep hot in the oven. Serve piping hot with the chicken pieces.

CHICKEN LIVERS AND SQUASH EN BROCHETTE
YIELD: ENOUGH TO SERVE 6

2 Medium-size winter squash, peeled and seeded
(or 2 medium-size summer squash)
2½ Pounds chicken livers
12 Preserved kumquats, cut in half
Garlic Butter (see page 194), melted
Hot cooked rice

Directions: Trim squash and cut into 1-inch cubes. Parboil winter squash 3 minutes. Thread skewers alternately with squash cubes, chicken livers and halved kumquats; baste with hot garlic butter. Broil on both sides, turning once, until the livers are cooked on the outside but still slightly pink inside. Serve at once over hot rice, topping each serving with a spoonful or two of hot basting butter.

SQUASH AND LIVERS CÔTE D'AZUR
YIELD: ENOUGH TO SERVE 6

6 Tablespoons butter
2 Medium-size summer squash, coarsely chopped
3 Medium-size tomatoes, peeled, seeded and
coarsely chopped
2½ Pounds chicken livers
¾ Cup white wine
Hot, cooked rice or buttered, trimmed toast
6 Scallions, each with 3 inches green top, finely chopped

Directions: Heat 2 tablespoons of the butter in a small skillet over medium flame and quickly sauté the squash and tomatoes until most of the liquid evaporates. Remove from the heat and set aside.

In a heavy saucepan heat the remaining butter until very hot, then add the livers and sauté over high heat for 3 or 4 minutes. Remove the livers from the skillet and add the wine to the pan; cook over medium heat until slightly reduced, stirring to incorporate all the brown bits that cling to the bottom and sides. Return the livers to the skillet, stir in the reserved squash-tomato mixture and continue to cook only long enough for the vegetables and livers to heat through. Do not let the mixture boil. Serve over hot rice or buttered, trimmed toast. Garnish with finely chopped scallions.

FILOMENA'S VEAL AND SQUASH CASSEROLE
YIELD: ENOUGH TO SERVE 6

12 Small veal scallopini
   Salt and black pepper
   Flour
  3 Eggs, lightly beaten
  ½ Cup olive oil
  6 Tablespoons butter, cut in pieces
1¼ Cups dry white wine
  1 Oversize summer squash, peeled*
1½ Cups Ripe Tomato Purée (see page 194) or
    tomato sauce
12 Thin slices each prosciutto and mozzarella cheese
  ½ Cup grated Parmesan cheese

Directions: Arrange veal slices between two pieces of wax paper, flatten slightly, then season to taste with salt and pepper. Dip slices first in flour, then in beaten egg; quickly sauté, a few at a time, to a golden brown on both sides in 3 tablespoons of the olive oil, turning once.

Remove the veal from the skillet and set aside to keep warm. Discard the oil in the skillet; add the butter to the pan along with the wine and cook over medium heat, stirring frequently and scraping in the brown bits that cling to the sides and bottom of the pan. Lower the heat, return the veal scallops to the skillet and continue to cook for 3 minutes. Remove from the heat and set aside.

*If the seeds in your oversize squash are tough and inedible, substitute 2 tender medium-size squash or discard the hard seeds, coarsely chop the squash and sauté until golden, then spread evenly over the cooked veal scallops and proceed as directed in paragraph four.

Heat the remaining oil in another large skillet. Cut the squash into 12 ¼-inch slices; dredge the squash slices in flour, shaking off any excess, dip in the remaining beaten egg and cook to a golden brown on both sides in the skillet, turning once. Remove from the skillet and drain thoroughly on paper towels.

Preheat the oven to 375 degrees F.

To assemble the casserole, arrange veal scallops in a single layer over the bottom of a well-buttered shallow baking dish. Pour over the pan juices and tomato purée, then top each veal piece with a slice of sautéed squash. Cover each slice of squash with one slice each of prosciutto and mozzarella, sprinkle Parmesan over all and bake for 10 minutes, or until the cheese is bubbling and brown. Serve hot.

ZUCCHINI-STUFFED VEAL ROLL ITALIA
YIELD: ENOUGH TO SERVE 6

    2 Medium-size zucchini
    3 Whole thin veal slices, cut from center of veal leg
    ½ Pound each very thinly sliced mortadella,
        prosciutto and salami
    2 Cloves garlic, peeled and minced
    ¼ Cup fine bread crumbs
    ¼ Cup finely chopped scallions
    1 Tablespoon minced fresh basil or generous ½
        teaspoon dried
    3 Tablespoons olive oil
     Salt and black pepper
5 or 6 Strips country-cured bacon
    2 Cups Ripe Tomato Purée
      (see page 194)

½ Cup dry vermouth
1 Tablespoon minced fresh parsley
1½ Teaspoons minced fresh basil or
    ¼ teaspoon dried
1 Teaspoons each finely chopped
    onion and celery leaves

Directions: The zucchini should be of uniform thickness throughout their lengths, with no bulbous ends. Scrub and trim the vegetables, then set aside.

Pound the veal slices to a thickness of $\frac{1}{16}$ inch and arrange side by side on wax paper so that each slightly overlaps its neighbor, then pound the overlaps well until the 3 slices become 1 large slice of uniform thickness. Arrange the mortadella, prosciutto and salami slices in overlapping rows over the length of the veal.

Using your fingers, work the garlic into the bread crumbs and sprinkle over the meat. Top with the scallions and 1 tablespoon basil, sprinkle with olive oil and season to taste with salt and pepper. Arrange the squash along the center of the veal; then, starting at one end and using the wax paper as a guide, carefully roll up the veal without dislodging zucchini slices. Tie the roll securely in several places with string. Set the roll in a baking pan and cover with the bacon strips.

Preheat oven to 350 degrees F.

Combine the purée, vermouth, parsley, onion, celery leaves and 1½ teaspoons basil in a small saucepan and season to taste with salt and pepper. Simmer the mixture for 5 minutes and pour over the rolled-up veal. Bake for 1 hour, basting occasionally with the sauce.

Remove the bacon and string after taking from the oven and transfer the roll to a heated serving platter. Pour the sauce remaining in the pan over all and cut the meat into slices before serving hot, garnished with minced fresh parsley.

ZUCCHINI-STUFFED VEAL MARENGO
YIELD: ENOUGH TO SERVE 8

1 Four-pound piece veal shoulder, trimmed of all
    bones and cartilage
2 Medium-size zucchini, trimmed and finely chopped
1 Small onion, peeled and finely chopped
8 Tablespoons butter
8 Slices white bread, trimmed
3 Tablespoons minced fresh parsley
1 Teaspoon salt
½ Teaspoon rosemary
¼ Teaspoon black pepper
2 Carrots, scraped and finely chopped
2 Ribs celery, trimmed and finely chopped
1 Medium-size onion, peeled and finely chopped
3 Cups consommé
2 Teaspoons cornstarch

Directions: Place the meat on a flat surface and pound lightly until it forms a large rectangle about 1 inch thick.

Sauté the zucchini and small onion in the butter until the onion is soft. Meanwhile, use your fingers or a blender to break the bread into fine crumbs.

Combine the zucchini and onion (with the butter in which they were cooked) and bread crumbs, parsley and seasonings in a large bowl. Blend thoroughly and spread evenly over the top surface of the veal, then roll up the veal, jelly-roll fashion, and tie securely in several places with string.

Preheat oven to 350 degrees F.

Place the chopped carrots, celery and medium-size onion on the bottom of a large roasting pan. Set the veal on top and pour consommé over all. Cover the pan and bake in the preheated oven for 1½ hours, or until the veal tests tender when pricked with a fork. Remove the cover during the last half-hour of cooking to brown the top of the veal.

Transfer the veal to a platter after taking from the oven, cut off the strings and allow the roll to cool to room temperature.

If you prefer, prepare a gravy to serve with the meat. Skim and discard the fat from the liquid in the pan, then transfer both liquid and vegetables to a saucepan. Mix the cornstarch with 2 cups consommé and stir into the vegetable mixture. Bring to a boil, stirring constantly, and cook until smooth.

To serve, cut the meat into thin slices and serve with gravy on the side.

OVERSIZE SQUASH STUFFED WITH LAMB
YIELD: ENOUGH TO SERVE 4

1 Oversize squash, cut in half lengthwise
1 Teaspoon salt
¼ Cup olive oil
¾ Cup Ripe Tomato Purée (see page 194)
1 Large onion, peeled
1 Green pepper, trimmed
1¼ Pounds chopped lean lamb
2 Tablespoons each minced parsley and dill
¼ Teaspoon each allspice and black pepper
2 Tablespoons butter
¼ Cup bread crumbs
3 Tablespoons Parmesan cheese

Directions: If the squash seeds are hard, scoop them out and discard them. Scoop out remaining soft pulp and set aside to drain. Take care to leave ½ inch sides of the squash intact.

Sprinkle the pulp of each squash half with ½ teaspoon salt and turn each upside down to drain for 15 minutes. Using paper towels, carefully squeeze the excess moisture from the squash shells and reserved pulp. Sauté the shells in ¼ cup olive oil and set aside. Finely chop the reserved pulp, the onion and green pepper, and sauté vegetables in the oil remaining in the pan. Add the lamb (and a bit of butter if necessary) and the parsley, dill, allspice and pepper. Cook for 10 minutes, stirring occasionally.

Preheat oven to 375 degrees F.

Drain off excess fat and stir ½ cup tomato purée into the lamb mixture. Season to taste and simmer for 5 to 10 minutes, or until the mixture is fairly thick. Spoon the lamb into the squash shells, top each with 2 tablespoons tomato purée, arrange in a shallow gratin dish and bake 15 to 20 minutes or until well heated. Mix the bread crumbs and cheese, and sprinkle a generous amount over each filled squash half. Dot with butter and place under broiler until nicely browned. Serve immediately.

TURKISH STUFFED SUMMER SQUASH
YIELD: ENOUGH TO SERVE 6

6 Small-to-medium-size yellow squash or zucchini
  Salt
6 Tablespoons vegetable oil
2 Medium-size onions, peeled and finely chopped
10 Medium-size mushrooms, finely chopped
1½ Cups cooked chopped lamb
1 Tablespoon each minced fresh mint and thyme leaves
¾ Cup currants
½ Cup pine nuts
3 Tablespoons uncooked rice
2 Tablespoons tomato sauce or catsup
  Salt and black pepper
  Beef broth or bouillon
1 Cup yogurt or sour cream
1½ Tablespoons tomato paste

Directions: Cut the squash in half; scoop out the seeds and pulp, leaving the walls of the shells ½ inch thick. Sprinkle both the hollowed-out shells and the pulp with salt, and let stand for 10 minutes, then pat dry with paper towels. Set shells aside. Discard any large seeds and coarsely chop any large pieces of pulp.

Heat oil in a large skillet and sauté squash pulp, onions and mushrooms for 10 minutes, adding more oil if necessary to keep vegetables from sticking.

Add lamb and herbs to sautéed vegetables; cook until lightly browned, breaking up any large pieces with a fork. Add the currants, pine nuts, rice and tomato sauce. Season to taste with salt and pepper, and cook over low heat, stirring frequently, for 5 minutes.

Preheat oven to 350 degrees F.

Spoon lamb and vegetable mixture into squash shells and set the shells in a deep, rectangular baking dish. Pour in enough broth to bring the liquid level halfway up the sides of the squash shells; cover and bake for 1 hour.

Set shells on a serving dish. Combine the yogurt with 1 cup of the liquid left in the baking dish and mix in the tomato paste. Season the sauce to taste with salt and pepper, and spoon over the stuffed shells. Serve warm or cold.

SAVORY WINTER SQUASH WITH SAUSAGE STUFFING
YIELD: ENOUGH TO SERVE 6

3 Medium-size winter squash, cut in half and seeded
¾ Pound sausage meat
2 Medium-size onions, peeled and finely chopped
⅓ Cup corn bread cubes (white bread will do if corn bread is difficult to obtain)
⅓ Cup fine dry bread crumbs
⅛ Teaspoon allspice
⅓ Cup warm water
  Salt
1 Egg, lightly beaten
  Melted butter

Directions: If a long squash, such as Butternut, is being used, you might want to cut a V-shaped notch down the neck to provide more stuffing per portion. Finely chop the squash removed from the neck.

Crumble the sausage meat into a large skillet and fry until light brown. Pour off all but 2 tablespoons fat. Add the onions (and the finely chopped squash mentioned above) and sauté for 5 minutes. Mix in the bread cubes, bread crumbs, allspice, water and salt to taste. Mix well with your fingers, breaking up any large sausage pieces. Stir the egg into the stuffing.

Preheat oven to 350 degrees F.

Fill the squash cavities with the stuffing and arrange the squash halves on a baking sheet. Use crushed aluminum foil to keep the halves from tipping. Bake for 1 to 1½ hours or until tender, brushing occasionally with melted butter.

SUMMER SQUASH AND HAM AU GRATIN
YIELD: ENOUGH TO SERVE 6 TO 8

4 Medium-size tomatoes, peeled
1 Cup coarsely chopped scallions
4 Tablespoons butter
2 Medium-size zucchini, thinly sliced
  Salt
1 Pound cooked ham, cut in ½-inch cubes
½ Pound sharp Cheddar cheese, grated
2 Cups heavy cream
1 Teaspoon cornstarch
3 Tablespoons coarse dry bread crumbs
2 Tablespoons Parmesan cheese

Directions: Squeeze the seeds from each tomato and cut the pulp into ½-inch pieces. Arrange the tomato pieces in a colander and set aside to drain.

Meanwhile, sauté the scallions in the butter for 2 minutes; add the zucchini slices, sprinkle the mixture with salt to taste and continue to cook, stirring once or twice, until the zucchini slices are just translucent (about 5 minutes). Remove from heat and set aside.

Butter a 3-quart gratin dish and spread some of the zucchini mixture over the bottom. Top with a layer of tomatoes, then cover with a layer of ham. Continue to build layers until all the vegetables and ham are used, ending with the ham.

Preheat oven to 400 degrees F.

Place the Cheddar cheese in a medium-size saucepan. Combine the cream and cornstarch and add to the cheese. Simmer the mixture over medium heat, stirring frequently, until the cheese melts and the sauce is well blended. Add salt to taste and pour over the vegetables and ham. Mix together the bread crumbs and Parmesan cheese, spread evenly over the top of the casserole and bake in the preheated oven for 35 to 40 minutes, or until the top is bubbly and golden. Serve hot.

STIR-FRIED BEEF WITH SUMMER SQUASH
YIELD: ENOUGH TO SERVE 6

Stir-frying is an imaginative way to enhance the flavor and color of all vegetables, and summer squash is no exception. To make sure that your zucchini, summer yellow, patty pan squash, etc., will arrive at the table fresh, the trick is to shorten the cooking time needed by cutting them into even-sized pieces and blanching them briefly, just prior to cooking.

1 Pound flank steak or other lean beef,
    partially frozen
2 Tablespoons each soy sauce
    and sherry
1 Tablespoon cornstarch
1 Tablespoon granulated sugar
2 Pounds summer squash
6 Scallions, each with 3 inches green top, cut on
    the bias into ½-inch slices
 3 Slices fresh ginger root, minced
⅓ Cup vegetable oil
 1 Teaspoon salt
 1 Cup beef broth or bouillon

Directions: Using a very sharp knife, slice the beef very thinly across the grain while still partially frozen. Combine soy sauce, sherry, cornstarch and sugar in a flat shallow bowl; add the meat and toss lightly to coat all surfaces. Allow to stand for 15 minutes, stirring occasionally. Place in colander set over a plate. Reserve all marinade.

Meanwhile, cut the squash into ¼-inch slices or thin pieces of equal shape and thickness, and pat thoroughly dry with paper towels.

Heat a wok or large skillet until hot enough for a drop of water to sizzle and bounce over its surface. Add half the oil, then add the beef slices and stir-fry rapidly for a minute or two; cook only until the meat loses its red color.

Remove meat from pan and add the remaining oil, salt and ginger root. Stir-fry for a few seconds, add the squash and scallions, and continue to stir-fry until the slices or pieces are heated through and coated with oil.

Add broth and reserved marinade to pan; cover and cook over medium heat until the squash is tender but still "crunchy." Return beef to pan and cook for 1 minute more. Serve hot over rice.

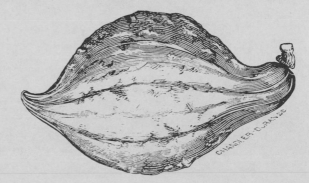

SUMMER SQUASH FRITTATA
YIELD: ENOUGH TO SERVE 4 TO 6

2 Very small zucchini or yellow summer squash
  (or 1 of each), thinly sliced
1 Cup finely diced cooked ham
4 Tablespoons olive oil
2 Cloves garlic, peeled and crushed
8 Eggs, lightly beaten
  Salt
¾ Cup sour cream

Directions: Blanch the squash with *boiling* water. Let stand 5 minutes. Drain well, then blot dry with paper towels. In a 9-inch skillet or omelet pan sauté the ham for a few seconds in 3 tablespoons oil. Add half the garlic and the squash slices and cook, stirring occasionally, until the vegetables start to brown. Add the remaining tablespoon of oil, pour the eggs over all and cook over *low* heat without stirring until the eggs are set on the bottom but still a little runny on top. Slide the pan under the broiler until the top is set. Season to taste with salt and serve hot, topped with sour cream flavored with garlic.

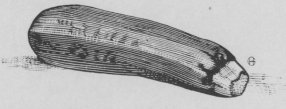

SUMMER GARDEN QUICHE
YIELD: ONE 10-INCH QUICHE

1 Recipe Double-Crust Pie Pastry (see page 193)
1 Oversize summer squash, peeled, seeded and
  cut in ½-inch dice
1 Tablespoon salt
4 Scallions, each with 3 inches green top, cut into
  ½-inch slices
¾ Cup vegetable oil
6 Strips lean country-cured bacon, coarsely chopped
3 Large ripe tomatoes, peeled, seeded and
  coarsely chopped
3 Eggs
1½ Cups Ripe Tomato Purée (see page 194)
2 Tablespoons each chopped fresh thyme leaves
  and basil
  Salt and black pepper
  Dijon-type mustard
1 Cup grated Swiss cheese

Directions: Prepare and refrigerate pastry.

Spread squash cubes on paper towels and sprinkle on all sides with the salt. Let stand 10 minutes, then rinse in cold water and squeeze dry. Discard any large seeds.

Sauté squash cubes and scallions in hot oil until squash is lightly browned on all sides. Remove from pan with a slotted spoon and drain on paper towels. Discard oil and brown bacon pieces in the same pan. Remove bacon pieces with a slotted spoon and set aside, then sauté tomatoes in the same pan until the liquid evaporates.

Beat eggs and stir in cooled squash cubes, scallions, bacon, tomato, tomato purée, herbs, and salt and pepper to taste.

Preheat oven to 375 degrees F.

Roll out pastry and use to line a 10-inch quiche mold or pie plate; crimp the edges and lightly prick entire bottom surface with a fork. Prebake for 10 minutes on the middle rack of the oven.

Brush the bottom of the quiche shell with mustard, sprinkle with half the cheese and fill with the squash-and-egg mixture. Sprinkle with remaining cheese and bake at 375 degrees F. on the middle rack of the oven for 20 to 25 minutes, or until the top is set. Serve warm, *not hot.*

SUMMER SQUASH–CAMEMBERT QUICHE

YIELD: ENOUGH TO SERVE 4

1 Recipe Double-Crust Pie Pastry
    (see page 193)
  Rice
4 Thin slices ham cut into julienne
2½ Tablespoons butter
2 Very small zucchini or yellow summer squash
5 Scallions, each with 3 inches green top, coarsely
    chopped
1 Cup soft Camembert
¼ Cup grated Parmesan cheese
4 Eggs
1½ Cups heavy cream
  Pinch each nutmeg, thyme and white pepper

Directions: Roll out the crust and line a 9-inch pie or quiche pan. Prick the bottom of the shell well and chill thoroughly.

Preheat oven to 400 degrees F.

Line the crust with waxed paper, fill with uncooked rice and bake for 12 minutes. Remove the paper and the rice, and bake the crust 10 minutes more or until it is lightly browned.

Lower oven temperature to 375 degrees F.

Brown the ham in the butter, then remove and set aside. Cut the squash into thin slices and sauté, along with the scallions, for 4 minutes or until just tender. Drain the vegetables well, spoon them evenly over the bottom of the crust, spread with Camembert and top with the Parmesan and ham. Beat the eggs with the cream, add the seasonings and pour the mixture over the cheese. Bake for 30 minutes or until the custard is set.

EAST END SUMMER QUICHE
YIELD: 1 10-INCH QUICHE

1 Recipe Double-Crust Pie Pastry (see page 193)
2 Small yellow summer squash, thinly sliced
2 Small zucchini, thinly sliced
1 Large onion, peeled and chopped
1 Teaspoon each minced fresh parsley and rosemary
2½ Tablespoons butter
1 Cup grated Swiss cheese
4 Eggs
1 Cup heavy cream
1 Cup milk
½ Teaspoon salt
   Dash each ground nutmeg and black or
     cayenne pepper

Directions: Prepare and refrigerate pastry. Meanwhile, sauté squash slices, onion and herbs in butter until the onion is transparent; remove with a slotted spoon and set aside.

Preheat the oven to 375 degrees F. Roll out pastry and use to line a 10-inch quiche mold or pie plate; crimp the edges and lightly prick the entire bottom surface with a fork. Prebake for 10 minutes on the middle shelf of the oven.

Combine the cheese, eggs, cream, milk and seasonings. Arrange squash slices over bottom of partially baked pastry shell and pour cheese-egg mixture over squash. Bake at 375 degrees F. on the middle rack of the oven for about 25 to 30 minutes, or until the quiche is set and a knife inserted in the center comes out clean. Serve warm or at room temperature.

RATATOUILLE QUICHE
YIELD: ONE 10-INCH QUICHE

1 Medium-size summer squash, peeled and cut
   into ½-inch dice
1 Small eggplant, peeled and cut into ½-inch dice
1 Tablespoon salt
¾ Cup vegetable oil
1 Large sweet onion, peeled and coarsely chopped
1 Green pepper, parboiled for 8 to 10 minutes,
   then seeded and chopped
1 Small zucchini, cut in small dice
1 Clove garlic, peeled and crushed
2 Teaspoons thyme leaves
½ Teaspoon granulated sugar
   Salt and black pepper
3 Eggs
1½ Cups Ripe Tomato Purée (see page 194)
1 Recipe Double-Crust Pie Pastry (see page 193)
   Dijon-type mustard
¾ Cup grated Swiss cheese

Directions: Arrange squash and eggplant cubes on paper towels and sprinkle with salt. Let stand 15 minutes, then turn, salt and let stand 15 minutes more. Rinse in cold water and pat dry.

Sauté squash and eggplant cubes in hot oil until lightly browned on all sides. Remove from pan with a slotted spoon and drain on paper towels. Discard all but 3 tablespoons of the oil and in it sauté onion and green pepper. Add small zucchini, garlic, thyme, and sugar; cook until vegetables are tender. Add salt and pepper to taste, then remove from heat and cool.

Beat the eggs and stir in tomato purée and cooled cooked vegetables.

Preheat oven to 375 degrees F.

Roll out pastry and use to line a 10-inch quiche pan or pie plate; crimp edges and lightly prick entire bottom surface with a fork. Prebake for 10 minutes on the middle rack of the oven.

Brush the bottom of the quiche shell with mustard and fill with the squash-and-egg mixture. Sprinkle with cheese and bake on the middle rack of the oven for 20 to 25 minutes, or until the top is set and a knife inserted in the center comes out clean. Cool 5 minutes before serving warm.

ZUCCHINI CHEESE PUDDING
YIELD: ENOUGH TO SERVE 4 TO 6

---

4 Small zucchini, thinly sliced
1 Tablespoon minced fresh thyme
2 Tablespoons butter
4 Eggs
1 Cup milk
½ Cup heavy cream
¾ Cup grated Parmesan cheese
1 Cup grated Swiss cheese
  Tabasco sauce to taste
60 Soda crackers

Directions: Preheat oven to 350 degrees F.

Sauté the zucchini and thyme in the butter until the squash is tender. Beat the eggs, milk, heavy cream, Parmesan and Tabasco until thoroughly mixed. Arrange a layer of crackers in a well-buttered 9″ by 9″ ovenproof dish. Top with half

each egg mixture, squash slice and Swiss cheese. Repeat this layering.

Let stand 20 minutes, then bake about 35 to 40 minutes, or until puffy and nicely browned. Serve hot.

OMELETS
YIELD: ENOUGH TO MAKE 1 OMELET
TO SERVE 2

The art of omelet-making may seem a bit tricky at first, but the basic technique is easy to master if you start on a small scale and begin with omelets only large enough for two. When serving more than two, proceed in the same manner, but make a succession of small omelets.

BASIC RECIPE
5 Eggs
2 Tablespoons water
  Salt and black pepper
1 Teaspoon butter

Directions: Beat eggs and water together and season to taste with salt and pepper. Heat butter to sizzling in an omelet pan or skillet over medium flame. Quickly pour in egg mixture and rapidly stir with a fork in a circular motion, lifting cooked part of omelet so that any uncooked egg runs underneath. As soon as eggs are set on the bottom but still soft and creamy on top, press the pan handle down and let omelet slide toward you and halfway up side of pan. Immediately flip omelet over toward the center of the pan, tilt pan in opposite direction and let the folded omelet slip out of the pan on the side away from the handle, right onto a waiting plate.

OMELET VARIATIONS

MEDITERRANEAN OMELET

Sauté 1 coarsely chopped small zucchini, 1 peeled and coarsely chopped onion and 1 large tomato peeled, seeded and coarsely chopped, in 2 tablespoons butter. Season with fresh herbs, salt and pepper to taste. Cook the omelet as directed in the Basic Recipe (see page 120) until the eggs are set on the bottom but soft and creamy on top. Arrange 2 or 3 tablespoons vegetable filling along center, then flip over, fold and slide from pan.

SUMMER SQUASH CHEESE OMELET

Sauté 1 small sliced yellow squash in 1½ tablespoons butter until soft. Remove with slotted spoon and set aside to keep warm. Prepare the omelet as directed in the Basic Recipe (see page 120). When the eggs are set on the bottom but still soft and creamy on top, spoon some of the squash along the center, sprinkle with grated Parmesan or shredded Swiss cheese, flip, fold and slide from pan.

TOMATO-ZUCCHINI OMELET DOMINI

YIELD: ENOUGH FILLING FOR 3 SMALL OMELETS

Ingredients listed in Basic Recipe (see page 120) plus:
1½ Cups diced zucchini
⅓ Cup chopped cooked country-cured bacon
1 Tablespoon minced onion
2 Tablespoons butter
2 Medium-size ripe tomatoes, peeled, seeded and finely chopped
¼ Teaspoon granulated sugar

Directions: Sauté zucchini, bacon and onion in butter for 3 minutes. Lower heat, cover pan and cook for 4 minutes longer. With a slotted spoon, remove mixture from pan and set aside to keep warm. Add tomatoes to pan, sprinkle with sugar and cook over low heat, stirring, until most of the moisture evaporates. Remove tomatoes from pan and stir into reserved vegetables and bacon.

Prepare omelet mixture and cook according to directions until eggs are set but still soft and creamy. Spoon some of the zucchini filling along center, then flip, fold and slide omelet from pan.

POTATO-SQUASH CHEESE OMELET

Substitute 2 small peeled and thinly sliced potatoes for half the squash. Cook the potatoes without browning them. Remove and set aside. Arrange the potato slices over the squash and proceed as in Summer Squash Cheese Omelet (see page 121).

SQUASH RATATOUILLE BAKED WITH EGGS
YIELD: ENOUGH TO SERVE 6

Oversize summer squash are completely at home in this unusual version of an unusual dish. Serve hot or cold . . . it is superb either way.

1 Oversize summer squash, peeled and cut into ½-inch dice
1 Small eggplant, peeled and cut into ½-inch dice
1 Tablespoon salt
2 Large green peppers, seeded
2 Large sweet onions, peeled and coarsely chopped
1 Cup vegetable oil
6 Large ripe tomatoes, peeled, seeded and finely chopped
3 Large garlic cloves, peeled and crushed
1 Tablespoon fresh thyme leaves
1½ Teaspoons granulated sugar
¼ Teaspoon paprika
4 Tablespoons wine vinegar
6 Hard-cooked eggs, cut in quarters

Directions: Spread squash and eggplant cubes on paper towels, sprinkle with salt and let stand 15 minutes, then turn, salt and let stand 15 minutes more. Rinse in cold water and pat dry with paper towels.

Boil the peppers for 5 minutes, then rinse under cold water. Pat dry and cut into ½-inch strips. Sauté with the onions in 2 tablespoons oil for 15 minutes, or until vegetables are tender but not brown. Set aside.

In a large skillet, sauté squash and eggplant cubes in ¾ cup hot oil until lightly browned on all sides.

Preheat oven to 375 degrees F.

Simmer the tomatoes with 2 tablespoons oil, garlic, thyme and sugar, until most of the liquid has evaporated.

Stir together the squash, onions, peppers, tomato mixture, paprika and vinegar; spoon into an oven-proof baking dish. Arrange egg quarters on top, sprinkle each with a few drops of oil and bake for 15 minutes.

EGGS BAKED IN ZUCCHINI
YIELD: ENOUGH TO SERVE 6

6 Medium-size zucchini, grated
½ Teaspoon salt
4 Tablespoons butter
3 Scallions, each with 3 inches green
    top, minced
6 Eggs
2 Cups Basic White Sauce
    (see page 189)
2 Tablespoons grated Parmesan cheese

Directions: Sprinkle the grated zucchini with the salt, allow to stand for 5 minutes, then squeeze the zucchini between towels until all moisture is wrung out.

Preheat oven to 350 degrees F.

Heat 3 tablespoons butter in a skillet and sauté the zucchini and scallions for 5 minutes, stirring frequently. Remove from heat and spread vegetable mixture over the bottom of a shallow 10-inch square baking dish. Using a large spoon, make 6 evenly spaced depressions in the zucchini mixture and carefully break 1 egg into each. Dot each egg with ½ teaspoon butter and bake for 30 minutes, or until the egg whites are barely firm and the yolks are still soft. Top each egg with ⅓ cup white sauce and sprinkle with grated cheese; slide under the broiler only long enough to brown the cheese. Serve at once.

ZUCCHINI-EGG CASSEROLE PARMESAN
YIELD: ENOUGH TO SERVE 4 FOR LUNCH

1 Medium-size zucchini, cut in ¼-inch slices
3 Tablespoons melted butter
    Salt and pepper to taste
10 Medium-size mushrooms, quartered
3 Tablespoons vegetable oil
1 Green pepper, with pith and seeds removed
1 Tablespoon minced hot pepper
1 Small onion, peeled and finely chopped
4 Eggs
¼ Cup light cream
3 Tablespoons grated Parmesan cheese

Directions: Plunge the zucchini slices in boiling salted water to cover for 1 minute only. Drain well. Toss the zucchini slices with the melted butter and a generous amount of salt and pepper. Arrange the slices evenly in the bottom of a 10-inch glass pie plate. Sauté the mushrooms until tender in 2 tablespoons hot oil and set aside. Coarsely chop the green pepper and sauté until tender in the remaining oil along with the hot pepper and onion. Spoon the cooked vegetables over the zucchini slices.

Preheat oven to 450 degrees F.

Beat the eggs and cream together, pour over the vegetables and sprinkle with the Parmesan cheese. Bake 15 to 20 minutes, or until eggs are just set and top is lightly browned.

SQUASH FLOWER FRITTERS
YIELD: ABOUT 2 DOZEN FRITTERS

16 to 20 Summer squash flowers or enough to make
2 cups when coarsely chopped (male
flowers are best)
2 Cups all-purpose flour
3 Teaspoons baking powder
1 Teaspoon granulated sugar
1 Egg
½ Cup water
¼ Cup milk
Vegetable oil
Salt

Directions: Sift together the flour, baking powder and sugar. Beat together the egg, water and milk. Stir the liquid ingredients into the dry ingredients, then beat until the batter is smooth and stiff.

Stir in the chopped flowers and drop the batter by tablespoons into ¼-inch-deep hot oil. Fry 2 to 3 minutes on each side, flattening each fritter slightly with the back of a spoon. When the fritters are golden brown, remove them from the oil, drain on paper towels, sprinkle with salt and serve immediately.

BEER-BATTER SQUASH FRITTERS

3 Medium-size summer or winter squash, peeled, seeded
and cut into strips 2½ inches by ½ inch
¼ Cup olive oil
3 Cloves garlic, peeled and crushed
1 Cup all-purpose flour
⅓ Teaspoon salt
1 Cup beer
1 Teaspoon vegetable oil
Vegetable oil for frying
Salt to taste

Directions: Parboil the squash strips until *barely tender*. Do not overcook. The vegetable should still have a bit of "crunch." Drain well and marinate in olive oil mixed with garlic.

Sift together the flour and salt, add the beer and 1 teaspoon oil, and stir until the batter is smooth. Strain if necessary to remove lumps, cover and let the batter stand for several hours at room temperature.

Drain the squash strips thoroughly, coat each well with batter and fry in several inches of oil heated to 375 degrees F. Drain on paper towels, salt to taste and serve immediately.

SUNNY SUMMER SQUASH PANCAKES
YIELD: ENOUGH TO SERVE 6

Substitute other summer squash for zucchini in these recipes, but peel and seed them before grating.

---

3 Medium-size zucchini
1 Small onion, peeled
¼ Cup all-purpose flour
2 Eggs
½ Teaspoon salt
  Dry bread crumbs
  Butter or vegetable oil for frying
  Sour cream

Directions: Grate the squash and squeeze between towels until quite dry. Grate onion. Combine the grated vegetables with the flour, eggs, salt and enough bread crumbs to make a fairly stiff batter. Heat butter or oil to a depth of ½ inch in a large skillet and add the batter by tablespoonfuls, pressing each pancake flat with the back of a spoon. Fry until golden brown on both sides, turning once. Serve hot or cold, with sour cream.

FARM-STYLE POTATO-SQUASH PANCAKES
YIELD: ENOUGH TO SERVE 6

---

1 Medium-size summer squash
1 Large Spanish onion, peeled
3 Large eggs
2 Tablespoons chopped fresh chives
½ Teaspoon salt
  Dash white pepper
3 Large Idaho potatoes, peeled

Directions: Wash, trim and finely grate the summer squash. Grate the onion, then set both vegetables aside to drain thoroughly.

Beat together the eggs and combine with the chives, salt and pepper.

Grate the potatoes, blot briefly in paper towels, then stir into the egg mixture. Stir in the reserved squash and onion.

Heat a lightly buttered griddle and, using a slotted spoon, drop the batter, a spoonful at a time; cook each pancake until it is brown and crisp on both sides, turning once. As each pancake is finished, set it aside to keep warm. Serve hot, with sour cream or applesauce on the side.

VALLEY-OF-GOD'S-PLEASURE SQUASH PIE
YIELD: ENOUGH TO SERVE 4 TO 6

This is one of the most delicate and delicious vehicles for displaying your summer squash.

---

3 to 4 Medium-size summer squash, sliced
1 Cup water
3 Eggs
1 Teaspoon granulated sugar
½ Teaspoon salt
⅛ Teaspoon each cinnamon, ginger and
    nutmeg
  Pinch each freshly ground black pepper
    and mace
1 Cup heavy cream
¼ Cup sherry
½ Recipe Double-Crust Pie Pastry
  (see page 193)

Directions: Place squash slices in a large saucepan, add the water, then cook over medium heat, stirring occasionally, until most of the water evaporates. Purée the cooked squash in a food processor or blender, or force through a fine sieve.

Lightly beat the eggs and add to the squash purée; add the sugar, salt, spices, cream and sherry, and mix until well blended.

Preheat oven to 425 degrees F.

Roll out the pie pastry and use it to line a 7½-inch pie plate. Flute pastry edges. Spoon the squash mixture into the crust and bake for 15 minutes. Reduce heat to 350 degrees F. and bake for 30 minutes longer, or until a knife blade inserted in the center of the pie comes out clean.

SUMMER SQUASH SOUFFLÉ CONTESSA DI POMPEII

YIELD: ENOUGH TO SERVE 6

A good basic soufflé.

1½ Cups peeled and grated green or yellow summer squash
4 Tablespoons butter
3 Tablespoons all-purpose flour
1 Cup cold milk
    Salt
½ Teaspoon curry powder
4 Egg yolks
5 Egg whites

Directions: Squeeze all moisture from grated squash and sauté in 1½ tablespoons of the butter until very soft. Remove from heat and set aside.

In a heavy saucepan set over medium heat, melt remaining butter and blend in flour and curry powder. Stir in milk, season to taste with salt and cook, stirring constantly, until sauce thickens slightly.

Remove pan from heat and fold in cooked squash. Beat in the egg yolks, one at a time, until all have been incorporated. Allow mixture to cool.

Preheat oven to 350 degrees F.

Beat egg whites until they stand in stiff peaks and fold gently into squash mixture. Turn at once into well-buttered soufflé or other deep baking dish and bake for 35 minutes, or until top of soufflé is puffy and lightly browned.

To make a less crusty soufflé, set dish in a pan of hot (not boiling) water while it bakes.

(Also delicious without curry seasoning.)

WINTER SQUASH SOUFFLÉ

Follow directions for Summer Squash Soufflé (see page 126), but substitute 1½ cups Best Winter Squash Purée (see page 142) for summer squash.

SOUFFLÉ VARIATION I
ZUCCHINI-TOMATO SOUFFLÉ
YIELD: ENOUGH TO SERVE 6

Sauté 1 medium-size peeled and very finely minced zucchini in 1½ tablespoons butter until very soft. Combine with 1 cup Ripe Tomato Purée (see page 194). Add to soufflé mixture after removing pan from heat and before beating in egg yolks, then continue as directed.

SOUFFLÉ VARIATION II:
ZUCCHINI-MUSHROOM SOUFFLÉ
YIELD: ENOUGH TO SERVE 6

Sauté 1 medium-size peeled and grated zucchini (squeezed dry) and ¾ cup finely minced mushrooms in 2 tablespoons butter until vegetables are soft. Cool to room temperature. Fold these into soufflé mixture, then beat in egg yolks and proceed as directed for Summer Squash Soufflé (page 126).

ZUCCHINI-STUFFED CREPES NAPOLI
YIELD: ENOUGH TO SERVE 6

2 Medium-size zucchini
6 Tablespoons butter
2 Eggs
1½ Cups grated Parmesan cheese
1 Cup each finely chopped cooked ham and mozzarella cheese
1 Teaspoon fresh minced thyme leaves
½ Teaspoon Dijon-type mustard
  Pinch ground nutmeg
  Salt
2 Cups Basic White Sauce (see page 189)
  Crepes (see page 188)

Directions: Rinse and trim the zucchini, then shred coarsely and set aside to drain well. Heat 2 tablespoons butter and sauté the vegetable until barely tender. Remove from heat and transfer to a large bowl. Beat the eggs lightly and add to the zucchini, along with 1 cup of the Parmesan cheese and the ham, mozzarella, mustard and nutmeg. Season with salt to taste and bind the mixture with ¼ cup of the white sauce, blending all ingredients thoroughly.

Preheat oven to 375 degrees F.

Place 2 tablespoons of the zucchini mixture in the center of each crepe and roll up the crepes. Spoon the remaining white sauce evenly over the bottom of a shallow baking dish and arrange the stuffed crepes on top. Sprinkle with the remaining Parmesan cheese and dot with the remaining butter. Bake in the preheated oven for 20 minutes, or until the surface is golden brown and bubbly. Serve immediately.

ZUCCHINI ROLLS WITH THREE-CHEESE FILLING
YIELD: ENOUGH TO SERVE 6

1 Cup loosely packed, coarsely grated mozzarella cheese
½ Cup grated Parmesan cheese
⅓ Cup ricotta cheese
2 Eggs
1 Tablespoon each finely chopped fresh parsley and prosciutto
  Salt and black pepper
1 Egg white
4 Tablespoons all-purpose flour
1 Teaspoon baking powder
⅛ Teaspoon salt
⅔ Cup milk
1 Tablespoon vegetable oil
6 Plump zucchini, about 6 inches long and 3 inches in diameter, peeled
8 Tablespoons olive oil
4 Tablespoons butter
  Flour
  Minced fresh chives

Directions: Mix together to a smooth paste the cheeses, one of the eggs, and the parsley and prosciutto; season to taste with salt and pepper. Beat the egg white until it stands in stiff peaks and fold thoroughly into the cheese mixture. Refrigerate until well chilled.

Combine the flour, baking powder and ⅛ teaspoon salt, and sift together into a small bowl. Add the milk and vegetable oil, and beat until the batter is smooth.

Cut the zucchini in half lengthwise; then, starting from the cut surface of each half, cut lengthwise slices about ½ inch thick. Blot the slices on paper towels.

Heat half the olive oil and butter in a large skillet. Dip the zucchini slices first in flour, shaking off any excess, then in the prepared batter, and sauté to a golden brown on both sides, turning once. Use remaining oil and butter as needed for frying. Drain briefly on paper towels.

Preheat oven to 375 degrees F.

Spread about 2 tablespoons of the chilled cheese mixture on each zucchini slice. Roll up the slices loosely and set them, seam sides down, in a lightly buttered baking pan. Bake for 15 minutes, or until the cheese mixture melts and the squash is heated through. Top with Ripe Tomato Purée (see page 194). Sprinkle with minced chives and serve hot.

SQUASH KEPTETHAKEA
YIELD: ENOUGH TO SERVE 6 TO 8

These tiny squash-and-beef balls are an interesting variation on the Greek original.

2 Four-inch-long zucchini, finely grated
1½ Pound ground round steak
1 Medium-size onion, peeled and finely chopped
1 Egg, lightly beaten
3 Slices dry toast, trimmed
1½ Tablespoons each olive oil and lemon juice
2 Tablespoons each minced mint leaves and parsley
1 Large clove garlic, peeled and crushed
¼ Teaspoon each black pepper and cinnamon
  Salt to taste

Directions: Drain the squash well, then squeeze it dry in paper towels. Mix the squash, ground steak, onion and egg. Soak the toast in water, squeeze dry and mix, along with the remaining ingredients, into the squash-meat mixture. Refrigerate 30 minutes. Shape into balls slightly smaller than a 25-cent piece, roll the balls lightly in flour and sauté in butter until golden brown on all sides. Serve hot, with cold Yogurt Dipping Sauce if desired (see page 194).

SUMMER SQUASH KNISHES

PASTRY RECIPE
2 Cups sifted all-purpose flour
1 Teaspoon baking powder
½ Teaspoon salt
2 Eggs, beaten
1 Tablespoon salad oil
2 Tablespoons water
  Additional flour and/or water
    as needed

Directions: Sift together the flour, baking powder and salt, and mound it on a wooden surface. With your fist, make a well in the center of the flour and into it pour the eggs, oil and water. Use your fingers to work the liquid ingredients into the flour, adding a bit more flour if the dough is too sticky or a bit more water if the dough will not hold together. Work until the dough is smooth. Let stand 1 hour. On a lightly floured board roll out the dough to form a thin sheet. Cut large or small rounds or squares to suit your preference, place a spoonful of filling on one half of each, fold the other half

over, moisten the edges and press firmly together. Arrange on a well-oiled baking sheet and bake at 400 degrees for 15 to 20 minutes, or until browned and crisp.

SQUASH-AND-POTATO FILLING FOR KNISHES

2 to 3 Small zucchini, finely grated (enough to make
    2 cups)
1 Medium-size onion, peeled and coarsely chopped
3 Tablespoons rendered chicken fat or butter
1 Cup mashed potatoes
1 Tablespoon beaten egg
  Salt and black pepper to taste
¼ Teaspoon powdered sage (optional)

Directions: Drain the squash well, then squeeze dry in paper towels. Sauté the onion and squash in the chicken fat until the onions are lightly browned. Remove the pan from the heat, and stir in the potatoes and then the egg and seasonings. The filling should be at room temperature or chilled when used.

SQUASH-AND-MEAT FILLING FOR KNISHES

Follow recipe for Squash-and-Potato Filling for Knishes, but substitute 1 cup chopped beef for one of the squash and 1 cup cooked buckwheat groats for the mashed potatoes.

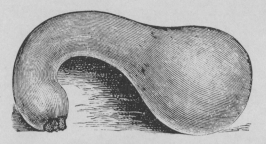

RATATOUILLE
YIELD: ENOUGH TO SERVE 6

1 Medium-size eggplant, peeled and cut in ½-inch cubes
  Salt
4 Medium-size onions, peeled and coarsely chopped
½ Cup olive oil
3 Green peppers, seeded and chopped
5 Small zucchini, cut in ½-inch slices
5 Ripe tomatoes, peeled, seeded and chopped
1½ Cups chopped celery
1 Large clove garlic, peeled and crushed
1 Tablespoon each minced fresh basil and marjoram
  Salt and black pepper to taste

Directions: Arrange eggplant cubes in a single layer on paper towels. Sprinkle with salt, let stand 15 minutes, then turn, salt and let stand 15 minutes more. Rinse in cold water and dry.

In a large skillet sauté the onions in the oil until soft and transparent. Lower the heat, add the peppers and eggplant, and cook for 5 minutes, stirring occasionally. Mix in the zucchini, tomatoes and celery; cover the skillet and allow the vegetables to simmer over low heat for 50 minutes. Stir in the garlic and seasonings, and cook 5 minutes more. Serve hot or cold.

SCALLOPED POTATOES WITH SUMMER SQUASH GRUYÈRE
YIELD: ENOUGH TO SERVE 4 TO 6

1½ Pounds potatoes, peeled
1 Medium-size zucchini
1¼ Cups heavy cream
10 Tablespoons grated Gruyère cheese
  Salt and black pepper

Directions: Preheat oven to 350 degrees F.

Cut the potatoes and zucchini into ⅛-inch slices. Pour ¼ cup cream into a flameproof baking dish and arrange ¼ of the sliced potatoes over the bottom. Sprinkle with 2 tablespoons grated cheese and season to taste with salt and pepper, then add ¼ of the squash slices. Continue to build layers in the same way until all the vegetables are used, but do not add any cheese to the top layer.

Set the baking dish into a larger baking pan; add enough boiling water to bring the water level halfway up the pan's sides and bake for 1½ hours. Pour the remaining heavy cream over the vegetables and bake for 30 to 40 minutes more, or until the potatoes are tender. Just before serving, sprinkle the top of the casserole with the remaining grated cheese and place under the broiler for 3 minutes, or until the cheese turns bubbling and golden. Serve hot.

SCALLOPED POTATOES WITH WINTER SQUASH

Follow directions for Scalloped Potatoes with Summer Squash, but substitute 1 medium-size Butternut squash, peeled, seeded and sliced, for the summer squash.

SISTER ENDICOTT'S SCALLOPED SQUASH

YIELD: ENOUGH TO SERVE 6

---

6 to 8 Small summer squash cut in ⅓-inch slices
5 Tablespoons butter
⅓ Cup minced chives
1 Cup fine dry bread crumbs
½ Teaspoon salt
⅛ Teaspoon each black pepper and grated nutmeg
½ Cup heavy cream
3 Tablespoons grated Cheddar cheese

Directions: Preheat oven to 450 degrees F.

Sauté the squash slices in the butter until they begin to brown, stirring frequently. Stir in the chives and remove pan from the heat. Transfer the vegetables to a deep baking dish.

Mix the bread crumbs with the salt, pepper and nutmeg, and toss half of them with the squash. Pour the cream over all, top with the remaining crumbs and the cheese, and bake until the crumbs and cheese are brown and the squash is bubbling hot. Serve immediately.

SCALLOPED SUMMER SQUASH SLICES

YIELD: ENOUGH TO SERVE 6

Serve this old-time country favorite as a vegetable dish or over toast points as hearty luncheon fare.

---

6 to 8 Small summer squash, cut into ¼-inch slices
3 Tablespoons butter
4 Strips country-cured bacon, minced
2 Medium-size onions, peeled and coarsely chopped
1½ Cups Basic White Sauce (see page 189)
1 Teaspoon caraway seeds
2 Cups Garlic Bread Crumbs (see page 194)

Directions: Sauté the squash slices in the hot butter until barely tender. Remove with a slotted spoon and set aside to drain.

Preheat oven to 350 degrees F.

Fry the bacon for 2 minutes, add the onions and cook until transparent. Stir in the squash. Spoon a layer of squash into a glass baking dish, spread with ½ cup white sauce and sprinkle with ¼ teaspoon caraway seed and ½ cup garlic crumbs. Repeat this process until all the ingredients are used, ending with layers of white sauce, seeds and crumbs. Bake for 20 minutes or until bubbling hot.

ZUCCHINI SLICES IN HOLLANDAISE–SOUR CREAM SAUCE
YIELD: ENOUGH TO SERVE 6

6 Very small zucchini, thinly sliced
　Salt
1 Small onion, peeled and grated
¼ Cup lemon juice
¾ Cup Hollandaise Sauce (see page 190)
¾ Cup sour cream
2 Tablespoons minced chives

Directions: Sprinkle the squash slices with salt, weight with a plate and set aside for 20 minutes. Pour off any accumulated liquid, toss the zucchini and grated onion with the lemon juice and marinate for 3 hours. Drain the slices once more and arrange them in a shallow dish. Mix the hollandaise and sour cream, pour the sauce over the zucchini, sprinkle with chives and serve with slices of buttered pumpernickel.

TOMATO–SUMMER SQUASH CASSEROLE WITH MOZZARELLA CHEESE
YIELD: ENOUGH TO SERVE 6

1 Oversize squash, peeled and seeded if necessary
1 Tablespoon salt
½ Cup all-purpose flour
1 Cup olive oil
½ Pound mozzarella cheese, thinly sliced
3 Onions, peeled and coarsely chopped
6 Large tomatoes, peeled, seeded and coarsely chopped
1 Tablespoon currants

1 Tablespoon minced fresh basil
1 Teaspoon minced fresh thyme
1 Teaspoon granulated sugar
⅛ Teaspoon allspice
⅓ Cup grated Parmesan cheese

Directions: Cut the squash into ½-inch slices, sprinkle them with salt and let stand 15 minutes. Blot dry with paper towels, dust lightly with flour and sauté in ¾ cup hot oil until browned on both sides. Drain on paper towels. Cover the bottom of a flameproof casserole with a layer of the squash slices, then cover with a layer of mozzarella and another layer of squash.

Preheat oven to 350 degrees F.

Heat the remaining oil and sauté the onions until transparent. Add the tomatoes, currants, basil, thyme, sugar and allspice, and cook over medium heat until slightly thickened. Spoon the tomato mixture over the squash, top with Parmesan cheese and bake, covered, for 25 minutes. Remove the cover and brown under the broiler. Serve hot.

SAUTÉED PEPPERS AND SUMMER SQUASH MILANO
YIELD: ENOUGH TO SERVE 6

2 Sweet red peppers, with seeds and pith removed
2 Sweet green peppers, with seeds and pith removed
3 Tablespoons olive oil
2 Tablespoons butter
2 Medium-size summer squash, cut in ⅓-inch-thick slices
2 Medium-size onions, peeled and sliced
3 Cloves garlic, peeled and crushed
⅛ Teaspoon dry mustard
4 Tablespoons Basic Vinaigrette/French Dressing (see page 190)

Directions: Cut the peppers into ⅓-inch-thick slices. Heat the olive oil and butter in a large skillet. Sauté the peppers, squash, onions and garlic until onions become translucent. Season the dressing with the mustard, shake well and toss with the vegetables until well mixed. Serve hot, at room temperature or cold.

SUMMER SQUASH PURÉE
YIELD: ENOUGH TO SERVE 6

2 Pounds summer squash, peeled and seeded if necessary

Directions: Any kind of summer squash will make a tasty purée. Simply chop the squash, place in a saucepan over low heat and simmer gently, stirring frequently, until the vegetable is soft and all liquid has evaporated. Purée in a food processor or blender, or force through a fine sieve or food mill. Chill quickly and freeze as is. To reheat, place in a saucepan over low heat with a bit of butter, then season to taste with salt and black pepper and the herbs of your choice.

ZUCCHINI STRIPS WITH LEMON-CLAM SAUCE
YIELD: ENOUGH TO SERVE 6

6 to 8 Small zucchini, cut lengthwise into ½-inch-thick fingers
5 Tablespoons butter
3½ Tablespoons lemon juice
1 Cup minced clams, including some of the clam liquid
Salt and black pepper

Directions: In a skillet sauté the zucchini fingers until just tender in 3 tablespoons butter. Use a slotted spoon to transfer the squash pieces to a heated serving platter; keep them warm in a slow oven. Melt the remaining 2 tablespoons butter in the skillet, stir in the lemon juice, clams and clam liquid, and simmer until sauce is slightly reduced, (about 3 minutes).

Pour off any liquid that has accumulated on the platter, spoon the hot clam sauce over the zucchini and serve at once.

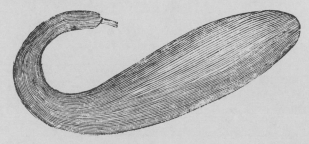

SUMMER SQUASH MEDLEY IN CREAM
YIELD: ENOUGH TO SERVE 6 TO 8

2 Carrots, peeled and thinly sliced
2 Tablespoons butter
1 Each medium-size zucchini, patty pan and
    crookneck squash, sliced
3 Leeks, cut in ½-inch pieces
½ Cup heavy cream
¼ Teaspoon salt
    Pinch each sugar and nutmeg
    Black pepper
1 Tablespoon minced fresh chives

Directions: Sauté the carrots in the butter until nearly tender, then add the squash and leeks and continue to cook, stirring occasionally, for 5 to 10 minutes, or until the squash is tender but still has a bit of "crunch." Using a slotted spoon, remove the squash from the pan and set aside.

Blend the cream, salt, sugar, nutmeg and pepper to taste into the remaining vegetables; cook over medium heat until the cream thickens a bit and clings to the vegetables. Return the squash to the pan and cook only long enough to reheat. Serve hot, garnished with chives.

POTATO-AND-CHEESE-STUFFED SUMMER SQUASH
YIELD: ENOUGH TO SERVE 6

6 Six-inch zucchini
1 Medium-size onion, peeled and minced
4 Tablespoons butter
1 Cup Béchamel Sauce (see page 189)
1 Cup mashed potatoes
¼ Cup grated Parmesan cheese
    Bread crumbs

Directions: Slice off the top third of each zucchini lengthwise. Simmer squash in hot water for 10 minutes. Refresh in cold water and drain. Carefully scoop pulp from each bottom section, leaving shells with walls ½ inch thick. Mince this pulp and the pulp from the top sections. Discard the remaining top skin. Invert the bottom shells on paper towels.

Preheat oven to 450 degrees F. Squeeze the moisture from the minced zucchini and sauté, along with the onion in the butter, until the onion is transparent. Stir in the béchamel sauce, the mashed potatoes, 2 tablespoons grated cheese and enough bread crumbs to somewhat stiffen the mixture. Blot the zucchini shells with paper towels and pipe the potato mixture into each. Sprinkle with grated cheese and bake 25 minutes or until nicely browned.

SUMMER SQUASH IN DILLED SOUR CREAM SAUCE
YIELD: ENOUGH TO SERVE 6

6 Six-inch zucchini, cut in ¼-inch slices
5 Scallions, each with 3 inches green top, coarsely
    chopped
2 Tablespoons each butter and vegetable oil
1 Clove garlic, peeled and crushed
1 Cup sour cream
1 Cup hot Basic White Sauce (see page 189)
2 Tablespoons minced fresh dill
1 Teaspoon lemon juice
1½ Tablespoons minced chives

Directions: Sauté the squash and scallions until barely tender in the hot butter and oil. Add the crushed garlic and mix well. Keep warm.

Mix the sour cream, white sauce and dill, and heat until steaming. *Do not boil.* Stir in the lemon juice. Arrange the vegetables on a serving platter and spoon the sauce over all. Garnish with chives and serve hot.

ZUCCHINI PROVENÇALE
YIELD: ENOUGH TO SERVE 6

2 Medium-size zucchini, peeled and cut into
  ½-inch dice
1 Large onion, peeled and thinly sliced
1 Medium-size sweet green pepper, seeded,
  trimmed and chopped
¼ Cup olive oil
3 Large tomatoes, peeled, seeded and cut in eighths
2 Cloves garlic, peeled
  Salt and pepper to taste
3 Tablespoons grated Parmesan cheese

Directions: Preheat oven to 450 degrees F.

In a skillet sauté the zucchini for 5 minutes in 2 tablespoons oil. Remove with a slotted spoon and transfer to an ovenproof casserole. Add the remaining oil to the skillet and sauté the onion and green pepper until the onion is lightly browned. Add the tomatoes, garlic, salt and pepper, and simmer for 15 minutes. Discard the garlic, pour the tomato mixture over the squash and bake until the zucchini is tender. Sprinkle with Parmesan cheese and bake for 10 minutes until lightly browned. Serve hot.

SUMMER SQUASH IN EGG CREAM SAUCE
YIELD: ENOUGH TO SERVE 6

Summer squash tastes even more delectable when served with this lovely, light cream sauce freshened with mint.

6 to 8 Small summer squash cut into fingers or ¼-inch
       slices
  1 Cup heavy cream
  ½ Teaspoon salt
  ⅛ Teaspoon granulated sugar
1½ Teaspoons chopped fresh mint
  2 Tablespoons butter
  2 Egg yolks, lightly beaten
    Pinch ground nutmeg

Directions: Simmer the squash pieces in a little salted water until barely tender.

Stir the cream, salt, sugar and mint into the melted butter and simmer for 8 to 10 minutes or until slightly thickened. Stir the egg yolks a bit at a time into the cream sauce, then heat for 1 minute more, stirring constantly. Do not allow to boil. Drain the hot squash pieces well, arrange on a hot serving plate and top with the cream sauce. Sprinkle a bit of nutmeg over all. Serve immediately.

NEAPOLITAN SUMMER SQUASH PARMESAN

YIELD: ENOUGH TO SERVE 6 TO 8

This is one of the most delicious vegetable recipes I know of.

---

1 to 2 Oversize squash
    Olive oil (or half olive oil, half cooking oil)
    1 Sixteen-ounce can Italian tomatoes packed in thin tomato purée (if these are not available, bolster the tomato juice in the can of tomatoes with 2 additional tablespoons tomato paste)
    2 Tablespoons tomato paste
    ½ Cup water
    1 Teaspoon granulated sugar
    3 Tablespoons olive oil
    ⅛ Teaspoon thyme
    1 Teaspoon fresh fennel
    ¾ Cup grated Parmesan
    1¼ Cups fine bread crumbs
    2 Large cloves garlic, peeled and minced
    2 Tablespoons minced parsley
    Salt and black pepper to taste
    ½ Pound mozzarella cheese, thinly sliced

Directions: Peel the squash if skin is tough. Cut squash into ½-inch slices. Cover with boiling water (this partially cooks the slices). Drain well. Heat olive oil to a depth of ⅛ inch in a large skillet (or two) and lightly brown the squash slices on both sides. Season to taste with salt and pepper.

Purée Italian tomatoes with their juice, tomato paste, water, sugar and 3 tablespoons olive oil. Bring to a boil, then add thyme and fennel, and simmer until the sauce is the consistency of a thin purée.

Mix by hand, or whirl in a blender or food processor, the Parmesan, bread crumbs, garlic and parsley.

Preheat oven to 400 degrees F.

Arrange half the squash slices in a shallow oven-proof dish (preferably one that will grace your table, since the squash will be served in this baking dish). Sprinkle half the Parmesan–bread crumb mixture over the squash slices, and top with half the tomato sauce and 6 or 8 slices of mozzarella cheese. Repeat the layers, using the remaining squash, Parmesan–bread crumb mixture, tomato sauce and mozzarella. Bake for 20 minutes, or until ingredients in *the center* of the dish are bubbling and the mozzarella is melted.

SUMMER SQUASH MOUSSE WITH BÉCHAMEL SAUCE
YIELD: ENOUGH TO SERVE 6

4 Small summer squash (zucchini is best), peeled and
　　seeded if necessary
1 Tablespoon butter
1 Tablespoon all-purpose flour
½ Cup milk
3 Eggs, well-beaten
　Generous pinch each nutmeg and marjoram
　Salt and pepper to taste
　Béchamel Sauce (see page 189)

Directions: Cut the squash into thick slices and cook
in water to barely cover until just tender. Drain and
purée.

Preheat oven to 350 degrees F.

Melt the butter in a small skillet and stir in the
flour until well-blended. Add the milk all at one
time and bring to a boil, stirring constantly. Remove
the skillet from the heat and beat in the eggs until
the mixture is smooth. Beat in the squash purée
and seasonings, and turn into a buttered mold.
Place the mold in water and bake for 45 minutes,
or until firm on top. Unmold and serve with Béchamel Sauce.

CURRIED SUMMER SQUASH MOUSSE

Follow directions for Summer Squash Mousse, but
add 1 teaspoon (or more to taste) curry powder
when you add the flour.

BROILED MARINATED ZUCCHINI SLICES
YIELD: ENOUGH TO SERVE 6

6 Small zucchini, cut in ¼-inch slices
1 Cup Basic Vinaigrette/French Dressing (see page 190)
　Garlic Butter (see page 194)
　Bread crumbs

Directions: Toss the zucchini slices in the dressing
and marinate in the refrigerator overnight. Drain
the slices and arrange on a greased broiling rack.
Brush with garlic butter, sprinkle lightly with bread
crumbs and broil until golden brown. Serve hot.

SUMMER SQUASH TEMPURA
YIELD: ENOUGH TO SERVE 6

Tempura Batter:
　1 Egg
　1 Cup water
　1 Cup all-purpose flour
　6 Small-size summer squash, cut in ⅓-inch slices
24 Butterflied shrimp or scallops (optional)
　Vegetable oil for frying

Directions: Beat the egg and water together lightly.
Add the flour, 1 tablespoon at a time, stirring up
and over with chopsticks (or a spoon). Do not
overmix; the batter should be lumpy.

Dip squash pieces in batter, drain off excess and fry, one piece at a time, in hot, deep oil (350 to 375 degrees F.) until golden brown. This will take about 2 minutes. Drain on paper towels and serve immediately.

Seafood may be prepared in the same fashion as squash.

WINTER SQUASH TEMPURA

Follow directions for Summer Squash Tempura (see page 138), but substitute for the summer squash peeled and seeded winter squash cut into ¼-inch pieces.

FARM COUNTRY BATTER-FRIED SQUASH
YIELD: ENOUGH TO SERVE 6

1 Large summer or winter squash, peeled and seeded
  Salt
1½ Cups all-purpose flour
⅛ Teaspoon salt
3 Eggs
1 Cup milk
  Vegetable oil for frying

Directions: Cut the squash into ¼-inch slices. Parboil winter squash 5 minutes. Arrange slices in a single layer on paper towels and sprinkle with salt. Allow to stand for 5 minutes, then blot well with paper towels.

Sift together the flour and ⅛ teaspoon salt. Beat in the eggs and add the milk, stirring only long enough to thoroughly moisten the batter.

Dip squash slices in the batter, one at a time, and fry in 1 inch of hot oil until golden brown on both sides, turning once. Drain briefly on paper towels before serving hot.

NUT-FRIED SQUASH
YIELD: ENOUGH TO SERVE 6

1 Large summer or 1 medium-size winter squash,
    peeled and seeded
  Vegetable oil for frying
2 Eggs
2 Teaspoons water
1½ Cups finely chopped walnuts, pecans or almonds

Directions: Use a French-fry cutter to cut the squash into serving-size pieces, or cut into ½-by-2-inch sticks by hand. Cover winter squash with boiling salted water and allow to stand for 20 minutes.

Heat oil to a depth of ½ inch in a skillet. Beat eggs together with 2 teaspoons water. Drain squash sticks well and pat dry. Dip first in beaten egg and then in nuts; fry to a crisp golden brown in the hot oil. Drain briefly on paper towels before serving hot.

COPY-RIGHTED 1887 BY J.J.H. GREGORY O.M. HEAD

OLD NEW ENGLAND STEAMED VEGETABLE PUDDING
YIELD: ENOUGH TO SERVE 6 TO 8

8 Tablespoons butter (1 stick)
6 Eggs
1 Cup prepared summer or winter squash,
    chopped and cooked
½ Cup chopped cooked spinach
½ Cup minced mushrooms, sautéed in
    1 tablespoon butter
6 Slices bread
    Heavy cream
2 Tablespoons each grated Parmesan cheese and
    minced fresh parsley
½ Cup dry bread crumbs
    Salt and black pepper

Directions: Cream the butter until light and fluffy. Separate the eggs; reserve the whites and add the yolks to the creamed butter, beating until the mixture is light and smooth. Squeeze all cooking liquid from the squash and spinach before measuring, then add these vegetables, along with the mushrooms, to the creamed mixture. Moisten the bread slices with as much cream as necessary, squeeze out any excess and add the bread to the vegetable mixture. Stir in the cheese, parsley, bread crumbs and salt and pepper to taste.

Thoroughly grease a tubular pudding mold and pour in the batter. Secure a piece of aluminum foil over the top of the mold; set on the lid. Cover lid tightly with foil tied with string. Place the mold in a deep kettle and encircle its top and bottom with crushed pieces of aluminum foil to keep it upright in the kettle. Pour in enough boiling water to reach ¾ of the way up the sides of the mold. Cover the kettle and allow the mold to steam for 1½ to 2 hours, adding more boiling water as necessary to keep the water level at its original depth.

To test for doneness, press the top of the pudding lightly with your fingers. If the top springs back, loosen all edges of the pudding, set a serving plate over the mold and turn upside down, then shake once. If the top feels sticky and soft, re-cover as before and continue to steam until the pudding tests done.

FRIED CURRIED SQUASH STICKS
YIELD: ENOUGH TO SERVE 6

2 Cups grated summer or winter squash, squeezed
    dry in paper towels
4 Tablespoons butter
2½ Tablespoons all-purpose flour
6 Eggs
1 Cup milk
3 Tablespoons grated Parmesan cheese
1 Teaspoon each salt, granulated sugar and
    curry powder
1 Cup fine cracker crumbs
    Vegetable oil for frying

Directions: Sauté the squash in 2 tablespoons butter until the vegetable is tender. Spread on paper towels to drain and cool. Melt 2 tablespoons butter in the top of a double boiler, add the flour and stir until smooth. Beat 4 eggs well, then beat them into the manié along with the squash, milk, cheese, salt, sugar and curry powder. Cook over hot water until the mixture is thick enough to hold its shape. (If the eggs used were large, a few teaspoons of bread crumbs may be beaten in to stiffen the paste to the desired consistency.)

Pour a 1-inch-thick layer of the paste into a well-buttered baking pan and chill it thoroughly. A few minutes prior to serving, cut the paste into short strips and dip each in beaten remaining eggs, then in cracker crumbs, then in egg and crumbs again. Deep-fry the strips in hot (375 degrees F.) oil until golden brown. Drain briefly on paper towels and serve very hot, with Yogurt Dipping Sauce (see page 194).

COUNTRY CREAMED SQUASH
YIELD: ENOUGH TO SERVE 4 TO 6

3 Tablespoons butter
¾ Cups heavy cream
1¼ Cups milk
2 Medium-size summer or winter squash (peeled
   and seeded if necessary), sliced
   Flour
¾ Teaspoon salt
⅛ Teaspoon each nutmeg and
   white pepper

Directions: Melt the butter in a large, heavy skillet, add the cream and milk, and heat to steaming over the lowest possible flame. Do not boil. Coat the squash pieces lightly with flour and slip them into the hot liquid one at a time until evenly distributed. The liquid should barely cover the squash. Sprinkle with half of each of the seasonings and simmer, without boiling, for 30 minutes.

Turn the slices carefully, sprinkle with the remaining seasonings and simmer for 30 minutes more, again without boiling. Serve hot.

GARDEN VEGETABLES IN CREAM
YIELD: ENOUGH TO SERVE 6

4 Very small zucchini or yellow summer squash,
   cut into lengthwise strips ½ inch thick
4 Carrots, scraped and cut into lengthwise strips
   ⅓ inch thick
12 Scallions, each with 3 inches
   green top
4 Tablespoons butter
3 Cups young peas
⅓ Cup water
1 Cup heavy cream
   Generous pinch nutmeg
   Salt and black pepper

Directions: Sauté the zucchini and carrot strips for 4 minutes in the butter. Add the whole scallions, the peas and the water. Cover and simmer until the vegetables are tender. Add a very little water if necessary to prevent the vegetables from scorching. In a small saucepan reduce the cream slightly; season with nutmeg and salt and pepper to taste. Arrange the peas in a mound in the center of a small platter, surround with the remaining vegetables and pour the cream over all. Serve immediately.

BEST WINTER SQUASH PURÉE
YIELD: ABOUT 3 TO 4 CUPS

Winter squash is often used (both for home use and commercially) as a substitute for pumpkin. Although most winter squash varieties perform equally well as pumpkin substitutes, Butternut and Buttercup are best for this purpose. The flavor of these is superior to pumpkin, and with smaller seed cavities there is less waste.

3-to-4-Pound winter squash
   Butter
   Pinch each salt and ground cloves
    (if desired)

Directions: Preheat oven to 350 degrees F.

Scoop out and discard seeds and stringy fibers. Set the cleaned pieces in a large roasting pan. Add hot water to a depth of ½ inch and bake for 1½ to 2 hours, or until the pulp is tender.

Scrape out pulp and purée it in a food processor or blender, or force through a fine strainer or food mill. Stir in butter, salt and cloves to taste. Refrigerate, freeze (see pages 59–61 and 62–63) or reheat and serve hot.

SCALLOPED WINTER SQUASH AND APPLES
YIELD: ENOUGH TO SERVE 6

3 Medium-size winter squash, peeled, seeded and sliced
4 McIntosh apples, peeled, cored and sliced
3 Tablespoons brown sugar
⅓ Teaspoon salt
¼ Teaspoon each cinnamon and grated nutmeg
⅛ Teaspoon mace
3 Tablespoons butter
¼ Cup freshly squeezed orange juice

Directions: Preheat oven to 350 degrees F.

Simmer the squash slices until tender in water to cover. Drain well. Arrange a layer of squash slices in the bottom of a buttered casserole. Cover with a layer of apples. Mix the sugar, salt, cinnamon, nutmeg and mace, and sprinkle some of the mixture over the apple slices. Dot with bits of butter. Continue to build alternating layers, ending with a layer of apples. Sprinkle with orange juice and brown sugar, and bake 50 minutes.

SQUASH-NUT PANCAKES

1 Cup Best Winter Squash Purée (see page 142)
2 Eggs, lightly beaten
½ Cup all-purpose flour
¼ Teaspoon baking powder
1¼ Teaspoons salt
½ Teaspoon granulated sugar
¼ Teaspoon cinnamon
  Pinch cloves
¾ Cup finely chopped pecans
¾ Cup bread crumbs
  Vegetable oil for frying

Directions: Beat together the purée and eggs. Sift together the flour, baking powder, salt, sugar and spices. Stir the dry ingredients into the squash mixture. Mix the nuts and bread crumbs, and spread them over a sheet of waxed paper. Spoon a tablespoon of the batter onto the nuts and bread crumbs, turn to coat the other side and flatten the pancake slightly. Fry in 1 inch hot (375 degrees F.) oil until golden on both sides.

SOUR CREAM–SQUASH PANCAKES
YIELD: 12-16 PANCAKES

4 Cups grated winter squash
1 Medium-size onion, peeled and grated
1 Large egg, lightly beaten
3½ Tablespoons all-purpose flour
⅓ Teaspoon salt
  Pinch granulated sugar
3 Tablespoons sour cream
⅓ Cup vegetable oil

Directions: Squeeze the squash between paper towels to remove excess moisture. Mix with the onion, egg, flour, salt, sugar. Stir in the sour cream.

Heat the oil in a skillet and fry small pancakes to crispy brown on both sides, turning only once. Serve plain, with applesauce or cold sour cream.

SWEET POTATO–SQUASH SOUFFLÉ
YIELD: ENOUGH TO SERVE 6 TO 8

1⅓ Cups Best Winter Squash Purée (see page 142)
1⅓ Cups cooked and mashed sweet potatoes
5 Tablespoons butter
4 Tablespoons orange liqueur
½ Cup plus 2 tablespoons hot milk
5 Eggs
1½ Teaspoons grated lemon zest*
¾ Teaspoon salt
  Pinch each ground mace and nutmeg

Directions: Place the squash purée and sweet potatoes in a large bowl. Stir the butter and orange liqueur into the hot milk and add to the vegetable mixture, beating until smooth. Separate the eggs, reserving the whites; beat in the egg yolks and continue to beat while adding the lemon zest and spices.

Preheat oven to 400 degrees F. Beat egg whites until they form stiff peaks and gently fold into sweet potato–squash mixture. Pour into a well-buttered soufflé or other deep baking dish and bake for 30 to 40 minutes, or until the soufflé is lightly browned and puffy on top. Serve immediately.

*The thin outer skin of the fruit, with none of the bitter white underskin included.

PINEAPPLE–WINTER SQUASH CASSEROLE

YIELD: ENOUGH TO SERVE 4 TO 6

2 Medium-size winter squash, peeled, seeded and cut into
   ½-inch thick slices
  All-purpose flour
1 Large can crushed pineapple
¼ Teaspoon ground nutmeg
2 Tablespoons butter
2 Tablespoons light brown sugar

Directions: Cook squash slices in water to cover until tender. Drain the slices well, blot between paper towels and dust *lightly* with flour.

Preheat oven to 350 degrees F.

Arrange a layer of squash slices in the bottom of a well-buttered casserole, top with a few tablespoons of crushed pineapple and a sprinkle of nutmeg. Continue to arrange alternate rows of squash and pineapple, ending with a layer of pineapple. Pour the pineapple juice remaining in the can into the casserole. Dot with butter and sprinkle with sugar. Bake 45 minutes. Serve hot.

SHERRIED CREAMED WINTER SQUASH

YIELD: ENOUGH TO SERVE 4 TO 6

2 Medium-size winter squash, peeled, seeded and
   cut into ½-inch dice
3 Cups hot Basic White Sauce
   (see page 189)
2 Tablespoons sherry
¾ Cup shredded blanched almonds
1½ Tablespoons butter

Directions: Cook squash pieces in water to barely cover until tender. Drain well and combine with the white sauce and sherry. Turn into a baking dish, dot with butter and sprinkle with almonds. Brown lightly under broiler. Serve immediately.

SWEET-AND-SOUR WINTER SQUASH SLICES

YIELD: ENOUGH TO SERVE 4 TO 6

2 Medium-size winter squash, peeled, seeded
   and thinly sliced
  Water
3 Tablespoons butter
1 Tablespoon cornstarch
2 Tablespoons granulated sugar
3 Tablespoons vinegar
  Salt and black pepper
1½ Tablespoons minced parsley

Directions: Cook the sliced squash in salted water to barely cover until tender. Drain well and reserve the cooking liquid. Melt the butter and stir into it

1½ cups cooking liquid and the cornstarch. Cook over medium heat, stirring constantly until the sauce thickens. Stir in the sugar, vinegar, salt and pepper to taste, and adjust the degree of sweet and sour to suit your taste. Add the squash slices and continue cooking until they are heated through. Serve hot sprinkled with parsley.

DILLED SWEET-AND-SOUR WINTER SQUASH SLICES

Prepare as above, but add 2 tablespoons minced fresh dill when you melt the butter.

FLUFFY BAKED STUFFED WINTER SQUASH
YIELD: ENOUGH TO SERVE 4

2 Medium-size winter squash, split in half
  lengthwise and seeded
2½ Tablespoons melted butter
2 Eggs, separated
⅛ Teaspoon each grated nutmeg and
  cayenne pepper
Salt and black pepper to taste
2 to 3 Tablespoons heavy cream
Garlic Bread Crumbs
  (see page 194)

Directions: Preheat oven to 350 degrees F.

Brush the tops of the squash with melted butter, cover with waxed paper and bake until tender (about 1 hour). Scoop out most of the pulp, leaving the shells intact. Mash the pulp and whip it with the egg yolks, 2 tablespoons melted butter, the seasonings and enough cream to make a soft but not runny mixture.

Beat the egg whites until they are stiff but not dry, fold into the squash mixture and spoon into the reserved squash shells. Sprinkle with garlic crumbs and bake 30 to 40 minutes, or until the filling is hot and the tops are nicely browned. Serve hot.

SUGARED WINTER SQUASH WITH CANDIED GINGER
YIELD: ENOUGH TO SERVE 4 TO 6

2 Medium-size winter squash, split in
  half and seeded
7 Tablespoons butter
7 Tablespoons light brown sugar
7 Tablespoons fresh orange juice, strained
3 Tablespoons minced candied ginger
  Salt
  Melted butter

Directions: Preheat oven to 350 degrees F.

Heat the butter, sugar and orange juice in a small saucepan. Stir over low heat until the sugar is dissolved and add the ginger. Brush the cut sides of the squash with the sugar-butter syrup. Divide remaining syrup between the four squash cavities. Sprinkle the squash lightly with salt and arrange on a shallow baking sheet. Add ½ inch water to the bottom of the pan and bake the squash 1¼ hours, or until tender, brushing frequently with melted butter. Serve hot.

RUMANIAN WINTER SQUASH
YIELD: ENOUGH TO SERVE 4 TO 6

2 Medium-size winter squash, peeled and seeded
3 Tablespoons butter
1 Large onion, peeled and coarsely chopped
1½ Tablespoons all-purpose flour
2 Tablespoons minced fresh dill
1⅓ Cups cold water
½ Teaspoon salt
1 Tablespoon lemon juice
⅔ Cup heavy cream

Directions: Cut the squash into strips ¼ inch wide and 2 inches long. Melt the butter in a large skillet and sauté the onion until golden. Stir in the flour until well blended, add the dill, the water and salt, and stir constantly over medium heat until thick, pressing out lumps with the back of a spoon. Add the squash pieces, cover and cook 1 hour or until tender. Stir in the lemon juice and then the cream. Reheat and serve hot.

BRANDIED AND BAKED WINTER SQUASH
YIELD: ENOUGH TO SERVE 4 TO 6

2 Medium-size winter squash, peeled and seeded
¾ Cup light brown sugar
¼ Cup melted butter
¼ Cup apricot brandy
½ Teaspoon each ground cinnamon and nutmeg
¼ Teaspoon salt
1 Cup milk

Directions: Cut the squash into ½-inch thick slices and cook until tender in water to cover.

Preheat oven to 400 degrees F.

Mash the squash and beat in the sugar, butter, brandy, seasonings and milk. Spoon into a buttered casserole, sprinkle with sugar and bake 20 minutes.

DEEP-FRIED JULIENNE WINTER SQUASH
YIELD: ENOUGH TO SERVE 4 TO 6

2 Medium-size winter squash, peeled and seeded
Vegetable oil
Salt

Directions: Cut the squash into julienne the size of matchsticks. Drain well and dry thoroughly between paper towels. Fry in deep fat (395 degrees F.) until crisp and nicely browned. Drain briefly on paper towels, sprinkle with salt and serve hot.

DEEP-FRIED WINTER SQUASH SLICES
YIELD: ENOUGH TO SERVE 4 TO 6

2 Medium-size winter squash, peeled and seeded
Vegetable oil
Salt

Directions: Cut the squash into ½-inch thick slices and cook in water to cover until just tender. Drain the slices and dry thoroughly between paper towels. Deep-fry until golden brown on all sides. Drain briefly on paper towels, sprinkle with salt and serve hot.

SUMMER SQUASH SALAD MIMOSA
YIELD: ENOUGH TO SERVE 6

6 to 8 Small yellow summer squash or zucchini (or half
    and half)
8 Flat anchovy fillets, drained and cut in eighths
    Basic Vinaigrette/French Dressing (see page 190)
3 Hard-cooked egg yolks

Directions: Cut the squash into thin slices and blanch
in boiling water. Drain well, blot on paper towels
and toss with the anchovy pieces and dressing.
Chill well and top with sieved egg yolks.

MARINATED BEET AND SUMMER SQUASH SALAD
YIELD: ENOUGH TO SERVE 6

4 Medium-size beets, cooked, peeled and thinly sliced
1 Sweet red onion, peeled and thinly sliced
½ Cup olive oil
6 Tablespoons tarragon vinegar
1 Tablespoon granulated sugar
4 Small yellow summer squash (or zucchini, or a
    combination), cut into ¼-inch slices
2 Tablespoons minced dill
¾ Cup sour cream
    Salt and black pepper
3 Scallions, each with 3 inches green top,
    coarsely chopped

Directions: Toss together the beets and red onion
with ¼ cup olive oil, 3 tablespoons vinegar and 1
tablespoon sugar. Refrigerate for at least 2 hours.
In another bowl toss together the squash slices,
the remainder of the oil and vinegar, and the dill.
Refrigerate for at least 2 hours. Just prior to serving, drain the squash and toss all the vegetables
together with the sour cream. Season to taste with
salt and pepper, adding additional sugar and vinegar if desired for a more distinctive sweet-and-sour
taste.

SUMMER GAZPACHO SALAD
YIELD: ENOUGH TO SERVE 6

2 Spanish onions, peeled and thinly sliced
1 Medium-size zucchini
1 Medium-size cucumber
4 Medium-size ripe tomatoes
2 Cups dry bread crumbs
¼ Cup Garlic Butter (see page 194)
  Salt and black pepper
1 Cup garlic-flavored Basic Vinaigrette/French Dressing
  (see page 190)

Directions: Cover the sliced onions with ice water and allow to soak for 30 minutes. Meanwhile, trim the zucchini and cucumber, and cut into thin slices. Peel and thinly slice the tomatoes. Arrange vegetables on paper towels and chill well. Sauté the bread crumbs in garlic butter until golden brown.

Drain the onions and pat dry. In a large glass bowl arrange alternate layers of onion, zucchini, cucumber and tomato slices, sprinkling each of the layers with the garlic bread crumbs and salt and pepper to taste before adding the next. Pour the dressing over all and serve immediately.

DILLED ZUCCHINI SALAD
YIELD: ENOUGH TO SERVE 6

8 Very small zucchini
  Basic Vinaigrette/French Dressing
    (see page 190)
  Salad greens
¼ Cup each minced fresh parsley
    and dill

Directions: Rinse and trim the zucchini and cut into ½-inch slices. Place in a saucepan with water to cover and cook, uncovered, from 5 to 6 minutes, or until the zucchini is tender but still firm. Drain immediately and allow to cool to room temperature, then gently toss with as much dressing as necessary to coat all the slices. Set aside for 1 hour.

Just before serving, arrange crisp salad greens over the bottom and sides of a salad bowl. Heap in the marinated zucchini slices and garnish with parsley and dill. Serve at once.

WATERCRESS, SUMMER SQUASH AND CHERRY TOMATO SALAD
YIELD: ENOUGH TO SERVE 6

40 Cherry tomatoes
 3 Small unpeeled zucchini or yellow summer squash
 1 Bunch watercress
½ Cup sour cream
¼ Cup mayonnaise
 1 Tablespoon each minced fresh dill, chives, lemon juice
     and prepared horseradish
   Salt and black pepper

Directions: Pour boiling water over the tomatoes; allow to stand for a minute or two, then drain and carefully peel. Cut the squash into thin slices.

Arrange the watercress leaves over the bottom of a salad bowl. Add the tomatoes and squash, and chill well.

Just before serving, mix together the sour cream, mayonnaise, dill, chives, lemon juice and horseradish. Season to taste with salt and pepper. Pour over the salad and serve at once.

AUNT SUE'S MARINATED TOMATO-ZUCCHINI SALAD
YIELD: ENOUGH TO SERVE 6 TO 8

6 Small zucchini (about 1½ inches in diameter)
4 Medium-size ripe tomatoes
1 Green pepper, seeded
6 Scallions, each with 3 inches green top
  Basic Vinaigrette/French Dressing (see page 190)

Directions: Cut zucchini into paper-thin slices, tomatoes into ½-inch wedges, and green pepper into very thin rings. Chop scallions. Toss all ingredients in dressing and marinate in refrigerator for 1 hour.

MARINATED TOMATO-ZUCCHINI-ANCHOVY SALAD

Peel and thinly slice 1 sweet onion. Drain 12 large flat anchovies and cut in quarters. Follow directions as given above, tossing the onion with the other vegetables. Garnish with anchovy pieces and serve cold.

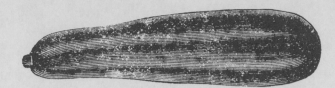

SALADE MONA
YIELD: ENOUGH TO SERVE 6

2 Very small zucchini, cut into ¼-inch slices
3 Medium-size tomatoes, peeled and sliced
4 Cooked artichoke bottoms, cut
    into ½-inch cubes
¾ Cup Basic Vinaigrette/French Dressing
    (see page 190)
¾ Cup mayonnaise
3 Hard-cooked eggs, peeled and
    neatly sliced
1 Tablespoon capers
1 Teaspoon each minced fresh chervil, tarragon,
    chives and parsley

Directions: Blanch the zucchini slices for 5 minutes in boiling water to cover. Drain well and dry between paper towels. Toss the slices with ¼ cup French dressing.

Arrange the tomato slices and artichoke pieces neatly over the zucchini and pour the remaining ½ cup French dressing over all. Marinate 30 to 40 minutes and drain well. Arrange the tomato slices on a serving plate and top them with zucchini slices nicely arranged. Cover the top with a thin layer of mayonnaise and garnish with artichoke cubes, egg slices, capers, and the herbs.

CANTALOUPE, ZUCCHINI AND CUCUMBER SALAD
YIELD: ENOUGH TO SERVE 6

1 Small ripe cantaloupe, peeled, seeded and cut
　　into bite-size, ¼-inch slices
2 Small zucchini, cut into ⅛-inch slices
1½ Cups Basic Vinaigrette/French Dressing
　　(see page 190)
2 Small cucumbers, cut into ⅛-inch slices
½ Cup sour cream
2 Teaspoons onion juice
　　Salt
1½ Tablespoons minced chives
1 Bunch watercress

Directions: In separate bowls toss cantaloupe and zucchini slices in French dressing and marinate in the refrigerator for 1 hour. Sprinkle cucumber slices with salt and refrigerate for 1 hour.

Mix sour cream, onion juice and salt to taste. Drain cantaloupe, zucchini and cucumber slices, and toss with the sour cream mixture. Arrange on a bed of watercress leaves, sprinkle with chives and serve immediately.

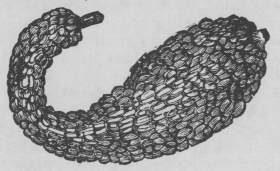

ZESTY TOMATO, ZUCCHINI AND CUCUMBER SALAD
YIELD: ENOUGH TO SERVE 6 TO 8

4 Very small zucchini, sliced
4 Small cucumbers, sliced
　　Salt
1 Tablespoon tarragon vinegar
2 Tablespoons oil
4 Medium-size tomatoes, peeled, sliced and seeded
4 Scallions, each with 3 inches green top, cut
　　in ¼-inch slices
1 Cup mayonnaise
2 Hard-cooked egg yolks

Directions: Sprinkle the squash and cucumber slices with salt and set them aside for 1 hour. Drain well and toss with the vinegar and oil. Drain well again. Arrange the tomato slices over the cucumber and squash slices and spread with mayonnaise. Garnish with scallion slices and egg yolk pressed through a sieve.

ZUCCHINI CIRCLE SALAD

1 Recipe Zucchini Circles with Horseradish Cream
　　(see page 85)
1 Small head lettuce, shredded
1 Cup chilled mayonnaise
1 Cup chilled sour cream
2 Tablespoons minced chives
1 Clove garlic, peeled and minced
2 Drops green food coloring

Directions: Arrange chilled zucchini circles on shredded lettuce. Mix mayonnaise, sour cream, 1 tablespoon chives, the garlic and food coloring. Pipe the salad dressing attractively over the salad. Serve immediately, sprinkled with the remaining chives.

SUMMER SQUASH, SPINACH AND TARRAGON SALAD
YIELD: ENOUGH TO SERVE 6

2 Small zucchini or yellow summer squash, thinly sliced
2 Cups fresh spinach leaves, with stems removed
3 Plum tomatoes, peeled and quartered lengthwise
½ Cup finely chopped fresh parsley
5 Tablespoons minced fresh tarragon leaves
⅓ Cup olive oil
3 Tablespoons lime juice
1 Teaspoon salt
2 Cloves garlic, peeled and minced

Directions: Place squash slices, spinach, tomatoes and herbs in a large salad bowl. Chill. Combine the remaining ingredients and blend thoroughly, then pour over the vegetables. Toss well and serve at once.

COUNTRY GARDEN VEGETABLE SALAD
YIELD: ENOUGH TO SERVE 12

This marvelous salad remains at the peak of perfection for several days and is so versatile that the wise cook prepares an ample amount . . . hence this generous recipe.

4 Small zucchini, cut into ⅓-inch cubes
4 Medium-size potatoes
4 Medium-size beets
1½ Cups shelled peas
4 Medium-size carrots, scraped and cut into ⅓-inch dice
2 Medium-size cucumbers, peeled, seeded and cut into ⅓-inch dice
8 Scallions, each with 3 inches green top, coarsely chopped
2 Cups Basic Vinaigrette/French Dressing (see page 190)
1 Cup mayonnaise
1 Cup sour cream
Salt and black pepper

Directions: Preheat oven to 375 degrees F.

Blanch the zucchini for 8 minutes in boiling water to cover. Drain well and dry between paper towels. Cool. Cook the potatoes in their skins until tender. Drain, peel and cut into ⅓-inch cubes. Cool. Bake the beets for about 40 minutes, or until tender. Peel, cool and cut into ⅓-inch cubes. Cook the peas and carrots separately in salted water until tender. Drain and cool. Sprinkle the cucumber cubes with salt, weight with a heavy plate and set aside 15 minutes. Drain well and press between paper towels to extract additional moisture. Toss all of the vegetables with the French dressing and marinate for several hours or overnight, tossing occasionally. Drain the vegetables and toss them with the mixed mayonnaise and sour cream. Season to taste with salt and pepper. Chill.

DILLED COUNTRY GARDEN VEGETABLE SALAD

Prepare Country Garden Vegetable Salad as directed (see page 152), but mix ¼ cup minced fresh dill with the mayonnaise and sour cream. Garnish with hard-cooked egg slices and capers.

PICKLED HERRING AND VEGETABLE SALAD
YIELD: ENOUGH TO SERVE 6

Prepare one-half recipe Dilled Country-Garden Vegetable Salad as directed. Mix 1 jar pickled herring in cream sauce (cut the herring and onions into ½-inch pieces) with the mayonnaise and ½ cup sour cream. Continue as directed.

COUNTRY GARDEN VEGETABLE SALAD WITH MUSTARD CREAM

Prepare Country Garden Vegetable Salad as directed (see page 152), but substitute 2 tablespoons yellow prepared mustard for 2 tablespoons of the sour cream. Garnish with julienne strips of cooked ham and chopped chives.

DILLED CHICKEN AND VEGETABLE SALAD
YIELD: ENOUGH TO SERVE 6

Prepare one-half recipe Dilled Country Garden Vegetable Salad as directed. Toss 3 cups boned, cooked chicken with the mayonnaise. Substitute 1 cup whipped cream for the sour cream. Fold the whipped cream gently into the finished salad. Garnish as directed.

SHRIMP AND VEGETABLE SALAD
YIELD: ENOUGH TO SERVE 6

Prepare one-half recipe Dilled Country Garden Vegetable Salad. Toss the vegetables with two dozen shelled and cleaned shrimp, each cut in half lengthwise. Garnish as directed.

COUNTRY GARDEN VEGETABLE SALAD IN TOMATO SHELLS
YIELD: ENOUGH TO SERVE 6

Use one-half recipe Country Garden Vegetable Salad (see page 152) to fill 6 tomato shells prepared as follows:

Plunge the tomatoes first in boiling water for a few seconds, then in cold water, and slip off the skins. Cut a slice from the top, scoop out the pulp and seeds, turn upside down to drain for 45 minutes and chill. Place the stuffed tomatoes on lettuce leaves and garnish with watercress sprigs. Serve cold.

SHRIMP AND VEGETABLE SALAD IN TOMATO SHELLS

Stuff tomato shells with Shrimp and Vegetable Salad. Serve cold.

DILLED CHICKEN AND VEGETABLE SALAD IN TOMATO SHELLS

Stuff tomato shells with Dilled Chicken and Vegetable Salad. Serve cold.

RATATOUILLE IN TOMATO SHELLS
YIELD: ENOUGH TO SERVE 6

1 Recipe Ratatouille
   (see page 130)
6 Firm tomatoes
   Salt

Directions: Chill the ratatouille. Cut a slice from the top of each tomato and scoop out the pulp and seeds. Sprinkle the cavities with salt and turn upside down on paper towels to drain. Stuff the tomato shells with ratatouille and chill for 2 or 3 hours. Serve cold.

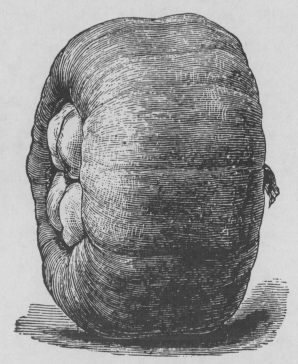

SUMMER VEGETABLE SALAD
YIELD: ENOUGH TO SERVE 6 TO 8

3 Cups well-washed watercress or other salad
   greens, drained
2 Small yellow summer squash, cut in ¼-inch slices
2 Small zucchini, cut in ¼-inch slices
1 Small cucumber, peeled and sliced
2 Small carrots, peeled and cut into thin strips
1 Green pepper, seeded and cut in ½-inch slices
1 Red pepper, seeded and cut in ½-inch slices
12 Radish roses
12 Cherry tomatoes, cut in half
12 Scallions, each with 3 inches green top, cut in
   ½-inch slices
   Basic Vinaigrette/French Dressing (see page 190)

Directions: Arrange the watercress or greens over the bottom of a large salad bowl. Top with squash, zucchini and cucumber slices, and decorate with carrot and pepper strips radiating outward from the center. Set the radish roses and cherry tomato halves around the edge of the bowl and sprinkle the sliced scallions over all. Refrigerate. Toss with dressing just before serving.

SUMMER VEGETABLE BOWL

Prepare all vegetables as directed in Summer Vegetable Salad, but omit the lettuce or greens and leave the scallions whole. Arrange the vegetables attractively over cracked ice. Serve with Basic Vinaigrette/French Dressing, or a variation (see page 190), on the side.

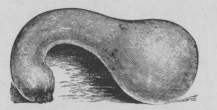

VEGETABLES À LA GRECQUE
YIELD: ENOUGH TO SERVE 8

1 Each very small zucchini and yellow summer squash, sliced
1½ Cups each cauliflower flowerets, small artichoke hearts, sliced carrots, small white onions, mushrooms or any other small vegetables or vegetable pieces you may wish to include
½ Cup olive oil
3 Tablespoons each tarragon vinegar and lemon juice
2 Large cloves garlic or 3 smaller ones, peeled
¾ Teaspoon each salt and whole black peppercorns
1 Bay leaf
1 Sprig each fennel, thyme and tarragon
   Bouquet garni

Directions: Prepare the vegetables for eating. In a small saucepan bring to a boil the oil, vinegar, lemon juice, garlic, salt, peppercorns, bay leaf, fennel, thyme, tarragon and the bouquet garni. Add the vegetables with enough water to barely cover. Cook until the vegetables are just tender, then remove with a slotted spoon to a serving dish and set aside. Simmer the cooking liquid until it is reduced by half. Remove the bouquet garni and strain the sauce over the vegetables. Cool to room temperature, then chill.

CHILLED SUMMER SQUASH MOUSSE
YIELD: ENOUGH TO SERVE 6

2 Medium-size summer squash, peeled and seeded if necessary
⅛ Teaspoon Tabasco sauce
1 Tablespoon lemon juice
½ Cup mayonnaise
1 Tablespoon prepared horseradish
1 Envelope unflavored gelatin
1 Cup whipped cream
2 Drops green food coloring
   Salt and black pepper
1 Very small zucchini, thinly sliced
1 Tablespoon Basic Vinaigrette/ French dressing (see page 190)
   Watercress

Directions: Cut all of the squash (except the small zucchini) into ½-inch-thick slices and blanch in boiling water to cover for 8 minutes. Drain well, then purée and chill. Mix the purée with Tabasco, lemon juice, mayonnaise and horseradish. Soften 1 envelope gelatin in 1 tablespoon cool water, then add 1 tablespoon hot water to dissolve and fold thoroughly into the squash mixture along with the whipped cream, food coloring and salt and pepper to taste.

Pour into a chilled timbale mold and refrigerate until firm. Meanwhile, marinate the thin zucchini slices in dressing. Unmold the mousse on a chilled platter, decorate the top with the marinated zucchini slices and surround with watercress. Serve cold.

SUMMER SQUASH SLAW
YIELD: ENOUGH TO SERVE 6 TO 8

1 Small head cabbage
2 Small summer squash
3 Tablespoons granulated sugar
¾ Teaspoon salt
1 Teaspoon poppy seeds
3 Tablespoons lemon juice
2 Tablespoons milk
1 Tablespoon prepared yellow mustard
1 Cup mayonnaise
2 Tablespoons minced chives

Directions: Remove and discard the tough outer leaves and hard core from the cabbage. Finely shred or grate the cabbage and the squash into separate bowls and drain each well.

Combine the sugar, salt, poppy seeds, lemon juice, milk, mustard and mayonnaise, and mix well. Refrigerate the two bowls of vegetables and the dressing separately for several hours. Quickly drain the vegetables well once more and mix them with the dressing. Adjust the seasonings, sprinkle with chives and serve cold.

VEGETABLE MEDLEY SLAW
YIELD: ENOUGH TO SERVE 6 TO 8

2 Small summer squash
1 Small head cabbage
1 Each small sweet red and green pepper, seeded, trimmed and finely chopped
10 Black olives, pitted and chopped
1 Medium-size carrot, scraped and grated

¼ Large Spanish onion, peeled and minced
3 Scallions, each with 3 inches green top, coarsely chopped
¾ Cup granulated sugar
1 Cup mayonnaise
1 Cup mild vinegar
¾ Teaspoon salt

Directions: Shred or grate squash, drain well and refrigerate overnight. Remove and discard the tough outer leaves and hard core from the cabbage. Finely shred or grate the cabbage, drain well and mix with remaining ingredients. Refrigerate overnight.

Prior to serving, drain the squash again and mix with coleslaw. Adjust the seasonings to suit your taste and serve cold.

FARM-STYLE CHESTNUT AND WINTER SQUASH SALAD
YIELD: ENOUGH TO SERVE 6

2 Medium-size winter squash, peeled, seeded and cut into ½-inch dice
2 Cups boiled and peeled chestnuts
1 Cup Unboiled Salad Dressing (see page 190)
4 Scallions, each with 3 inches green top, cut in ¼-inch slices

Directions: Simmer the squash pieces until just tender in salted water to cover. Do not overcook. Drain and chill. Coarsely chop the chestnuts. Toss the squash, chestnuts, dressing and scallions. Serve cold.

SOURDOUGH* VEGETABLE BREAD
YIELD: 2 LOAVES

These unusual and delicious sourdough loaves can double as both bread *and* vegetable. Just spread the rolled-out dough with the seasoned and cooked squash filling and roll up, then bake and serve hot with melted butter.

    1 Cup Sourdough Starter (see page 188), at least
        1 week old
1½ Tablespoons sugar
    2 Cups milk
5½ Cups all-purpose flour
    2 Cups finely chopped summer squash
    1 Cup finely chopped onion or scallion
    3 Cloves garlic, peeled and minced
        Oregano, dill, thyme, sage, etc., to taste
    3 Tablespoons butter or vegetable oil
¾ Teaspoon baking soda
2¼ Teaspoons salt
    1 Cup grated cheese

Directions: The day before you bake the bread, mix the week-old starter with the sugar and milk. Stir in 3½ cups flour, 1 cup at a time. The dough will be fairly moist. Cover with a dishtowel and set in a warm, draft-free place overnight to rise.

To prepare filling, sauté the squash, onion, garlic and spices to taste in the butter or oil. Remove from the heat and set aside in a strainer or colander to cool and drain.

*This filling is equally delicious when rolled up with any fairly stiff-doughed white bread.

Sprinkle the baking soda over the risen dough and mix in thoroughly. Add the salt and ½ cup flour, then turn out onto a floured board. Knead in the remaining flour, ½ cup at a time, until the dough is fairly stiff and no longer sticks to the board (use a bit more flour if the dough still feels sticky). Continue to knead for 10 minutes.

Preheat oven to 375 degrees F.

Divide the dough into two parts. Roll each piece into a rectangle ½-inch thick. Spread with the cooled filling, sprinkle with grated cheese and roll up, pinching seams and ends closed.

Arrange the loaves on greased baking sheets and bake for 55 minutes. Serve hot with melted butter.

MARILYN HILLMAN'S SQUASH BREAD
YIELD: ONE 10-INCH CAKE

½ Cup butter
    1 Cup firmly packed light brown sugar
    2 Eggs
¾ Cup cooked winter squash or yellow summer squash,
        minced
    2 Cups sifted cake flour
½ Teaspoons salt
½ Teaspoon baking soda
½ Teaspoon baking powder
½ Teaspoon each ground cinnamon, nutmeg, allspice and
        ginger
½ Cup plain yogurt
½ Cup chopped walnuts or pecans
¾ Cup golden raisins

Directions: Preheat oven to 325 degrees F.

Cream the butter, add the sugar, and cream again until light and fluffy. Beat in the eggs, one at a time, until well incorporated. Sift together dry ingredients and stir in alternately with the yogurt and squash, mixing well after each addition. Mix until batter is smooth and stir in the nuts and raisins. Turn into a greased 10-inch tubular spring-form pan and bake 1 hour, or until bread springs back when lightly pressed in the center. Cool 5 minutes, release spring-form, remove bread and cool on a rack for 30 minutes.

GOOD 'N' SWEET WINTER SQUASH BREAD
YIELD: 2 LOAVES

```
  1 Cup grated winter squash
  ¾ Cup yellow corn meal
  ½ Cup honey
  ⅓ Cup molasses
  ¼ Cup light brown sugar
  7 Tablespoons butter or cooking oil
  ¾ Cup buttermilk (or sour milk)
  ½ Teaspoon salt
  1 Teaspoon ground cinnamon
  ¼ Teaspoon ground nutmeg
  ⅛ Teaspoon allspice
    Grated zest* of two oranges
  ½ Cup water, at wrist temperature
  2 Packages dry active yeast
  2½ Cups whole wheat flour
3 to 4 Cups all-purpose flour
  ⅔ Cup currants
```

Directions: Simmer the squash in water to cover until just tender. Drain the squash and reserve the cooking liquid. In a large bowl mix the squash, 1 cup cooking liquid, corn meal, honey, molasses, brown sugar, butter, buttermilk, salt, the spices and the zest. Cool to room temperature. Soften the yeast in ½ cup water and stir, along with the whole wheat flour, into the squash mixture. Cover with a towel and let rise for 35 minutes in a warm, draft-free place.

Stir 1 cup all-purpose flour into the dough. Place an additional cup flour on a kneading board and turn the dough onto it. Knead until this flour has been incorporated into the dough. Repeat the process, kneading in enough flour a cup at a time to produce a stiff dough. Knead in the currants with the last cup of flour you use. Knead vigorously for 8 minutes longer.

Place the dough in an oiled bowl and turn once to grease the top. Cover and let rise 45 minutes in a warm, draft-free place. Punch down the dough, turn it over, cover and let rise again for 50 minutes. Punch down the dough, divide it in half and roll each half into a long rectangle, 8 inches wide. To form a loaf, begin at the short end and roll up the dough tightly to produce an 8-inch loaf. Turn the ends under, place each loaf in an oiled loaf pan, cover and let rise until doubled in bulk (about 50 minutes). Bake 1 hour in an oven preheated to 325 degrees F. Use a sharp knife to loosen the sides of the loaves, remove from the pans and cool on a wire rack.

*The thin outer skin of the fruit, with none of the bitter white underskin included.

ZUCCHINI BREAD
YIELD: 1 LOAF

1 Cup grated zucchini
2 Eggs
¼ Cup honey or maple syrup
2 Tablespoons granulated sugar
½ Cup corn oil
2¼ Cups all-purpose flour
¾ Teaspoon baking soda
2 Teaspoons baking powder
¾ Teaspoon each salt and ground cinnamon
¾ Cup each currants and coarsely chopped walnuts
1 Tablespoon grated orange zest*

Directions: Set zucchini aside to drain well. Squeeze dry.

Preheat oven to 325 degrees F.

In a large bowl beat the eggs until light and fluffy. Add the honey, a little at a time, beating well after each addition. Beat in the sugar and oil. Sift together flour, baking powder, salt and cinnamon, and add to the egg mixture alternately with the grated zucchini. If the batter seems too dry, add a small amount of milk or water.

Stir in the currants, walnuts and zest, and bake in a loaf pan for 45 to 55 minutes.

WINTER SQUASH ROLLS
YIELD: ABOUT 2 DOZEN

1 Cup each milk and water
½ Cup firmly packed brown sugar
1½ Teaspoons salt
4 Tablespoons butter, softened
1 Package dry active yeast
¼ Cup lukewarm water
¼ Teaspoon granulated sugar
1 Whole egg plus 2 egg yolks
 (at room temperature)
1 Cup Best Winter Squash Purée
 (see page 142)
1 Teaspoon grated lemon zest*
8 Cups all-purpose flour

Directions: In separate small saucepans, scald the milk and bring the water to a boil.

Place the brown sugar and salt in a large mixing bowl. Cut the butter into bits and add to the bowl. Stir in the scalded milk and boiling water until the butter is melted, then set aside to cool to lukewarm.

Meanwhile, sprinkle the yeast over the ¼ cup lukewarm water, add the granulated sugar and allow to dissolve for 10 minutes.

Beat the whole egg and egg yolks lightly with a fork and stir into the milk-butter-sugar mixture. Add the yeast mixture, squash purée and grated lemon rind, and combine the ingredients thoroughly.

Add enough of the flour, ½ cup at a time and incorporating each addition well before adding the

*The thin outer skin of the fruit, with none of the bitter white underskin included.

next, to make a soft, sticky dough that comes clean from the sides of the bowl. Cover the dough and allow to rise in a warm, draft-free place for 1½ hours, or until the dough doubles in bulk.

Punch down the dough. Lightly butter your hands and pinch off egg-size pieces of dough, placing each piece in a buttered 3-inch muffin cup. Cover the muffin tins lightly and allow the rolls to rise for 30 minutes, or until double in bulk.

Preheat oven to 375 degrees F.

Bake the rolls for 15 to 20 minutes, or until golden brown on top. Serve warm with butter.

If you prefer, this recipe will produce two attractive *loaves* of bread with multi-puffed tops that resemble dinner rolls. Simply arrange the egg-size pieces of dough side by side in two buttered loaf pans. Let rise 45 minutes, or until the dough reaches the tops of the pans. Bake 45 to 55 minutes, or until golden brown. Slice or pull apart and serve as rolls.

WINTER SQUASH BISCUITS
YIELD: ABOUT 2 TO 2½ DOZEN

1 Cup Best Winter Squash Purée (see page 142)
¾ Cup milk
8 Tablespoons (1 stick) butter, melted
5 Cups sifted all-purpose flour
2 Tablespoons granulated sugar
4 Teaspoons baking powder
½ Teaspoon salt

Directions: Preheat oven to 450 degrees F.

Beat the squash until light, fluffy and free from lumps; combine with the milk and melted butter. Mix together the dry ingredients and sift again into a large bowl. Blend in the squash mixture, stirring until the dough comes away cleanly from the bowl.

Turn out the dough on a lightly floured pastry board and knead gently for about 1 minute, then roll out to ½-inch thickness. Dip the edges of a 2-inch round cookie cutter or glass in flour and cut rounds from the dough. Arrange on a lightly greased baking sheet; bake for 15 minutes, or until biscuits are lightly browned.

SWEET-EATIN' SQUASH MUFFINS
YIELD: 1 DOZEN

1 Cup winter squash, peeled, seeded and
 cut in ¼-inch dice
4 Tablespoons butter
⅓ Cup granulated sugar
½ Teaspoon lemon extract
1 Cup all-purpose flour
1 Teaspoon baking powder
 Salt
½ Cup milk
2 Egg whites

Directions: Preheat oven to 325 degrees F.

Roll squash pieces between paper towels to extract excess moisture. Beat the butter until it is fluffy, then cream in the sugar until the mixture is puffy and lemon-colored. Stir in the lemon extract. Sift the flour, baking powder and a pinch of salt together, and add alternately with the milk to the creamed butter and sugar. Beat the egg whites with ⅛ teaspoon salt until they form a stiff peak. Fold gently into the batter. Dust the squash pieces lightly with flour and carefully stir into the batter. Grease a muffin tin and fill each cup ⅔ full. Bake 25 to 30 minutes, or until *very* lightly browned. Cool on wire racks.

WINTER SQUASH–PECAN STUFFING
YIELD: ABOUT 6 CUPS

---

3 Cups dry bread crumbs (corn bread crumbs may be substituted for all or part of these)
⅓ Cup hot water
1 Cup Best Winter Squash Purée (see page 142)
1 Large onion, peeled and finely chopped
3 Ribs celery, finely chopped
1 Cup chopped pecans
2 Tablespoons butter
1 Teaspoon poultry seasoning
½ Teaspoon salt
1 Egg, lightly beaten

Directions: Place the bread crumbs in a large bowl and sprinkle with the hot water. Stir in the squash purée. Sauté the onion, celery and pecans in the hot butter. Add the poultry seasoning and stir the vegetables thoroughly into the crumb mixture. Season with salt and stir in the egg.

WINTER SQUASH STUFFING
YIELD: ABOUT 8 CUPS

---

2 Cups Best Winter Squash Purée (see page 142)
4 Tablespoons butter
1 Large onion, peeled and finely chopped
1 Cup diced celery
5–6 Cups stale bread cubes
2 Eggs, lightly beaten
1¼ Teaspoons salt
1 Teaspoon poultry seasoning
⅛ Teaspoon black pepper
2 Tablespoons minced chives

Directions: Spoon the squash purée into a large bowl. Melt the butter in a skillet and sauté the onion and celery until tender. Soak the bread in cold water and squeeze out the excess moisture. Place the vegetables and the bread in the bowl with the squash. Add the eggs, salt, poultry seasoning, pepper and chives, and stir to thoroughly blend all ingredients.

DILLED ZUCCHINI AND MUSHROOM STUFFING

YIELD: ABOUT 8 CUPS

2 Medium-size zucchini, cut in
  ½-inch dice
1 Pound mushrooms, sliced
1 Large onion, peeled and coarsely
  chopped
4 Tablespoons butter
3 Cups soft bread crumbs
3 Tablespoons minced fresh dill
1 Teaspoon salt
½ Cup heavy cream

Directions: Sauté the zucchini, mushrooms and onion in the hot butter. Toss the vegetables with the bread crumbs, dill and salt. Sprinkle with the cream and toss again.

HAM AND CANDIED ZUCCHINI STUFFING

YIELD: ABOUT 10 CUPS

3 Cups Candied Zucchini, drained (see page 173)
½ Pound cooked ham, cut into ½-inch cubes
⅓ Cup Candied Zucchini syrup (see page 173)
⅓ Cup sweet sherry
1 Cup currants
2½ Cups dry bread crumbs
1 Tablespoon minced fresh thyme
⅛ Teaspoon ground cloves
½ Teaspoon salt

Directions: Place the zucchini, ham, syrup, sherry, and currants in a large bowl and marinate 1 hour. Toss the bread crumbs and spices with the ham and fruit. Sprinkle with additional sherry, hot water or syrup if the stuffing seems too dry.

SWEETS

While testing hundreds and hundreds of divers ways to utilize those redundant squash teeming on my garden vines, I tried all of the standard preserving methods ... canning, drying and freezing ... with vinegar, salt and, inevitably, sugar. My first encounter with the latter stemmed from a need, late of a Sunday evening, for candied fruit to grace a spur-of-the-moment Diplomat Pudding. Accustomed as I was to "thinking squash," the quincelike texture and color as well as the delicate flavor of zucchini seemed, suddenly, a logical answer. After all, the fruit/vegetable status of the pumpkin, the carrot and the tomato established a precedent. Why not candy squash? Why, indeed, not? The result was the most delectable Diplomat Pudding I ever prepared. Naturally, I tested further ... a cookbook author with a new toy. Candied zucchini, while not bound to become a staple food, is a treat you might also find it fun to try. Another delight, while you're being adventurous, is the use of winter squash in dessert recipes. This highly nutritious garden favorite lends an unusual, delicious flavor while it moistens and sweetens the cake, cookie or pudding you create. (The Squash Cheesecake alone is worth the price of admission.) Here are the recipes; all you need supply is that extra dollop of curiosity.

SQUASH CHEESECAKE WITH ORANGE GLAZE
YIELD: ENOUGH TO SERVE 12

A cheesecake prepared with winter squash may sound like a dish more to be avoided than savored, but this is one of the most delicately flavored, creamy desserts ever to grace a table. Prepare a day in advance of serving.

CRUST
1 Cup all-purpose flour
3 Tablespoons granulated sugar
¼ Teaspoon salt
6 Tablespoons butter
1 Large egg yolk (reserve the egg white)

Directions: Preheat oven to 350 degrees F. Sift dry ingredients together and cut in the butter until the mixture resembles coarse grain. Stir in the egg yolk until well mixed. Use fingers to press the dough over the bottom of an assembled 9-inch spring-form pan. Bake for 20 minutes. Cool in the pan.

CHEESE FILLING
32 Ounces cream cheese at room temperature
4 Eggs
1 Cup granulated sugar
1 Cup Best Winter Squash Purée (see page 142)
⅓ Teaspoon each salt and nutmeg
1 Teaspoon lemon extract
1½ Teaspoons vanilla extract

Directions: Preheat oven to 350 degrees F.
Cream the cheese in a mixer, food processor or blender, or work it with a spoon until it is very soft and smooth. Add the 4 eggs plus the reserved egg white one at a time, beating until smooth after each addition. Continue beating while you sprinkle in the sugar, and spoon in the squash purée. Add the salt, nutmeg, lemon extract and vanilla, and beat until thoroughly blended, stopping several times to scrape the bottom of the bowl. There should be no white bits of cream cheese discernible in the batter. Pour over the cool crust and bake for 1 hour and 15 minutes. Turn off oven heat, open oven door several inches and allow the cake to cool, in the oven, for 30 minutes.

SOUR CREAM TOPPING
1½ Cups sour cream
2½ Tablespoons granulated sugar
1½ Teaspoons vanilla extract

Directions: Thoroughly mix ingredients and spread over the top of the warm cake. Bake for 15 minutes at 300 degrees F. Turn off the oven heat, open oven door and allow cake to cool, in the oven, to room temperature. Refrigerate until thoroughly chilled. Meanwhile prepare the Orange Glaze.

ORANGE GLAZE
1 Cup orange juice
1 Cup granulated sugar
18 Very thin strips of orange peel with none of the bitter white underskin included
2½ Tablespoons cornstarch
¼ Cup water
   Orange coloring (optional)
20 Whole blanched almonds

Directions: Bring the orange juice, sugar and orange peel to a boil. Mix the cornstarch and water to a smooth paste and stir into the orange-juice mixture, stirring constantly over medium heat until the glaze is thick and clear. For a more intense color, add orange coloring. Spread this glaze over the cheesecake, and use the glazed orange peel and whole almonds to form almond flowers with orange-peel stems. Chill overnight.

WINTER SQUASH CAKE WITH PENUCHE ICING
YIELD: ONE 8-INCH 2-LAYER CAKE

½ Cup butter
1½ Cups granulated sugar
 2 Eggs, lightly beaten
¾ Cup Best Winter Squash Purée
    (see page 142)
1½ Teaspoons vanilla extract
2¼ Cups cake flour
 2 Teaspoons baking powder
 1 Teaspoon baking soda
½ Teaspoon each ground allspice and cinnamon
¼ Teaspoon each ground nutmeg and cloves
½ Cup sour milk
 2 Cups light brown sugar
⅓ Cup water
 1 Egg white
⅛ Teaspoon salt
12 Pecan halves

Directions: Cream the butter and sugar until fluffy, beat in the eggs and continue to beat until the mixture is very light and airy. Stir in the squash purée and 1 teaspoon vanilla extract.
Preheat oven to 350 degrees F.

Sift together the flour, baking powder, baking soda and spices, and add alternately with the sour milk, blending well after each addition. Divide the batter between two buttered and lightly floured 8-inch cake pans and bake about 45 minutes, or until the cake tests done. Cool on racks.

To prepare the icing: dissolve the sugar in the water, stir once, then continue to boil, without stirring, until the syrup reaches the soft-ball stage (or a candy thermometer registers 234 degrees F.). Beat the egg white with ⅛ teaspoon salt until frothy, then add the hot syrup in a thin stream, beating constantly. Continue to beat until the icing is thick enough to hold its shape. Stir in the remaining ½ teaspoon vanilla extract. Ice the tops and sides of the cake layers and decorate with pecan halves.

COPYRIGHT 1889 BY J.J.H.GREGORY.

SWEET 'N' SPICY SQUASH CAKE
YIELD: ENOUGH TO SERVE 10 TO 12

3 Cups all-purpose flour
2½ Teaspoons baking powder
1¼ Teaspoons baking soda
½ Teaspoon each ground allspice, cinnamon, cloves and
    nutmeg
10 Tablespoons butter, cut in small pieces
1¼ Cups granulated sugar
½ Cup light brown sugar
2 Eggs
½ Cup milk
¼ Cup orange juice
¾ Cup Best Winter Squash Purée (see page 142)
1 Teaspoon vanilla extract
    Butter-Cream Icing I or II (see page 192)

Directions: Preheat oven to 350 degrees F.

Sift together the flour, baking powder, baking soda and spices. Place the butter in a mixing bowl, sprinkle in the sugars and beat until fluffy. Add the eggs, one at a time, beating well after each.

Mix together the milk and orange juice; let stand for 5 minutes, then stir in the squash purée and vanilla extract. Add the milk and squash mixture to the creamed butter alternately with the sifted dry ingredients, a little of each at a time, beating until smooth after each addition.

Spoon the batter into a greased and floured tube pan and bake for 40 to 45 minutes; the cake is done when it springs back after pressing lightly with the fingers. Cool in the pan for 15 minutes, then turn out onto a wire rack and allow to cool to room temperature before frosting.

BANANA-SQUASH SPICE CAKE
YIELD: ENOUGH TO SERVE 8 TO 10

½ Teaspoon lemon juice
¼ Cup warm milk
⅓ Cup vegetable shortening
1 Cup granulated sugar
½ Cup Best Winter Squash Purée (see page 142)
1 Very ripe banana, mashed
1 Egg
2 Cups all-purpose flour
2 Teaspoons baking powder
½ Teaspoon baking soda
1 Teaspoon ground cinnamon
¼ Teaspoon each salt, allspice and ground nutmeg
¾ Cup finely chopped dates
1½ Cups finely chopped walnuts
¾ Cup peach jam or
    Butter-Cream Icing I or II (see page 192)
    (optional)

Directions: Stir lemon juice into milk and let stand for 10 minutes to sour. Meanwhile, beat the shortening until light and fluffy, then cream in the sugar. Add the purée and mashed banana to the creamed mixture, blending in thoroughly. Beat in the egg.

Preheat oven to 350 degrees F.

Sift together the flour, baking powder, baking soda and spices. Add the dry ingredients to the creamed mixture alternately with the soured milk, using a little of each at a time, and mixing well after each addition. Stir in the dates and 1 cup of the walnuts.

Pour the batter into a well-buttered 9-inch tube pan; bake for 1 hour or until the top springs back

when lightly pressed with the fingers. Cool in the pan for 10 minutes, then remove and cool on a wire rack. Spread peach jam over the cooled cake and sprinkle with the remaining finely chopped walnuts, or ice with Butter-Cream Icing.

DATE AND SQUASH SQUARES
YIELD: ABOUT 16

1 Cup finely grated summer squash
1 Cup finely chopped dates
3 Tablespoons rum, cognac or bourbon
2 Eggs
½ Cup granulated sugar
1 Cup sifted all-purpose flour
½ Teaspoon each baking soda and baking powder
1 Cup coarsely chopped walnuts or pecans plus 12 perfect halves

Directions: Squeeze squash very dry and combine with the dates in a small bowl. Sprinkle the mixture with rum and let stand.

Preheat oven to 350 degrees F.

Beat the eggs with a rotary or electric beater; add the sugar and continue to beat until mixture is well incorporated. Sift together remaining dry ingredients and add to the egg mixture, along with the walnuts. Drain the squash-date mixture well and stir into the batter until thoroughly mixed, then spread the batter evenly over the bottom of an 8- or 9-inch square baking pan; decorate with walnut halves and bake for 40 minutes. Cool for 10 minutes on a wire rack. Cut into squares with a sharp knife. Remove from the pan as soon as the squares have completely cooled.

SWEET SQUASH PANCAKES

Follow directions for Sour Cream–Squash Pancakes (see page 143), but omit onion, increase sugar to 2 tablespoons and season with nutmeg to taste.

MOLASSES-SQUASH COOKIES
YIELD: ABOUT 2 DOZEN

5 Tablespoons butter
¾ Cup each granulated sugar and molasses
⅔ Cup Best Winter Squash Purée (see page 142)
1 Egg
4 Cups sifted all-purpose flour
2 Teaspoons each baking soda and ground cinnamon
1 Teaspoon each ground cloves and nutmeg
½ Teaspoon each salt and ground ginger
⅓ Cup hot water

Directions: Preheat oven to 400 degrees F.

Beat the butter until fluffy, then add the sugar, about 2 tablespoons at a time, beating well after each addition. Stir in the molasses and squash purée. Beat the egg lightly and add to the creamed mixture, blending all ingredients thoroughly.

Combine the sifted flour with the baking soda and spices, and sift again. Add these dry ingredients alternately with the hot water, a little of each at a time, to the creamed mixture, blending well after each addition.

Drop the batter by tablespoonfuls on a well-greased cookie sheet. Bake for 10 to 12 minutes. Cool for 3 minutes before loosening and removing to a wire rack to cool further.

SQUASH DATE-AND-NUT COOKIES

Follow directions for Molasses-Squash Cookies (see page 169), but stir ½ cup *each* coarsely chopped dates and nuts into the finished batter. Bake as directed.

LANCASTER COUNTY APPLE–SQUASH– GRAHAM CRACKER PUDDING
YIELD: ENOUGH TO SERVE 6

2 Medium-size winter squash, peeled, seeded and sliced
5 Tablespoons cold butter
3 Cups applesauce
5 Tablespoons light brown sugar
2 Cups graham cracker crumbs
1¼ Cups cold sour cream, whipped cream or ice cream

Directions: Preheat oven to 375 degrees F.

Simmer the squash slices until tender in water to cover. Drain well. Grease a glass baking dish with 1 tablespoon butter. Spoon ¾ cup applesauce into the bottom of the dish. Sprinkle with 1 tablespoon brown sugar and ½ cup graham cracker crumbs, and dot with butter pieces. Top with squash slices. Continue to build layers in this manner, ending with applesauce, 2 tablespoons brown sugar, crumbs and the remainder of the butter. Bake for 1 hour. Serve hot with your choice of creams.

STEAMED SQUASH PLUM PUDDING
YIELD: ENOUGH TO SERVE 10-12

1 Cup grated squash (summer or winter)
1 Cup granulated sugar
3 Eggs
2 Cups sifted all-purpose flour
⅓ Pound fresh beef suet, minced
⅓ Pound each currants and raisins
⅓ Cup chopped pecans
¼ Cup chopped citron
½ Teaspoon each ground cinnamon, cloves and nutmeg
¼ Teaspoon salt
½ Cup heated brandy
    Hard Sauce (see page 192)

Directions: Drain the grated squash thoroughly and set aside.

Place sugar in a large bowl, add eggs and beat until well mixed. Add the flour, ½ cup at a time, beating well after each addition. Blend in the suet, currants, raisins, pecans, citron, squash, and spices. Cover with plastic wrap and chill overnight.

Grease and lightly flour a pudding mold and fill with the batter. Press the mixture down, then cover the mold with aluminum foil tied in place with string. Top with the lid of the mold and place on a rack in a deep kettle. Arrange crushed circles of aluminum foil around the top and bottom of the mold to keep it upright. Pour in enough boiling water to reach ¾ of the way up the sides of the mold. Cover the kettle and bring the water to a boil. Simmer the pudding for 4 hours, adding more water if necessary, then remove and transfer mold and all to a cake rack and allow to cool to room temperature. Chill overnight.

Return the mold to its rack in the kettle, pour in 1 inch boiling water and allow the pudding to steam, covered, for 1 hour, or until it tests done. The top should feel firm and should spring back when lightly pressed with the fingers.

To serve, loosen the pudding from its mold and invert on a flameproof platter. Pour the heated brandy over and ignite, spooning the flaming liquid over until the flames go out. Cut into slices and serve immediately with Hard Sauce.

BRANDIED AND BAKED WINTER SQUASH PUDDING
YIELD: ENOUGH TO SERVE 6

Follow directions for Brandied and Baked Winter Squash (see page 146), but increase the sugar to 1 cup and beat 2 eggs into the milk before adding it to the pudding. Top with slivered almonds and bake about 1 hour at 375 degrees F. The center of the pudding should be cooked through. Serve warm or chilled, with or without whipped cream.

WINTER SQUASH CUSTARD
YIELD: ENOUGH TO SERVE 6

1 Cup Best Winter Squash Purée (see page 142)
⅔ Cup light brown sugar
2 Eggs, lightly beaten
¼ Teaspoon each salt, ginger, cinnamon and nutmeg
1 Cup heavy cream
2 Tablespoons orange marmalade (mince the candied peel)
   Whipped cream

Directions: Preheat oven to 350 degrees F.

Mix together all ingredients in the order given. Pour into buttered custard cups, set in a pan of hot water and bake 50 to 60 minutes, or until a knife inserted in the center of the custard comes out clean. Top with whipped cream.

MOCK PINEAPPLE PIE
YIELD: ONE 10-INCH PIE

No one will ever guess that squash is the secret ingredient in this fruity pie.

1 Medium-size spaghetti squash, peeled, seeded and very finely chopped
1¾ Cups water
1½ Cups granulated sugar
⅛ Teaspoon nutmeg
   Juice and zest* of 2 small or 1 large lemon
½ Cup sour cream
½ Recipe Double-Crust Pie Pastry (see page 193)
   Whipped cream or sour cream, sweetened with maple syrup

Directions: Preheat oven to 425 degrees F.

Boil the squash in the water for 10 minutes. Mix in the sugar, nutmeg, lemon juice and zest and, finally, the sour cream. Line the pie plate with pastry and crimp the edges. Pour in the filling and bake for 20 minutes in the preheated oven, then lower the heat to 350 and bake 1½ hours longer. The pie is done when the filling has thickened and the squash is tender. Serve at room temperature with whipped or sour cream.

*The thin outer skin of the fruit, with none of the bitter white underskin included.

PENNSYLVANIA WINTER SQUASH PIE

YIELD: ENOUGH TO SERVE 6 TO 8

2 Cups Best Winter Squash Purée (see page 142)
4 Eggs
1¼ Cups granulated sugar
¾ Teaspoon grated orange zest*
½ Teaspoon ground cinnamon
4 Tablespoons butter
⅓ Cup orange liqueur
⅔ Cup heavy cream, at room temperature
1 Tablespoon cornstarch
½ Recipe Double-Crust Pie Pastry
  (see page 193)

Directions: Place the squash purée in the large bowl of your electric mixer. Separate the eggs, reserving the whites; add the yolks to the purée, along with the sugar, orange zest and cinnamon. Beat at medium speed for 5 minutes.

Preheat oven to 350 degrees F.

Melt the butter over hot water, then cool to room temperature. Add the butter and orange liqueur to the squash mixture and blend thoroughly. Stir in the cream. Beat the reserved egg whites until they form stiff peaks, sprinkle with the cornstarch and fold into the squash mixture.

Roll out the pastry and use it to line a deep 10-inch pie plate. Pour in the filling and bake for 1 hour. Chill before serving cold, topped with whipped cream if desired.

*The thin outer skin of the fruit, with none of the bitter white underskin included.

BEST-EVER FRUIT "MINCEMEAT" PIE

YIELD: ONE 9-INCH PIE

Perhaps your family will agree with mine that this is the best (and freshest-tasting) mincemeat pie they ever tried.

Double-Crust Pie Pastry (see page 193)
1 Quart Best-Ever Fruit Mincemeat (see page 184)
3 Tablespoons melted butter
2 Tablespoons lemon juice

Directions: Preheat oven to 425 degrees F.

Roll out dough and line a 9-inch pie plate with one crust. Pour the mincemeat into the crust, spoon the melted butter and lemon juice over all and cover with the top crust slashed in several places to allow steam to escape. Crimp the edges of the crust, bake 20 minutes, then lower the heat to 350 degrees F. and bake for 30 to 40 minutes more, or until the crust is golden brown.

CANDIED ZUCCHINI*
YIELD: 3 TO 4 QUARTS

Zucchini behaves very well as a fruit when it is first candied in sugar syrup. More succulent and milder-tasting than candied fruit peel, it is an excellent substitute for the latter in any number of recipes.

6 Very firm medium-size zucchini,
   peeled
2 Cups granulated sugar
¾ Cup water
1 Tablespoon lemon juice, strained

Directions: Cut the zucchini into ½-inch cubes and drop into a syrup made by boiling the sugar and water together for 5 minutes. Cook only until barely tender. Stir in the lemon juice. Chill in the syrup overnight.

DIPLOMAT PUDDING WITH CANDIED ZUCCHINI
YIELD: ENOUGH TO SERVE 10 TO 12

VANILLA CUSTARD
3 Cups milk
1 Cup granulated sugar
Two-inch piece of vanilla bean
6 Egg yolks

Directions: In the top of a double boiler bring the milk, sugar and vanilla bean just to the boiling

*Other summer squash varieties may also be candied with success, but most of them must be seeded as well as peeled before cooking.

point, but *do not boil.* Stir until the sugar is dissolved, then cool to room temperature. Beat in the egg yolks. Use half this mixture in the preparation of the pudding, then cook the remaining custard over hot water, stirring constantly, until it thickens enough to coat a spoon. Cool and chill.

TO ASSEMBLE THE PUDDING
½ Cup apricot jam
3 Packages split ladyfingers (approximately 50
   whole sponge fingers)
2 Cups Candied Zucchini
½ Cup sliced candied cherries
½ Cup each golden raisins and currants
¼ Cup chopped candied
   orange peel
¼ Cup Cointreau

Directions: Spread the jam over the bottom of an assembled 9-inch spring-form pan. Arrange a layer of *split* ladyfingers attractively over the jam. Sprinkle with ⅓ *each* of the candied zucchini, sliced cherries, raisins, currants, orange peel and Cointreau. Spoon a little vanilla custard over each ladyfinger.

Preheat oven to 325 degrees F.

Repeat the entire process until all of the ladyfingers, fruit and Cointreau and half the Vanilla Custard has been used. Cover the bottom and sides of the pan with several overlapping wrappings of aluminum foil. Bake for 1 hour.

Cover the pudding with a serving plate, invert and allow the pudding to settle on the platter. Decorate with candied fruit and serve with chilled custard and/or whipped cream on the side.

COUNTRY KITCHEN PUDDING
YIELD: ENOUGH TO SERVE 4 TO 6

14 Slices trimmed white bread
    (home-baked is best)
4 Tablespoons butter
¾ Cup Candied Zucchini (see page 173),
    coarsely chopped
5 Tablespoons currants
½ Cup marmalade (orange, lemon, lime or ginger,
    to suit your taste)
1¼ Cups milk
¾ Cup light cream
4 Eggs
⅔ Cup granulated sugar
½ Teaspoon ground cinnamon
⅛ Teaspoon ground nutmeg

Directions: Preheat oven to 375 degrees F.

Butter each slice of bread generously on one side. Line the sides of a buttered loaf pan with six slices of the bread, placing the buttered sides against the pan. Spread the remaining slices of bread with marmalade. Cover the bottom of the pan with bread slices (marmalade-spread sides up) and sprinkle with candied zucchini and currants. Top with 2 more slices of bread and continue the process until the pan is ¾ full. Beat together the milk, cream, eggs, sugar and spices, and pour over the bread in the pan. The milk mixture should soak into the bread and fill the pan only as deep as the bread layers. Bake about 1½ hours, or until the top is golden brown and the center is puffed. (This is prone to overflow, so it's best to place aluminum foil under the pan to catch the drippings.)

Bring to room temperature, then chill in the pan overnight. To unmold, soak the pan in hot water for 30 minutes, carefully loosen the sides with a sharp knife, turn onto a serving plate, chill and serve.

WHISKEY PUDDING WITH CANDIED ZUCCHINI
YIELD: ENOUGH TO SERVE 6

6 Egg yolks
2 Tablespoons all-purpose flour
2 Cups light cream
½ Cup whiskey
½ Cup Candied Zucchini (see page 173), finely chopped
¼ Cup candied orange peel, minced
2 Tablespoons sugar

Directions: Preheat oven to 400 degrees F.

Beat egg yolks until lemon-colored and stir in the flour. Gradually add the cream, whiskey, candied zucchini and orange peel and the sugar. Stir until the sugar is dissolved. Pour into buttered custard cups and bake about 20 minutes or until firm.

SOUR CREAM COFFEECAKE WITH CANDIED ZUCCHINI

1 Cup butter
1¾ Cups granulated sugar
2 Eggs, lightly beaten
2½ Cups sour cream
1 Teaspoon vanilla extract
2 Cups sifted all-purpose flour
1 Teaspoon baking powder
½ Teaspoon baking soda
⅛ Teaspoon salt
1 Teaspoon ground cinnamon
3 Cups Candied Zucchini (see page 173), well-drained
½ Cup finely chopped pecans
1 Cup dry macaroon crumbs

Directions: Cream the butter and 1¼ cups of the sugar until fluffy. Beat in thoroughly the eggs, 1 cup sour cream and the vanilla. Sift together the flour, baking powder, baking soda and salt, and stir the dry ingredients into the sour cream mixture a little at a time, until thoroughly incorporated.

Preheat oven to 350 degrees F.

Mix the cinnamon and remaining ½ cup sugar. Pour half the batter into a buttered 9-inch round cake pan and sprinkle half the cinnamon sugar over it. Top with 2 cups of the candied zucchini, the chopped nuts and the macaroon crumbs. Add the remaining batter, top the cake with the remaining cinnamon sugar and bake for 40 to 50 minutes, or until a toothpick inserted in the middle of the cake comes out clean.

Fold the remaining cup of candied zucchini into the remaining 1½ cups sour cream, sweeten to your taste and refrigerate until ready to serve. Serve the cake topped with the sour cream and zucchini.

CANDIED ZUCCHINI AND YOGURT FOOL
YIELD: ENOUGH TO SERVE 6

3 Cups cold Candied Zucchini (see page 173)
3 Cups cold thick yogurt
3 Tablespoons maple syrup
1 Cup cold mandarin orange segments

Directions: Drain the zucchini well and fold into it the yogurt and maple syrup. Serve immediately, decorated with mandarin orange segments.

VEGETABLE PATCH RELISH

YIELD: ABOUT 5-6 PINTS

3 Medium-size summer squash, peeled and seeded if necessary and cut into ½-inch dice
8 Medium-size green tomatoes, cut into ½-inch dice
2 Large onions, peeled and cut into ½-inch dice
1 Small head cauliflower, trimmed and cut into ½-inch dice
1 Each sweet green and red pepper, trimmed and cut into ½-inch dice
2 Cups each cut wax beans and green beans
2 Cups shelled lima beans
1 Tablespoon each minced fresh fennel, marjoram, thyme and mustard seed
1½ Cups noniodized salt
1½ Cups each granulated and light brown sugar
6 Cups cider vinegar

Directions: Toss the vegetables with the salt, cover and let stand overnight. Drain off any accumulated liquid, mix the vegetables with the remaining ingredients and boil over low flame until the vegetables are barely tender. Seal the relish in hot, sterilized jars. Process for 5 minutes in water bath canner (see page 68).

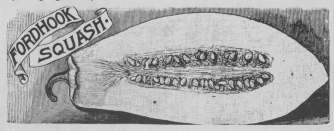

FORDHOOK SQUASH.

WINTER SQUASH–GREEN TOMATO RELISH

YIELD: 3 PINTS

12 Green tomatoes, seeded and finely chopped
¼ Cup noniodized salt
3 Medium-size winter squash, peeled, seeded and finely chopped
4 Cups cider vinegar
2 Large onions, peeled and finely chopped
1 Each red and green sweet pepper, seeded, trimmed and finely chopped
4 Cups granulated sugar
¼ Teaspoon each dry mustard and dried crushed red peppers
2 Teaspoons each mustard seed and celery seed
1½ Teaspoons each crushed black peppercorns, cardamom seed and whole cloves
Two-inch stick cinnamon

Directions: In a ceramic or glass bowl mix green tomatoes and salt, cover and let stand overnight. Drain the tomatoes and place in a large, stainless-steel kettle. Add the squash and vinegar, and cook over medium heat for 30 minutes. Stir in the onions, peppers, sugar, mustard, peppercorns, celery, mustard and cardamom seed. Tie the cloves and cinnamon in a cheesecloth bag and add to kettle. Lower the heat and simmer an hour or so, stirring occasionally, until relish is the consistency you prefer.

Discard spice bag and spoon the hot relish into hot, sterile jars, leaving ¼ inch headspace. Seal and place in boiling water in a water bath canner. When water returns to a boil, process for 5 minutes (see page 68). Remove jars and test seals. Arrange jars on a rack or towel and cool in a draft-free place. Store in a cool, dark storage area.

ZUCCHINI RELISH
YIELD: ABOUT 4 PINTS

6 Large zucchini, trimmed (and seeded if necessary)
4 Large onions, peeled
2 Green sweet peppers, seeded and trimmed
1 Red sweet pepper, seeded and trimmed
½ Cup non-iodized salt
3 Cups granulated sugar
2½ Cups vinegar
1 Cup water
2 Teaspoons each celery seed and turmeric

Directions: Coarsely chop the zucchini, onions and peppers by hand or, for a finer cut, put through a food chopper. Combine the vegetables in a large glass bowl. Stir the salt into enough ice water to cover the vegetables and allow to dissolve, then pour over the vegetables and allow to stand for 1 hour. Drain off the salted water, rinse the vegetables under cold running water and drain well. Set the vegetables aside.

Combine the sugar, vinegar, water and spices in a large saucepan and bring the mixture to a boil; continue to boil for 3 minutes. Add the vegetable mixture, reduce the heat to low and continue to cook for 10 to 15 minutes. Spoon into sterile pint or ½-pint jars. Seal and refrigerate for short-term storage.

SQUASH-BEET RELISH
YIELD: ABOUT 3 TO 4 PINTS

3 Medium-size summer squash, peeled and seeded if necessary and coarsely chopped
8 Medium-size cooked beets, peeled and finely chopped
2½ Cups granulated sugar
1 Cup grated horseradish
1 Tablespoon poppy seeds
1¼ Tablespoons salt
1 Teaspoon pepper
Mild vinegar

Directions: Toss squash and cooked beets together with sugar, horseradish, poppy seeds, salt, pepper and enough vinegar to cover. Let stand 1 hour, then pack into hot, sterilized pint jars and seal. Refrigerate.

SUMMER SQUASH–CORN RELISH
YIELD: ABOUT 6 PINTS

2 Medium-size summer squash, peeled (and seeded if necessary)
2 Each sweet red and green peppers, seeded and trimmed
2 Large onions, peeled
7 Large ripe tomatoes, peeled and seeded
5 Ears tender young corn, husked and with silk removed
2 Cups vinegar
1¾ Cups granulated sugar
4 Teaspoons noniodized salt
1½ Teaspoons each celery seed and mustard seed
¾ Teaspoon ground allspice
⅛ Teaspoon ground nutmeg

Directions: Coarsely chop all of the vegetables except the corn. Cut the corn from the cob and scrape cobs lightly with a dull knife to extract the milk. Boil remaining ingredients for 6 minutes in a large steel pan. Stir in the vegetables, return to the boil, then lower the heat and simmer for 1½ hours. Pack in hot, sterile jars, seal and process for 5 minutes in a boiling water bath (see page 68).

BRINED ZUCCHINI PICKLES
YIELD: 3 TO 4 QUARTS

7 Pounds very small zucchini
  (about 4 inches long)
¼ Cup whole mixed pickling spice
1 Bunch fresh or dried dill
4 Cloves garlic, peeled and quartered
1 Cup white vinegar
⅔ Cup noniodized salt
3 Quarts water

Directions: Wash zucchini thoroughly but handle gently to prevent bruising. Wipe dry. Cover the bottom of a 1-gallon pickle jar with 2 tablespoons pickling spice and a layer of dill. Fill with zucchini to within 3 inches of the top. Cover with the remainder of the pickling spices and dill, and the garlic. Mix the vinegar, salt and water well and pour over the zucchini. Cover with a heavy china or glass plate that fits *inside* the crock. Top with a weight to keep the pickles under the brine. A glass jar filled with water is excellent for this use; in any case, the weight should be china or glass, *not* metal. Cover loosely with a clean cloth.

Keep the pickles at room temperature. Scum may start to form after 3 to 5 days. Remove it as it forms. The pickles should not be stirred and should be kept completely covered with brine throughout the process. If necessary, make additional brine using the original proportions of vinegar. In 3 weeks the pickles will have a zesty flavor. Don't worry if there are white spots inside the pickles; these will disappear in processing.

The fermented brine will be cloudy due to yeast formation, but its flavor will be marvelous and therefore this should be strained and used to pack the pickles. If you prefer a clear brine, however, you may prepare some by mixing ½ cup salt and 1 quart white vinegar to 1 gallon of water.

Pack the pickles with some of the dill and garlic into clean, hot 1-quart jars. Do not pack the jars too tightly. Cover with boiling brine to within ½ inch of the top. Adjust jar lids and process in boiling water for 10 minutes. Remove jars and complete seals if necessary. Set jars upright, several inches apart, on a wire rack to cool.

PICKLED WINTER SQUASH
YIELD: 3 PINTS

1 Cup white vinegar
1 Cup dry white wine
½ Cup water
½ Cup olive oil
3 Tablespoons granulated sugar
3 Garlic cloves, peeled and crushed
1 Teaspoon salt
2 Sprigs each fresh tarragon and rosemary
1 Bay leaf
2 Medium-size winter squash, peeled, seeded
   and cut in ½-inch dice

Directions: Boil all ingredients, except the squash, for 5 minutes in a large saucepan. Add the squash pieces to this marinade, lower the heat, cover and simmer until the squash is barely tender. Chill the vegetable in the marinade and spoon into jars. Strain the marinade over all, seal the jars and store in the refrigerator for up to 3 weeks.

SUMMER SQUASH PICKLES FROM THE ORIENT
YIELD: 3 PINTS

1 Oversize squash, peeled, seeded and cut into
   bite-size ¼-inch-thick slices
  Salt
½ Cup rice vinegar
½ Cup granulated sugar
½ Cup soy sauce
4 Teaspoons dry mustard

Directions: Spread the squash slices on a plate, sprinkle with salt and set aside for 20 minutes. Squeeze dry between paper towels. Thoroughly mix the vinegar, sugar, soy sauce and dry mustard, and divide it evenly between 3 pint jars. Divide the squash slices evenly between the 3 jars, tighten the lids and rotate the jars until all the squash slices are coated with the marinade. Refrigerate overnight, or until needed. Serve cold.

ZUCCHINI PICKLES
YIELD: ABOUT 4 PINTS

5 Medium-size zucchini
3 Cloves garlic, peeled and minced
1 Cup noniodized salt
¼ Cup minced dill
2½ Cups granulated sugar
1 Tablespoon white pepper
1 Quart white vinegar

Directions: Rinse and trim the zucchini, then decorate them by using a sharp paring knife to make 4 or 5 regularly spaced lengthwise cuts about ⅛ inch deep in the outer skin of each vegetable. Cut the zucchini into ¼-inch slices. This will result in attractive slices with little notches in each. Place the slices in a large, deep bowl.

Work together the garlic, salt and dill until well integrated. Add to the zucchini, along with the sugar and white pepper. Toss gently until all slices are evenly coated, then allow to stand for 1 hour. Stir in the vinegar. The pickles are best when used immediately, although they will keep for a few weeks if refrigerated.

DILLED SQUASH SPEARS
YIELD: ABOUT 5 PINTS

20 Very small zucchini or yellow summer squash, cut lengthwise into spears ½ inch thick
1 Bunch fresh dill
5 Large cloves garlic, peeled
1 Quart cider or white wine vinegar
1 Pint water
5 Dill seed heads

Directions: Blanch the squash spears in boiling water for 5 minutes. Freshen in cold water, drain well and pack upright in hot sterilized pint jars with 1 clove garlic and several sprigs of fresh dill in each jar. Bring the vinegar, water and dill heads to a boil and quickly fill the jars. Seal. Process 5 minutes in water bath canner (see page 68).

SQUASH CATSUP
YIELD: ABOUT 2 CUPS

Here's a catsup with added crunch and zest.

2 Medium-size summer squash, peeled and seeded if necessary
1 Large onion, peeled
¼ Cup white vinegar
½ Teaspoon salt
¾ Cup catsup
⅛ Teaspoon black pepper

Directions: Finely grate the squash and onion into a large, shallow bowl. Stir in 3½ tablespoons of the vinegar and the salt. Place a plate topped with a heavy jar or can directly on the vegetables. Set aside for 1 hour. Pour off any accumulated liquid, reposition the plate and the weight, and drain. Repeat this process until no liquid remains. Mix the squash, catsup, 2 teaspoons vinegar and the pepper, spoon into a jar and refrigerate 2 days before using wherever relish is called for.

WINTER SQUASH–MANGO CHUTNEY
YIELD: ABOUT 4 PINTS

2½ Cups peeled and thinly sliced mangoes
2½ Cups peeled and thinly sliced winter squash
2½ Cups granulated sugar
1½ Cups light brown sugar
2 Small hot peppers
1 Cup cider vinegar
½ Cup golden raisins
¼ Cup dark raisins
¼ Cup finely chopped fresh ginger
2 Tablespoons each finely chopped garlic and salt
1 Teaspoon ground cloves

Directions: Place the mango and squash slices in a glass or porcelain bowl, sprinkle with the sugars, then toss lightly until all the slices are well coated with sugar. Cover and allow to stand overnight.

Drain the liquid from the bowl into a large saucepan, reserving the mango and squash slices. Seed the hot peppers and cut into thin slices crosswise; add them to the liquid in the saucepan along with all remaining ingredients. Simmer over low heat, stirring frequently, for 30 minutes. Add the reserved mango and squash slices, and continue to simmer for 30 minutes longer. Spoon into hot sterilized jars, cover tightly and refrigerate until needed.

SWEET 'N' SPICY WINTER SQUASH AND PEACH CHUTNEY
YIELD: ABOUT 6 PINTS

12 Plum tomatoes
 1 Medium-size winter squash, peeled, seeded and cut into ¼-inch-wide bite-size slices
 2 Cups vinegar
 5 Firm peeled peaches, cut into ½-inch dice
4½ Cups granulated sugar
 1 Cup dark raisins, minced
10 Cloves garlic, peeled and minced
 1 Large ginger root, peeled and thinly sliced
 2 Cups pitted dates
 4 Teaspoons salt
 3 Teaspoons cayenne pepper

Directions: Bake the whole tomatoes for 15 minutes in a 450-degree oven, then pull off the skins and cut off stem ends. In a stainless-steel kettle boil the whole tomatoes (and their juices) for 15 minutes with the squash and 1 cup of the vinegar. Boil the sugar and the remaining 1 cup vinegar for 5 minutes, stirring occasionally. Mix this syrup with the tomatoes and squash, add remaining ingredients and boil until the chutney is very thick, stirring frequently. Spoon into hot, sterile jars, seal and process for 5 minutes in boiling water bath (see page 68).

WINTER SQUASH–GREENGAGE CHUTNEY
YIELD: ABOUT 5 PINTS

 2 Medium-size winter squash, peeled, seeded and cut into ½-inch dice
 6 Firm greengage plums, peeled and cut into ¼-inch slices
 6 Large ripe tomatoes, peeled, seeded and quartered
 1 Cup currants
 2 Each sweet red and green peppers, seeded, trimmed and cut into ½-inch dice
 2 Large onions, peeled and cut into ½-inch dice
 1 Cup honey
 2 Cups granulated sugar
 1 Cup white vinegar
1¼ Teaspoons each curry powder, ground ginger and dry mustard
1½ Teaspoons salt
 ¾ Teaspoon ground allspice
 ⅓ Teaspoon cayenne pepper

Directions: Bring all ingredients to a boil in a large, stainless-steel pan. Lower the heat slightly and cook at a low boil, stirring occasionally, until the syrup is thick and just covers the fruit (about 1½ hours). Pack into sterile jars leaving no headspace. Seal and refrigerate for short-term storage or, for extended storage, process in boiling water bath for 5 minutes (see page 68).

SUMMER SQUASH–PEAR CHUTNEY
YIELD: ABOUT 4 PINTS

2 Medium-size summer squash, peeled, seeded
  and cut into ½-inch dice
6 Slightly underripe pears, peeled, seeded and
  cut into ½-inch dice
1 Small ginger root, peeled and thinly sliced
2¼ Cups granulated sugar
1 Cup white vinegar
1 Each red and green sweet pepper, seeded, trimmed
  and cut into ½-inch dice
12 Green plum tomatoes, cut into ¼-inch slices
2 Large onions, peeled and cut into ½-inch dice
1 Cup currants
1½ Teaspoons salt
1 Teaspoon each dry mustard and allspice

Directions: Bring squash, pears, ginger root, sugar
and vinegar to a boil in a stainless-steel kettle. Boil
over high heat for 15 minutes. Add remaining ingredients and cook at a low boil, stirring occasionally, for about 1 hour, or until the syrup is thick and
just covers the diced vegetables. Spoon into hot,
sterile jars, seal and process for 5 minutes in a
boiling water bath (see page 68).

ZUCCHINI-CUCUMBER CONSERVE

Small zucchini, finely chopped or finely ground
Small cucumbers, unpeeled but finely chopped
  or finely ground
Salt
Garlic, peeled and minced
White vinegar
Granulated sugar
Grated lemon zest*
Small onions, grated
Cayenne pepper
White pepper

Directions: Stir the zucchini and cucumbers together in a large stainless-steel kettle. Pour off any
accumulated liquid and measure the pulp. For
every quart of pulp mix in 1½ tablespoons salt. Set
aside for 1½ hours. Pour off all accumulated liquid
and measure the pulp once again. For every quart
of pulp add 2 cups vinegar, 1¼ cups sugar, 1 tablespoon lemon zest, 1 small onion, grated, and ¼
teaspoon *each* cayenne and white pepper. Boil
over low heat until the conserve is thick. Seal in
hot, sterilized jars and process in water bath
canner (see page 68).

*The thin outer skin of the fruit, with none of the bitter white
underskin included.

BEST-EVER FRUIT MINCEMEAT
YIELD: 2 QUARTS

While in a "testing frenzy," I folded some Candied Zucchini into fruit mincement, and the resulting pies were named "best ever" by the entire family.

½ Cup each golden and dark raisins
6 Medium-size McIntosh apples, peeled, cored and finely chopped
1 Cup Candied Zucchini (see page 173)
½ Cup each candied orange peel and orange marmalade
1¼ Teaspoons salt
1 Teaspoon each ground nutmeg, allspice, cinnamon and cloves
3½ Cups granulated sugar
½ Cup lemon juice
¼ Cup each dry sherry and brandy

Directions: Stir together all ingredients but the brandy. Seal tightly in quart jars and refrigerate 24 hours, turning several times. Stir in the brandy, reseal, and refrigerate for 24 hours longer. The mincemeat is "ready for pies" at this point, but it will keep at least 2 weeks if refrigerated.

SUMMER SQUASH MARMALADE

4 Medium-size summer squash, peeled, seeded and cut into ½-inch dice
4 Oranges, peeled and sliced
4 Lemons, peeled and sliced
4 Tablespoons each lemon and orange juice
4 Teaspoons each grated lemon and orange zest*
8 Cups granulated sugar

Directions: Boil over high heat the squash pieces, the orange and lemon slices, the juice and the zest with the sugar, stirring constantly, until the marmalade is thick and clear. Spoon into sterilized jars and seal with paraffin.

SQUASH PRESERVES

2 Medium-size winter squash (about 5 pounds), peeled and seeded
5 Lemons
1 Orange
8½ Cups granulated sugar
1 Stick cinnamon, broken into pieces
2 Tablespoons dark raisins

Directions: Cut the squash into uniformly thin slices (here is where your food processor can perform magic). Grate the thin outer skin, or zest, from the lemons and oranges, but include none of the bitter white underskin. Squeeze the juices from the fruits and discard the unused pith. In a large glass or

*The thin outer skin of the fruit, with none of the bitter white underskin included.

ceramic bowl sprinkle the squash slices with 5 cups sugar, the fruit zest and juices. Cover and let stand overnight.

Stir in the remaining 3½ cups sugar and the cinnamon, and cook over high heat until the syrup begins to thicken. Add the raisins and continue cooking, stirring frequently, until the preserves are very thick.

Spoon into hot, sterilized jars, fill with boiling syrup and seal.

SQUASH BUTTER
YIELD: SIX 8-OUNCE CROCKS

2 Medium-size winter squash, peeled,
    seeded and minced
1 Quart apple cider
2 Cups light brown sugar
1 Teaspoon each ground cinnamon,
    allspice and cloves

Directions: Place the squash and the cider in a large saucepan and cook over medium heat until tender. Purée in a food processor or blender, or force through a sieve.

Bring the brown sugar and squash purée to a low boil and cook for 40 minutes, stirring frequently to prevent scorching. Add the spices and cook over low heat, stirring constantly until the mixture reaches spreading consistency. Pour into hot, sterile jars and seal.

Note: To make a zesty sweet/sour steak sauce, substitute 2 cups cider vinegar for 2 cups of the cider.

SQUASH-RUM BUTTER
YIELD: THREE 8-OUNCE CROCKS

4 Medium-size winter squash, peeled, seeded and minced
2 Quarts water
3 Cups apple cider
2½ Cups pineapple juice
6 Cups light brown sugar
1 Teaspoon each ground cinnamon, allspice and cloves
9 Tablespoons light rum

Directions: Follow directions for Squash Butter, but add the pineapple juice along with the cider and measure 3 tablespoons rum into each hot, sterilized jar before filling with the squash butter.

CARROT–WINTER SQUASH BUTTER
YIELD: SIX 8-OUNCE CROCKS

3 Pounds carrots, scraped and finely chopped or ground
3 Pounds winter squash, peeled and finely chopped or
    ground
2 Tablespoons each ground cinnamon and ginger
1¼ Teaspoons allspice
2 Cups light brown sugar
    Juice and grated zest* of 5 lemons
2 Cups water

Directions: Mix the vegetables, spices, sugar, lemon juice and zest. Cover and let stand overnight. Add the water, boil and cook at a low boil until the vegetables are tender and the butter is the consistency you prefer. Pour into hot, sterile jars and seal.

*The thin outer skin of the fruit, with none of the bitter white underskin included.

SOURDOUGH STARTER
YIELD: 2 CUPS

Sourdough starter is a yeast that you can easily prepare right in your own kitchen. The only ingredients necessary are milk and flour; wild yeasts present in the air do the rest. Sourdough starter imparts a distinctive, zesty "sour" taste to any loaf.

2 Cups milk
2 Cups all-purpose flour

Directions: Measure 1 cup milk into a large glass or ceramic bowl. Cover with a dishtowel and let stand in a warm place for 2 days.

Measure 1 cup flour less 2 tablespoons, then stir into the soured milk only long enough to thoroughly moisten the flour. Cover the mixture and let stand for 4 to 5 days, or until mixture bubbles up to twice its original bulk. If mold forms and/or bubbles fail to appear by the fifth day, discard the milk-flour mixture and start over.

To double the starter, stir in 1 cup of milk and 1 cup of flour, then cover with a towel and let stand in a warm place for 3 hours.

Store the doubled starter in a ceramic crock or plastic container (never metal), loosely covered with plastic wrap. Use, give away or discard half the starter once a month, then double the remaining 1 cup starter as directed above. This guarantees that the starter will remain fresh, active and alive for years to come.

If desired, you may freeze the starter, using a plastic container; every 5 to 6 months, however, be sure to defrost it and discard half, then double as directed above and refreeze.

CREPES
YIELD: ENOUGH TO SERVE 6

These paper-thin French pancakes are delightfully easy to prepare and are versatile enough to serve with many delicious fillings.

4 Extra-large eggs
¾ Cup each milk and water
¼ Teaspoon salt
3 Tablespoons vegetable or peanut oil
1 Cup plus 2 tablespoons all-purpose flour
3 Tablespoons butter or oil

Directions: Beat the eggs lightly, then beat in the milk, water, salt, vegetable oil and flour, continuing to beat until the batter is well blended and free of any lumps. Refrigerate mixture for at least 2 hours.

Rub the inside of a 6-inch skillet or crepe pan with ½ teaspoon of the butter (or oil). Set pan over low heat for 1 minute, then remove and wipe pan with paper towels. Add another ½ teaspoon butter and repeat the process. This seasons the pan so the crepes won't stick.

Stir the cold crepe batter to make sure it is smooth and well mixed. Add ¼ teaspoon butter to the seasoned pan, tilting pan back and forth to coat bottom and sides evenly. The crepes should be very thin, yet hold together; have 2 to 3 tablespoons batter ready in a small ladle to add as soon as butter is hot enough. Experience—and the size of your pan—will help you determine exactly how much batter will be required each time.

Test to see whether pan is hot enough by flicking a few drops of water into it; if the water sizzles, add your measured crepe batter and rotate pan quickly around and from side to side so the mixture spreads evenly over the bottom surface.

As soon as bubbles appear throughout the batter, loosen one edge of the crepe with a spatula. If the bottom is light brown, turn the crepe over immediately to slightly brown the other side. Slide the crepe from the pan and set aside on a plate to keep warm.

Prepare subsequent crepes in the same manner, using about ⅛ teaspoon butter for each until the crepes no longer stick to the pan. If necessary to reheat the crepes, cover with moist cheesecloth and set on the middle rack of a warm oven.

FILLINGS FOR CREPES

Crepes adapt superbly to almost any kind of filling and will magically transform your leftovers into delectable main dishes. All you need do is spoon some of the filling down the center of each pancake and fold the edges over. If desired, top the crepes with Basic White Sauce, Curry Sauce (see page 190), Béchamel Sauce or Mornay Sauce, and slide under the broiler until piping hot.

BASIC WHITE SAUCE
YIELD: 2 CUPS

This "cold milk" white sauce assures you a silky smooth sauce every time.

4 Tablespoons butter
½ Cup all-purpose flour
2 Cups cold milk
½ Teaspoon salt
  White pepper

Directions: Melt the butter over medium heat in a heavy saucepan. Stir in the flour. When the mixture is smooth, remove from the heat and add the cold milk all at once, stirring until the mixture is well blended and free of lumps. Return to medium heat and cook, stirring continuously, until sauce is creamy and thick. Season with the salt and white pepper to taste.

When a thinner sauce is desired, increase the amount of milk by ½ cup. To make a thicker sauce, reduce the quantity of milk to 1¼ cups.

MORNAY SAUCE

Add ½ cup grated Swiss cheese and ⅓ cup grated Parmesan cheese to hot Basic White Sauce. Stir over low heat until cheeses melt.

BÉCHAMEL SAUCE

When preparing Basic White Sauce, sauté sliced onion in butter until soft, then discard onion and blend in flour. Substitute 1 cup cream for 1 cup of the milk and proceed as directed.

CURRY SAUCE

Melt butter as directed in Basic White Sauce (see page 189). Add flour and 1 teaspoon curry powder. Proceed as directed.

BASIC VINAIGRETTE/FRENCH DRESSING
YIELD: ABOUT 1 CUP

¼ Cup wine vinegar
⅛ Teaspoon salt
 Generous pinch black pepper
¾ Cup olive oil

Directions: Pour the vinegar into a shallow bowl. Lightly beat in the salt and pepper, then add the oil and continue to beat until all ingredients are well blended. A food processor or blender makes this a snap. Any unused dressing will keep in the refrigerator up to a week.

BASIC VINAIGRETTE/FRENCH DRESSING VARIATIONS

To vary the flavor and/or consistency of Basic Vinaigrette/French Dressing, add any of the following, singly or in combination:
 1 Teaspoon dry (or 2 tablespoons prepared) mustard
 1 Tablespoon minced fresh chervil, parsley or tarragon, or any mixture of these
 3 Tablespoons crumbled Roquefort or blue cheese
 1 Tablespoon minced fresh chives
 1 Hard-cooked egg, finely chopped

UNBOILED SALAD DRESSING
YIELD: ABOUT 1 CUP

4 Egg yolks
1 Tablespoon Dijon-type mustard
2 Tablespoons butter
¾ Cup white vinegar
3 Tablespoons honey

Directions: In the top of a double boiler beat together the egg yolks and mustard. Set over hot water, beat in the remaining ingredients and continue beating until the dressing thickens somewhat. Do not allow to reach too high a temperature or the dressing will curdle. Chill.

HOLLANDAISE SAUCE
YIELD: ABOUT 1½ CUPS

½ Pound (2 sticks) sweet butter
1 Cup hot water
6 Egg yolks
4 Teaspoons lemon juice
 Generous pinch each salt and white pepper

Directions: Melt butter over medium heat. Meanwhile, pour hot water into your blender bowl or the container of a food processor. Allow to stand 1 minute, then discard water.

Add egg yolks, lemon juice and seasonings to warmed bowl or container; whirl until well mixed. As soon as the butter is very hot, turn on the motor and add it through the blender top or container spout in a very thin but steady stream. Do not add the butter too quickly. When all the butter has been incorporated, turn off the motor. Serve at once.

SAUCE DIABLE
YIELD: ABOUT 1 CUP

⅓ Cup dry white wine
8 Peppercorns, crushed
2 Shallots, peeled and finely chopped
1 Cup brown sauce
1 Teaspoon Worcestershire sauce
½ Teaspoon minced fresh parsley

Directions: Combine the wine, peppercorns and shallots in a small saucepan and cook until the mixture reduces to a thick paste. Remove from heat and blend in the remaining ingredients. Serve with broiled meats or poultry.

HARD SAUCE
YIELD: ABOUT 1 CUP

8 Tablespoons (1 stick) sweet butter
1½ Cups confectioners' sugar
2 to 3 Tablespoons brandy, rum or whiskey

Directions: Beat the butter until light and fluffy, then gradually cream in the sugar. Add the brandy, rum or whiskey to taste and blend in thoroughly.

BUTTER-CREAM ICING I
YIELD: ENOUGH ICING FOR A 2-LAYER CAKE

4 Tablespoons butter
3½ Cups confectioners' sugar, sifted
4 Tablespoons heavy cream
1 Teaspoon almond extract

Directions: Cream butter, then blend in remaining ingredients, beating until smooth.

BUTTER-CREAM ICING II
YIELD: ENOUGH ICING FOR A 2-LAYER CAKE

8 Tablespoons (1 stick) butter
3½ Cups confectioners' sugar, sifted
3 Egg yolks
¼ Teaspoon ground nutmeg
1 Tablespoon rum, brandy or orange or lemon juice

Directions: Cream butter until light and fluffy. Beat in egg yolks, then blend in remaining ingredients, continuing to beat until the mixture is smooth. Chill well before spreading.

ORANGE BUTTER-CREAM ICING
YIELD: 2 CUPS OR ENOUGH FOR
4 DOZEN CUPCAKES OR 1 LARGE CAKE

1 Cup (2 sticks) butter
4 Egg yolks
4 Cups sifted confectioners' sugar
3 Tablespoons orange juice
1 Tablespoon lemon juice
1 Teaspoon grated orange zest*

Directions: Beat the butter until light and fluffy. Beat in the egg yolks, then blend in the remaining ingredients, beating until well blended and smooth. Refrigerate the icing if not used immediately.

*The thin outer skin of the fruit, with none of the bitter white underskin included.

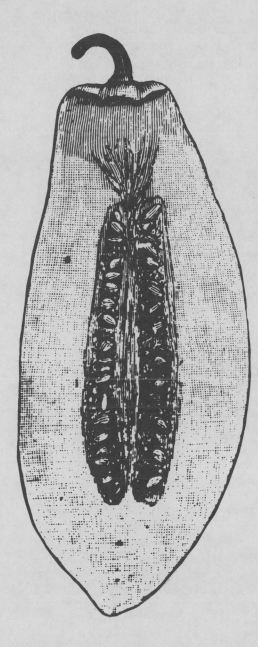
DOUBLE-CRUST PIE PASTRY
YIELD: ENOUGH PASTRY FOR A DOUBLE-CRUST PIE

---

2 Cups all-purpose flour
1 Teaspoon salt
12 Tablespoons vegetable shortening
6 to 8 Tablespoons ice water

Directions: Combine flour and salt; sift together into a large bowl.

Cut in shortening with 2 knives or a pastry blender, or whirl in food processor until mixture resembles coarse meal. Sprinkle with 6 tablespoons ice water, stir with a fork, then press into a firm ball. (If pastry crumbles, work in remaining ice water.) Chill 15 minutes.

Divide dough in half. Roll out each half on a lightly floured board. Do not overwork the dough.

CROUTONS
YIELD: ABOUT 3 CUPS

---

12 Slices leftover bread, with crusts trimmed
3 Tablespoons each vegetable oil and butter

Directions: Cut the bread into small cubes, then dry the cubes out in a slow oven. Sauté in the oil and butter, stirring frequently, until golden brown on all sides.

Serve with soups and salads.

GARLIC CROUTONS

Prepare bread cubes as directed for croutons. Add 1 clove peeled and finely minced garlic to the hot oil and butter, then stir in the bread cubes and sauté to a golden brown.

GARLIC BREAD CRUMBS

Prepare Garlic Croutons as directed (see page 193), then whirl into fine crumbs in a food processor or blender or crush with a rolling pin.

GARLIC BUTTER
YIELD: ABOUT ½ CUP

2 Large cloves garlic, peeled and
   minced
6 Tablespoons butter, softened

Directions: Mix together and spread on toasted French bread slices, or melt over low heat and use as a basting sauce.

YOGURT DIPPING SAUCE

1½ Cups cold yogurt
  2 Tablespoons minced dill
  2 Large cloves garlic, peeled
    and crushed

Directions: Mix ingredients well. Serve well chilled.

RIPE TOMATO PURÉE
YIELD: ABOUT 2 CUPS

The tomato season is right on schedule with summer squash, and the vegetables team up superbly in many dishes. When your tomato crop gets out of hand, turn excess fruits into this tasty purée. For hundreds of other useful, tested tomato recipes, see this book's companion volume, *The Tomato Book* (Vintage Books, Random House).

16 to 20 Fully ripe tomatoes
    1 Tablespoon butter or olive oil
   ½ Teaspoon granulated sugar

Directions: Wash the tomatoes and cut them in eighths. Heat the butter or oil in a large, heavy stainless-steel pan. Add the tomatoes and sugar, and cook uncovered over medium heat until the juices have evaporated. Purée the cooked tomatoes in a food processor or blender, then force through a strainer. If the purée is at all watery, return it to the pan and simmer until most of the juices have evaporated and the purée has a nice, thick consistency. Cool quickly and freeze at 0 degrees F., or use immediately.

Pumpkins are first cousins to squash—both stemming from the same branch of the Gourd family tree—and as fellow cucurbits their soil requirements and growing habits are practically identical. They respond enthusiastically to light, silky loam generously endowed with copious helpings of well-rotted manure or compost and an abundant supply of moisture. Like squash, pumpkins come in bush as well as vining varieties and, where space is a problem, can also be trained up trellises or fences or be interplanted with tall vegetables like corn and tomatoes. They are even subject to the same troublesome insects and diseases that occasionally plague their squash relatives but, being a bit more rugged, are better able to withstand these pests.

Sweet, dry, fine-grained pumpkin flesh can be used interchangeably with that of winter squash, and all recipes in this book that call for the winter variety have been tested with pumpkin and not found wanting. In addition to cooking, feel free to freeze, can, preserve or root-cellar store these stalwarts of the Halloween trade in the same manner you would winter squash. While squash seeds may be—and very occasionally are—roasted and consumed, there are some pumpkins grown expressly for their plump, delectable, easy-shelling or hull-less seeds. These are fun to grow, and the roasted seeds provide snappy and nutritious snacks or cocktail go-withs. And last, but not least, there is always the fun of *not* cooking pumpkins. It is particularly gratifying to have raised from infancy your own slightly weird jack-o'-lantern.

So many new hybrids have been developed in recent years that any variety's exact ancestry is almost impossible to trace. If you aren't already confused as to what constitutes pumpkins/squash/gourds, read the following. As single-season vegetables with only one slow-to-mature crop, pumpkins most resemble winter squash, yet horticulturally they are always classified along with summer squash as *C. pepo*. Two varieties—the cushaw and Japanese pumpkins—belong to the cucurbit species *C. mixta* and are frequently regarded by plant breeders as squash. The *C. maxima* squash varieties, however, which boast the biggest cucurbit specimens and might reasonably be expected to claim some pumpkins as members, can only point proudly to huge squash which "pass" for pumpkins.

The name "pumpkin" hails from *poumpon*, the French word for the vegetable, which in turn was probably derived from the Latin *pepo*. *Poumpon* entered the English language as *pompion* and the diminutive "kin" was tacked on. Fruits in general are large, averaging 10 to 20 pounds, but some are midget-size (5 to 7 pounds) and a few weigh in at close to 100 pounds. Shapes vary from oblate to circular to oblong, with the smooth, hard rinds ranging from lightly furrowed to deeply ribbed. Colors run the gamut from yellow-orange to hues of deep orange, although Cushaw and Lady Godiva are noted for their green and creamy yellow exteriors. Pumpkins are characteristically grown for their sweet delicious flesh, but Lady Godiva was developed for its remarkably flavorful, high-protein "naked," or hull-less seeds.

By all means, don't let limited garden space keep you from planting pumpkins. There are several ways of making room. Bush or semibush varieties like Cinderella, Spirit Hybrid and Funny Face all produce an abundance of small, cheerily colored fruits on vines that need no more than a 5- or 6-foot-square area for each plant, and Tricky Jack makes do with only 4 square feet. This is in decided contrast to those members of the pumpkin clan whose housing requirements are more extensive, but even these latter can often be accommodated. Some of the space-stretching methods outlined for squashes on page 26 also work for pumpkins. The highly ornamental as well as edible Japanese pumpkins put forth fruit on vines that can run up to 20 feet, but you can indulge your taste for Oriental cooking where space is at a premium simply by training the vines up a trellis or netting. The fruit should be kept from soil moisture anyway.

Pumpkins are slow to mature—average time between seeding and harvest is 3½ months—but be sure to wait until the ground has been thoroughly warmed by the late spring sun before planting. The idea is to plant soon enough for fruits to have time to mature before the first fall frost, but not so soon that their early growth will be nipped in the bud by an unexpected spring cold snap.

Pumpkins share the natural affinity of squash for warm weather, but they rarely do well in areas with long and intensely hot summers, preferring more northerly climates. Where the growing season is short and frosts arrive by mid-September, try the varieties that mature earlier or get your pumpkins off to a head start by seeding indoors or in a hotbed, using the methods for squashes detailed on page 23. You can also extend the growing season right in the garden bed by employing any of the protective techniques described on pages 32–33.

Pick the same sort of garden site for pumpkins as you do for squash plants. A light-textured, well-drained, organically rich area that receives a luxuriant daily allowance of sunlight is ideal. In planting seeds, follow the instructions on individual seed packets for seed depth and distance between hills. Generally, three or four seeds are planted in each hill, then all but one or two of the hardiest are removed once the seedlings are established. Distance between hills averages 6 to 8 feet.

To make sure that your pumpkin crop will reach maximum size, invigorate the soil in each planting hole with a shovelful or two of well-rotted manure or compost before setting in seeds. If, as sometimes happens, your plants respond with a frenzy of unchecked vine growth, make sure you pinch off all extra runners or you'll have an excess of foliage at the expense of fruit setting.

Pumpkins thrive on ample amounts of water just as squash do, so water them to the equivalent of 1 inch of water each week. Mulching (see pages 28–30) also has many benefits. A thick layer of any mulching material keeps the soil cool, moist and weed-free; fruit stays clean and off the ground, and is less susceptible to rotting. For information about control of insect pests and diseases, see pages 34–39 of the squash section.

As soon as each pumpkin plant has set its quota of fruit, pinch out the vine tips and remove any latecomers that appear. This measure spurs the fruit already launched to greater size and earlier ripeness. Pumpkins are ready to harvest whenever their rinds reach mature color, with no streaks of green. Should frost intervene before ripening is complete, a garage or some other cool, protected place makes a perfectly serviceable spot where ripening can continue.

Cut each specimen from its vine with a sharp knife, leaving 3 inches of stem. Handle them carefully to avoid bruising. Allow your pumpkins to cure off the ground, in the sun or on a shelf in a warm (80 degrees F.) room, for a week or ten days, to give the stem wounds and surface cuts time to heal.

To can or freeze pumpkin flesh or store the vegetables whole in a root cellar, follow directions for these procedures as detailed under winter squash (see pages 58–75).

PUMPKIN VARIETIES

VARIETY	DESCRIPTION	VARIETY	DESCRIPTION
Jonathan (75 days)	Also called White Cushaw, this variety can grow to 2 feet in length. Its sweet yellow flesh is tops for pies. (Shumway)	Early Sweet Sugar (95 days)	Bright orange fruits are 7 inches in diameter, with small seed cavities and fine-textured, sweet flesh that's superb for pies. (Gurney)
Funny Face (80 days)	This round, bright orange hybrid is a heavy yielder of uniform, 10-to-15-pound fruits. Semi-bush habit makes it ideal for small gardens. A good keeper. (Burgess, Gurney, Field, Jackson & Perkins, Olds, Shumway, Vesey)	New England Pie Pumpkin (95 days)	Small (5 to 7 pounds) and dark orange, the advantage of this variety over others of similar size is less stringy flesh. It's less sweet, too, but an excellent choice for pies. (Johnny's Selected Seeds)
Winter Luxury (85 days)	An old-fashioned type, but still considered one of the sweetest and best-flavored. Netted, light tannish-orange rind encloses golden-yellow flesh that's fine for pies and baked dishes. (DeGiorgi, Gurney, Shumway)	Jackpot (100 days)	The first hybrid pumpkin ever developed and still tops. Bright orange fruits are intermediate to large, average 10 inches in diameter. Yields heavily in less space than standard pumpkins. (A Harris development)
Cheyenne (95 days)	Small-size fruits grow on compact, bushy plants. Fine-grained, solid flesh is deep golden-yellow. (Farmer)	Rouge vif d'Étampes (100 days)	This deep-red French variety is globe-shaped, with bright orange flesh and small seed cavity. A good keeper. (Le Jardin du Gourmet)
Cinderella (95 days)	Early-maturing and excellent where growing season is short. This bush type produces 10-inch fruits, averaging 7 pounds each, in 6-foot-square area, making it ideal for small gardens. Prefers sandy, well-drained soil. (Burpee, Gurney, Nichols, Park)	Small Sugar (100 days)	Popular New England pumpkin and an all-purpose type. Fruits are round and slightly ribbed, about 7 inches in diameter, with rich orange flesh. A good choice for winter storage. (Burpee, Hart, Earl May, Nichols, Olds, Park, Roswell, Stokes, Vesey)

VARIETY	DESCRIPTION	VARIETY	DESCRIPTION
Spirit Hybrid (100 days)	An All-America Bronze Medal winner. One of the earliest of the large-fruited types, its bright orange oval fruits average 12 inches in diameter, weigh 10 to 15 pounds each. More compact than most pumpkin plants, it performs nicely even where summers are long and hot. (Burgess, Burpee, Field, Earl May, Hart, Olds, Park, Stokes)	Jack O' Lantern (110 days)	The blocky, rounded shape of this special selection of Connecticut Field makes it ideal for carving. Fruits average 10 to 15 pounds each and 8 to 12 inches in diameter. Orange-yellow flesh is tops for cooking, too. (Burgess, Burpee, DeGiorgi, Field, Gurney, Hart, Jackson & Perkins, Kelly, Le Jardin du Gourmet, Earl May, Olds, Park, Reuter, Roswell, Shumway, Stokes)
Streaker or Naked Pumpkin Seed (100 days)	Similar in size and shape to Small Sugar, this true pumpkin produces hull-less protein-rich seeds. (Nichols)	Jumbo (110 days)	Lives up to its name. Fruits can weigh in at 100 pounds, though they average 75. (Burgess)
Tennessee Sweet Potato (100 days)	Pear-shaped fruits are creamy white with green stripes. Flesh is creamy white, with sweet potato flavor when baked. (Shumway)	Lady Godiva (110 days)	This green pumpkin with mottled, yellow stripes was developed for its seeds rather than its flesh. Seeds are "naked," or hull-less, are high in protein and delicious raw or roasted. (Burpee, Gurney, Harris, Park)
Sugar Pie (100–108 days)	Fruits average 8 pounds and reach 10 inches in diameter. Flesh is sweet and fine-grained. An excellent keeper. (DeGiorgi, Farmer, Le Jardin du Gourmet, Roswell, Shumway)	Large Cheese (110 days)	My favorite both for beauty and for taste. Buff-colored fruits are meaty and flavorful. A good keeper. (DeGiorgi)
Tricky Jack (100 days)	Compact, 4-foot bushes produce deliciously fleshed fruits, with hull-less, edible seeds. Similar in size to Sugar Pie. (Farmer)	Spookie (110 days)	An improved variety of Small Sugar. Smooth, hard, bright-orange pumpkins reach 7 inches in diameter, weigh 5 to 6 pounds. High-quality flesh that's tops for pies. (DeGiorgi, Harris, Stokes)
Paris (105 days)	A French pumpkin variety and bright yellow-orange at maturity. Globe-shaped rind is slightly ribbed with yellowish webbing. A good keeper. (Le Jardin du Gourmet)		

VARIETY	DESCRIPTION
Triple Treat (110 days)	Bright orange, uniformly round fruits average 6 to 8 pounds, with thick, deep orange flesh that's superb for all purposes. Seeds have no hulls and make a fine snack whether raw or roasted. A good keeper. (A Burpee exclusive)
Golden Cushaw (112 days)	Golden yellow fruits weigh in at 12 pounds average, have curved necks and small seed cavities. Superb for all cooking purposes and a good keeper. (DeGiorgi)
Young's Beauty (112 days)	Uniformly round and intermediate-size fruits are ideal for the Halloween trade. Rich orange shells are moderately ribbed. (Farmer, Harris)
Connecticut Field (115 days)	This is the standard, all-purpose pumpkin that's popular with growers. Slightly ribbed, with a hard, smooth surface, the deep orange fruits weigh from 15 to 25 pounds each. (DeGiorgi, Farmer, Gurney, Earl May, Stokes, Vesey)
Big Max (120 days)	This pumpkin is guaranteed to make the biggest jack-o'-lantern you've ever see. It can grow to 100 pounds or more and measure 6 feet in diameter! A real state fair special, but plan on giving it lots of nutrients, moisture and, above all, space. Apricot-orange rind encloses yellow-orange flesh which is excellent for pies or canning. (Burgess, Burpee, Field, Gurney, Hart, Jackson & Perkins, Earl May, Northrup-King, Olds, Reuter, Stokes)

VARIETY	DESCRIPTION
Halloween (115 days)	Similar in size and flavor quality to Small Sugar and a heavy producer. Pumpkins are just the right size for carving. (Olds)
Howden's Field (115 days)	A Connecticut Field type, but larger, more uniform and more symmetrical. Extra-thick flesh makes it an excellent keeper. (Harris)
Striped Cushaw (115 days)	A crooknecked pumpkin variety whose curved neck and creamy yellow and green-striped skin may lead you to consider it a winter squash. Averaging 12 pounds in size, it's superb for baking, steaming or canning. (Field, Gurney, Earl May, Reuter, Roswell)
Big Tom (120 days)	A good all-purpose pumpkin of the old-fashioned, cornfield variety. Fruits are intermediate-size, averaging 18 pounds, with thick, orange-yellow, sweet flesh. Use for pies, canning, carving. (Burgess, Burpee, Hart, Reuter, Shumway, Stokes)
Mammoth King (120 days)	A giant, squash-type pumpkin that weighs in at up to 100 pounds or more, this variety also makes a good candidate for state fairs. Rind has an orange-salmon color, flesh is orange and fine-flavored. (Gurney, Hart, Nichols, Shumway)
King of Giants (120 days)	This variety can reach huge proportions, so it's only for very large gardens. High-quality flesh despite its size. (DeGiorgi)

JAPANESE PUMPKINS

VARIETY	DESCRIPTION	VARIETY	DESCRIPTION
Blue Kuri (90 days)	An extra-early variety whose smooth, grayish blue-green fruits average 4 to 5 pounds each. The thick orange-yellow flesh is very sweet and fine-grained. Good for short season areas and an excellent keeper. (Kitazawa)	Hybrid Baby Delica (90 days)	A heavy yielder and space-saver because of its habit of setting fruit close to the main stem. Rinds of the 2-to-2½ -pound fruits are very dark green with some lighter green streaking. Extra-early, fruits are ready for harvesting 25 days after flower set. Keeps fairly well. (Kitazawa)
		Orange Hokkaido (92 days)	Teardrop-shaped pumpkins of bright orange are small, about 2 to 3 pounds apiece, but their clear yellow flesh is superb for pies. (Johnny's Selected Seeds)
		Red Kuri (92 days)	Similar to Orange Hokkaido, but almost twice as big. Red-orange, slightly ridged fruits have flesh that's thick, sweet and dry. (Johnny's Selected Seeds)
		Green Hokkaido (95 days)	This vigorous Japanese variety is highly productive. Slate-green fruits are rounded, slightly ribbed, and about 3 to 4 pounds apiece. Yellow flesh is fiberless and extra-sweet. (Johnny's Selected Seeds)
		Chirimen (95 days)	A popular variety whose globe-shaped fruits are ribbed and heavily warted. The dark green rinds turn completely buff-orange at maturity, the yellow flesh is thick and sweet. (Kitazawa)

JAPANESE PUMPKIN SOUP
YIELD: ENOUGH TO SERVE 6 TO 8

1¼ Pounds pumpkin or winter squash
1 Medium-size potato, peeled and sliced
4 Cups water
¾ Teaspoon salt
3½ Cups heavy cream
1 Cup chopped lettuce
⅓ Cup each chopped sorrel and spinach
1 Small leek, trimmed and thinly sliced
3 Tablespoons butter
½ Cup fresh or frozen green peas
½ Cup cooked rice
2 Tablespoons minced fresh parsley

Directions: Peel and slice the pumpkin, scooping out and discarding all seeds and stringy fibers. Place the pumpkin and potato slices in a saucepan, add the water and salt, and simmer until tender. Purée the cooked vegetables, together with their liquid, in a food processor or blender, or force the vegetables through a fine sieve with the back of a spoon. Stir the cream into the purée.

Sauté the lettuce, spinach, sorrel and leek in the butter until the white of the leek is transparent; take care not to brown these vegetables. Add the sautéed vegetables to the soup, along with the peas and rice and additional cream if necessary to bring soup to the consistency you prefer. Simmer the soup for 10 minutes, stirring occasionally. Serve piping hot, garnished with the parsley.

FRIED JAPANESE PUMPKIN WITH PEANUT SAUCE
YIELD: ENOUGH TO SERVE 6

½ Small pumpkin, seeded
3 Tablespoons peanut butter
2 Tablespoons cornstarch
Vegetable oil
1½ Tablespoons miso paste
1½ Tablespoons rice vinegar
1 Teaspoon hot water
1 Tablespoon granulated sugar

Directions: Cut the unpared pumpkin into ¼-inch-thick, long, curved slices. Dust lightly with cornstarch and fry until tender and lightly browned on both sides. Serve hot with peanut sauce.

To prepare sauce: mix the peanut butter, miso, vinegar and sugar until smooth. Thin with the hot water if the paste seems too thick.

SUGAR PUMPKIN

204

HONEYED PUMPKIN BREAD
YIELD: 1 LOAF

Teatime calls for a treat of its own. What could be more tempting than buttered pumpkin bread that has been sweetened with honey and crunched with nuts and dried fruit?

1 Cup honey
¾ Cup milk
½ Cup granulated sugar
5 Tablespoons butter
2 Egg yolks
¾ Cup pumpkin purée
    (see page 142)
2¾ Cups all-purpose flour
1¼ Teaspoon baking soda
1 Teaspoon salt
1 Teaspoon each powdered cinnamon and
    powdered anise
¾ Cup each coarsely chopped walnuts and dates
½ Cup dried apricots soaked in hot water for
    5 minutes, then drained and chopped

Directions: Stir the honey, milk and sugar over medium heat until the sugar is dissolved. Cool for 10 minutes and then beat in the butter. Cool 10 minutes more and beat in the egg yolks and pumpkin purée. Sift the dry ingredients together and then sift them once more into the batter. Mix thoroughly. Fold in the fruit and nuts. Turn the batter into a buttered, floured bread pan. Bake at 350 degrees for 1¼ hours, or until cake tests done. Cool the bread in the pan for 15 minutes and then turn out on a rack to cool. Serve warm or at room temperature with sweet butter or cream cheese.

TRADITIONAL PUMPKIN PIE
YIELD: ENOUGH TO SERVE 6 TO 8

1½ Cups pumpkin purée (see page 142)
1 Cup dark brown sugar
½ Cup light brown sugar
5 Eggs
3 Cups milk
¾ Teaspoon each salt, ground cinnamon and ginger
½ Recipe Double-Crust Pie Pastry (see page 193)

Directions: Preheat oven to 400 degrees F.

Combine the pumpkin (or squash) purée, sugars, eggs and milk. Stir in the spices and mix all ingredients well. Line a 10-inch pie plate with the pastry and pour in the squash mixture. Bake for 1½ hours, or until a knife blade inserted in the center comes out clean.

RUM-SPIKED PUMPKIN AND NUT CAKE
YIELD: ENOUGH TO SERVE 10 TO 12

Nearly as high as an elephant's eye is this three-layer, rum-flavored pumpkin cake enhanced by golden raisins and pecans.

¾ Cup butter
1½ Cups granulated sugar
3 Eggs
1 Cup sour milk
1 Cup pumpkin purée (see page 142)
3⅓ Cups all-purpose flour
1¾ Teaspoons baking soda
¾ Teaspoon salt
3 Tablespoons dark rum
1¼ Teaspoons vanilla extract

1 Cup each golden raisins and pecans, coarsely chopped
1 Recipe Rum-Pumpkin Icing

Directions: Preheat oven to 350 degrees F.

Cream the butter until it is soft and lemon-colored. Add the sugar, a little at a time, and continue beating until well incorporated and fluffy. Beat in the eggs, one at a time, and beat for 4 minutes more. Sift the flour with the baking powder and the salt, and add to the batter (about ¼ at a time), alternately with milk. Stir in purée and rum, vanilla, raisins and nuts. Bake for 25 to 30 minutes, or until the cakes pull away from the sides of the pans. Cool.

Frost with Rum-Pumpkin Icing.

RUM-PUMPKIN ICING

3½ Cups confectioners' sugar
½ Cup butter, softened
3 Egg yolks
¼ Teaspoon nutmeg
1 Tablespoon each rum and pumpkin purée

Directions: Cream the sugar and the softened butter. Beat in the egg yolks, nutmeg, rum and purée. Chill well.

ROASTED PUMPKIN AND SQUASH SEEDS

One of the most delightful bonuses that accrues to winter squash and pumpkin gardeners is the seeds of these mature vegetables, which make an absolutely delicious, protein-rich snack. Some varieties —Eat-All among the squash and the pumpkins Triple Treat, Tricky Jack, Lady Godiva and Streaker —bear what are known as "naked," or hull-less seeds. These are delectable when raw, or they may be toasted or roasted if desired. Other varieties are easy to hull or may be roasted in the shell.

Squash or pumpkin seeds
Vegetable oil
Salt

Directions: Separate scooped-out seeds from the stringy fibers by washing under running water or picking off by hand. Spread on paper towels to dry in a warm, airy place for a day or two.

Preheat oven to 350 degrees F.

Toss seeds lightly with vegetable oil and arrange in a single layer on a cookie sheet. Roast in the preheated oven, stirring occasionally, until the seeds turn golden brown. Remove from the oven and salt to taste while seeds are still hot.

If desired, seeds may be toasted in a large skillet on top of your range. Simply heat 1 or 2 tablespoons vegetable oil and add the seeds. Stir gently or shake pan frequently while seeds are sautéeing; keep a mesh cover handy in case they "pop." As soon as the seeds are golden brown, drain briefly on paper towels and salt to taste.

GOURDS

Ever since the first gardener popped the first seeds into the first garden patch, lives of people everywhere have been closely linked to the plants and fruits of the Gourd family. From earliest times, numerous gourd varieties have provided the human animal with a steady and nutritious source of food. Gourds have been—and in many cultures still are—either cherished for their medicinal properties or venerated for their mystic powers. Some have served, through the ages, as household articles, tools and/or ceremonial objects. Hollowed-out gourds of all sizes have been pressed into service as containers for food and drink, cooking or storage vessels, floats for fishing nets, sponges for cleansing, rattles for children's play—even as pipes for peace-making and musical instruments for ritual dances. Gourd shapes have influenced and inspired pottery design since the first potter took to his (or her) wheel. Think of almost any common kitchen utensil, and chances are you can find its design equivalent among the fantastic shapes available.

Because the extensive Gourd family can count both edible and inedible species as members, sorting them out frequently results in considerable horticultural confusion. Squash, pumpkins, cucumbers and melons are, strictly speaking, gourds; but in this country they are rarely referred to as such, the term *gourd* being reserved solely for their inedible, purely ornamental kin. When today's gardener decides to grow gourds, he or she must turn to the flower rather than the vegetable pages of seed catalogs for varietal listings!

Yet there are gourds treasured as culinary delights in many parts of the world, particularly in the sunny, tropical countries of Southeast Asia, where gourd fruits grow to exquisite tenderness and succulence. These play a featured role in many East Asian cuisines, and are best known to American cooks as the Chinese winter melon, the Chinese fuzzy gourd, the Chinese bitter melon and the luffa, or Chinese okra. Worthy Gourd family members all, despite their names, these edible gourds have been upstaging more mundane vegetable crops in American gardens in recent years as creative American gardener-cooks rush to be the first on their block to meet the challenge of Oriental cookery by raising their own ingredients for wok, soup bowl or steamer.

Probably the most popular of these Oriental interlopers is the winter melon, not really a melon at all but properly a large East Asian wax gourd (*Benincasa hispida*). With its top re-moved and used as a lid, a whole winter melon can double as earth-born cooking pot or flam-boyant soup tureen for the Chinese favorite, Winter Melon Soup, a rich chicken broth laced with meat and vegetables. Or, if you don't fancy wrestling with the whole fruit, winter melon may be cut into bite-size portions and cooked with other ingredients as a flavorful addition to soup itself. Whether *in* or *as* soup, winter melon serves as a sit-up-and-take-notice introduction to any meal.

The winter melon actually goes by many names. To the Chinese, it is *Doan Gwa*; the Japanese call it *Togan, Tougan* or *Togwa*; in India it becomes *Zit-Kwa*. But in any language, the winter melon generally reaches 10 inches in diameter and can weigh in at a hefty 20 to 40 pounds when mature. In fact, the bigger the fruit, the more flavorful. In shape and size it is similar to an intermediate-size pumpkin, but with waxy, almost frosted greenish-white rind and delicately flavored, crisp-textured pale white flesh. A very exotic garden beauty indeed!

Winter melon is grown in much the same way as winter squash and pumpkins. Like them, it is a warm-weather-loving, annual vegetable with a definite preference for organically rich, well-drained soil and lavish amounts of sunshine. Its single crop needs plenty of time to mature (from 130 to 150 days) and planting should wait until the ground has been thoroughly warmed, but should not be so late that frost creeps in before harvest.

The winter melon sets fruit on a single-stalked vine, so a bit of special soil preparation is required. Once you've selected a suitably loamy, fertile spot for your plants, dig out a shallow trench and place two seeds, a few inches apart and 1½ inches deep, at 1-foot intervals along the trench's top ridge. As soon as the seedlings are established, thin out the weaker ones and leave their hardier siblings to stand 2 feet apart.

Plan on giving your plants lots of growing room—they love to spread and luxuriate, usurping your garden space with no regard for other garden vegetables. Mulching is also vital—despite their sturdy appearance, winter melons will rot if forced into continuous contact with moist soil. Surround each plant, even before it begins to run, with a 2-inch-deep layer of straw, salt hay or other bulky mulch material (see pages 28–30), and spread it along the trench and over any area where the vines may sprawl, for a distance of 6 to 8 feet. Be sure to rearrange the mulch to follow the vines should any suddenly switch direction.

Another way to keep the fruit of the winter melon dry and away from contact with soil moisture is to train the vine up a trellis or other stout garden structure (a method that enables home gardeners with limited space to grow the vegetable). The trick in successful vertical culture is to give each fruit some kind of extra support as it matures. Long, wide strips of cotton cloth, strapped round the fruits in a sling effect and securely tied to the structure, should brace them nicely.

Fertilize heavily as soon as fruits first form, and continue this routine, along with deep watering, at regular intervals as they mature. A winter melon is ready for harvest whenever its rind takes on a waxy appearance and a whitish powder shows up on the surface. Cut it from its

vine with a sharp knife, leaving 2 or 3 inches of stem, then allow it to cure in the sun on slatted boards or a thick pile of mulch material for one to two weeks, to give the stem time to harden and dry. If the weather is uncooperative, a warm (80 degrees F.) indoor spot makes a good substitute. *In either case, be sure to cure and store each melon in the exact position it took while growing!* Otherwise, the interior juices may shift and cause the fruit to spoil. To store, find a cool, dry cupboard or root cellar shelf where the humidity won't exceed 50 percent.

If you haven't the space to grow or store *Doan Gwa*, you might want to try planting *Mao Gwa*, known alternately as Chinese fuzzy gourd or little winter melon. This pear-shaped, small-scale version of winter melon is similar in flavor and texture to its bigger relative, is grown in the same manner, is ready to harvest much earlier and takes less growing space because vertical culture is a must.

Plant the seeds in thoroughly warm soil about 1 inch deep and 2 inches apart. Rows should stand 3 feet apart. When the seedlings are 3 inches high, thin them to stand 5 inches apart and begin a weekly application of half-strength fertilizer until the blossoms appear, increasing the fertilizer's strength once the fruits form. As soon as each vine is 1 foot long, tie it to its own sturdy pole with a soft cloth, affixing additional pieces of cloth as climbing proceeds. Harvest while still light green and about 4 to 6 inches long. To use *Mao Gwa*, peel off the fuzzy skin, then wash and cut into chunks or slices for steaming as a vegetable or for soup.

Bitter melon, or *Foo Gwa* in Chinese kitchens, is a clear, light green, wrinkled-skinned gourd (really a vegetable marrow) with a tangy flavor and fleshy texture more akin to cucumber or squash than to melon. Although it does best in rich soil, it will tolerate some degree of clay. It's also a natural climber, because the fruits must hang to mature properly, so plan on providing a set of cross-braced poles for your crop.

To help the seeds of *Foo Gwa* absorb water, scratch them a bit before setting them 3 inches apart and 1 inch deep in the top ridge of shallow trenches spaced 4 feet apart. Thin the plants to stand 1 foot apart as soon as the seedlings are 3 inches tall. Once the vines run to 1 foot long, tie each loosely to its own pole and fertilize once every two weeks.

The melons are mature when they are 4 to 6 inches long and about 2 inches in diameter. Their cool, quinine taste is an acquired one—the melons are, after all, bitter—but the bitterness seems to decrease somewhat with age. Also, the longer a fruit stays on its vine, the less cooking time is required. To prepare, the stem should be cut off, the fruit split lengthwise and the seeds removed. *Gwas* should be parboiled for several minutes (particularly young ones) to reduce some of their bitterness before stir-frying, stuffing or adding to soup. The skins of bitter melons need not be peeled.

Cee Gwa is the Chinese name for an okra-like, cucumber-sized fruit more familiar to Americans as the Luffa dishcloth gourd or sponge. This delicately flavored, slightly sweet vegetable may be eaten raw or cooked, but only in its immature, tender stage. Remove stringy ridges with a vegetable peeler and cut off ends. Allowed to mature on the vine, it can be transformed into durable organic scrubbers for the bath or a multitude of household uses.

Fruits of this gourd prefer hot, rich, moist soils for their growing medium. Where summers are short, you can get a jump on the growing season by seeding indoors or in a hotbed (see pages 20–23), about one and a half months before transferring to the garden bed. If seeding directly outdoors, find a sheltered, sunny exposure and set the seeds 1 inch deep and 3 inches apart in rows 3 feet apart. Thin to 6 inches apart when the seedlings are 3 inches tall, and fertilize frequently and water deeply throughout the growing season. Be sure to provide a pole for each vine, tying it loosely as it grows. Cross-bracing the poles will give extra support.

Like summer squash, Chinese okra plants will respond with heavy and continuous fruit production as long as harvesting is early and frequent. The fruits are tastiest and most tender when young, about 6 to 8 inches long. Plucked from their vines, shed of their ridges with a vegetable peeler and sliced like cucumbers, they impart a delicately sweet flavor to any salad. You may also cut the gwa into slices or chunks and use it for stir-frying, soups or stews.

If left too long on the vine, Chinese okra turns fibrous and bitter. Should production get out of hand, you can always turn the excess fruits into Luffa sponges. Simply cut them from the vines when they turn brown and leave them in the sun for a few days. As soon as they are papery and dry, cut off both ends and remove the seeds, then soak them in salty water, changing the water each day, until the remaining skin disintegrates. Bleach the sponges if you like before cutting them into desired lengths.

If you're the saving sort, seeds of all these gourds may be dried and stored for next year's crop.

EDIBLE GOURD VARIETIES

VARIETY	DESCRIPTION	VARIETY	DESCRIPTION
Lagenaria Longissima (65 days)	An edible gourd with the rich, full flavor of summer squash when picked half ripe. Stake for best results. To use, bake it Italian-style with fresh tomatoes, basil and olive oil topped with cheese. (Nichols)	Little Winter Melon (85 days)	Also known as Chinese Fuzzy Gourd, this plant produces succulent fruits that can substitute in recipes calling for Winter Melon. (Tsang & Ma)
Bitter Melon (80 days)	Similar in texture to squash, this 4-to-6-inch gourd has a podlike shape and ridged, bumpy green skin. The flavor is tangy but likable once you get used to it. (Tsang & Ma)	Luffa or Chinese Okra (90 days)	A ridged, elongated gourd whose tender and delicately sweet flesh when young has long been prized in China. Mature fruits make superb pot-scrubbers or sponges for bathing. (Glecklers, Johnny's Selected Seeds, Nichols, Shumway, Tsang & Ma)
Sweet Dumpling (80 days)	Also known as Vegetable Gourd. Ornamental, with flavor similar to squash. Fruits are small (7 ounces), skins are creamy white, striped or mottled with green. A good keeper. To use, stuff and bake as you would green pepper. (DeGiorgi, Gurney, Park, Sakata)	Winter Melon (130 to 150 days)	This is the granddaddy of edible gourds—a whopping-big (20 to 40 pounds) fruit used for that most famous of classic Chinese dishes, winter melon soup. A good keeper, store it where temperatures remain cool and humidity stays low. (Sakata, Tsang & Ma)

BITTER MELON SOUP
YIELD: ENOUGH TO SERVE 6

2¼ Cups thinly sliced skinned, boned chicken
7 Water chestnuts, thinly sliced
3 Leaves pickled cabbage, rinsed and
    thinly sliced
7½ Cups chicken broth or stock
1 Bitter melon, split lengthwise, seeded and
    thinly sliced
1 Clove garlic, peeled and speared with a toothpick
1 Tablespoon soy sauce
6 Small eggs

Directions: Add chicken, chestnuts and pickled cabbage to boiling chicken broth, lower heat, cover and simmer for 5 minutes. Stir in bitter melon and garlic, and simmer covered 10 minutes more. Add soy sauce, remove garlic and poach the eggs in some of the soup broth. Neaten the edges of the eggs and serve one in each bowl of soup.

STEAMED STUFFED BITTER MELON
YIELD: ENOUGH TO SERVE 6

3 Medium-size bitter melons
1 Tablespoon fermented black beans
    (Dow Sei)
2 Cloves garlic, peeled and minced
1 Teaspoon granulated sugar
2 Teaspoons soy sauce
¼ Pound ground pork
12 Shrimps, peeled, cleaned and minced

Directions: Slice off the stems of bitter melons, split them lengthwise and scoop out the seeds. (Or cut the melons in rounds and seed if you prefer.) Soak the fermented black beans, mash them and mix with the garlic, soy sauce, pork and shrimp to form a paste. Stuff the cavitites of the melons and arrange, stuffing side up, on an ovenproof platter in a steamer. If you lack a steamer, improvise with a large pot. Steam until the melons are tender and the stuffing thoroughly cooked.

STIR-FRIED BITTER MELON AND CHICKEN
YIELD: ENOUGH TO SERVE 6

2 Medium-size bitter melons
1 Tablespoon fermented black beans (Dow Sei)
2 Cloves garlic, peeled and minced
1 Teaspoon granulated sugar
1½ Tablespoons sherry
1 Small chicken, skinned and boned and cut into 1-inch
    chunks
3 Slices fresh ginger root, peeled
    and minced
½ Teaspoon salt
3 Tablespoons vegetable oil
1 Cup chicken broth or stock
1 Teaspoon cornstarch mixed with 2 tablespoons
    each water and soy sauce

Directions: Slice off the stems, split the bitter melons, scoop out the seeds and cut the flesh into 1-inch chunks. Parboil 3 minutes. Soak the fermented black beans, mash them and mix with the garlic, sugar, sherry and chicken. Heat the oil, add the salt, then the ginger root, and stir a few times. Stir-fry the chicken until just tender and set aside. Add the vegetable and stir-fry until heated through. Mix the broth, soy sauce and sugar, and add to the vegetables. Bring to a boil, then adjust the heat and simmer until the melon is not quite tender. Add the cornstarch mixture and cook until the sauce is thick and clear. Add the chicken and heat through. Serve immediately.

BRAISED SHRIMP BALLS WITH CHINESE OKRA
YIELD: ENOUGH TO SERVE 6 TO 8

2 Medium-size Chinese okra (Cee Gwa), scraped
¾ Pound shrimp, shelled, deveined and minced
¼ Pound ground fatty pork
1 Tablespoon sherry mixed with 1 tablespoon soy sauce
1 Teaspoon granulated sugar
½ Teaspoon salt
¾ Tablespoon cornstarch mixed with 2 tablespoons water
3 Tablespoons vegetable oil
1 Cup button mushrooms
½ Cup water
1½ Tablespoons soy sauce

Directions: Cut okra into ½-inch thick slices. Mix shrimp, pork, sherry and soy sauce mixture, sugar, salt and cornstarch paste. Form into walnut-size balls. Heat oil and brown shrimp balls lightly on all sides. Arrange okra slices and mushrooms at the bottom of the pan, top with shrimp balls, add ½

cup water and 1 tablespoon soy sauce, cover and simmer 10 minutes or until balls are thoroughly cooked.

WINTER MELON SOUP I
YIELD: ENOUGH TO SERVE 6

This soup is also delicious when prepared using a conventional Western jack-o'-lantern style pie pumpkin.

1 Whole winter melon
1 Three-and-a-half-pound chicken, skinned, boned and cut in ½-inch cubes
½ Cup diced Smithfield ham
1 Cup Chinese dried mushrooms
½ Cup dried lotus seeds
1 Cup diced fresh mushrooms
8 Cups chicken broth
½ Teaspoon salt
Black pepper

Directions: Scrub the melon's rind with a stiff brush to remove the waxy coating, then wash and pat dry. Cut 2 or 3 inches off the top portion and set aside. Remove and discard all seeds and stringy fibers, and scoop out some melon meat if necessary to make room for the soup (but not so much as to weaken the walls).

Soak mushrooms and lotus seeds in water for 30 minutes. Drain. Chop mushrooms. Place the chicken, ham, both kinds of mushrooms, and lotus seeds in a large saucepan. Add the broth, salt and pepper to taste and bring the mixture to a boil. Adjust the seasonings.

Line your largest heatproof bowl with a large

dishtowel, leaving the ends free; the towel will come in handy when lifting the melon from its cooking pot. Place a rack set on custard cups in the largest soup kettle you own (a canning kettle will serve nicely). Fill the kettle to a depth of 2 inches with hot water and set the bowl on the rack. Place the melon, cut side up, in the bowl and pour in the hot soup, then cover the melon with the reserved lid and bring up the ends of the towel to cover. If the kettle's own cover will not provide a tight fit, drape a large piece of aluminum foil over the melon, tie securely with string and set the kettle cover over. Steam for 3 to 4 hours, or until the melon meat is tender. To serve, lift the melon carefully from its cooking pot and set on a serving platter. Adjust seasonings. Ladle the soup into serving bowls, making sure to scoop out some of the melon meat along with the soup.

WINTER MELON SOUP II
YIELD: ENOUGH TO SERVE 6

1 One-pound slice winter melon
5 Cups chicken broth or stock
1 Cup abalone liquid
¾ Cup finely sliced abalone
½ Cup finely diced cooked Smithfield ham
1 Cup Chinese dried mushrooms, soaked, drained and diced
½ Cup fresh water chestnuts, peeled and sliced
½ Cup diced fresh mushrooms
1 Can lotus seeds
½ Teaspoon salt
Black pepper

Directions: Peel the winter melon slice, scoop out all seeds and stringy fibers, and cut crosswise into ¼-inch-thick slices.

In a large saucepan, bring chicken broth and abalone liquid to a boil. Add melon pieces, abalone, ham, both types of mushrooms, water chestnuts, lotus seeds, salt and pepper to taste. Cover and cook over low heat for 15 to 20 minutes, or until the melon pieces are tender. Adjust seasonings to taste and serve at once.

CHINESE FUZZY GOURD AND PORK SOUP
YIELD: ENOUGH TO SERVE 6

½ Pound fuzzy gourd (Mao Gwa)
⅓ Pound lean pork, thinly sliced
8 Dried black Chinese mushrooms
1 Cup fresh water chestnuts, peeled and sliced
7 Cups broth or stock
4 Scallions, each with 3 inches green top, thinly sliced
1½ Teaspoons granulated sugar
1 Teaspoon salt

Directions: Use paper towels to rub the fuzz from the gourd, then peel off the skin. Wash gourd well, cut it in half lengthwise, then into ¼-inch-thick slices. Soak the mushrooms in water for 30 minutes, then drain well and dice.

Bring broth to a boil, add the pork, lower the heat, cover and simmer 5 minutes. Add the gourd, mushrooms and water chestnuts. Add the sugar, salt and scallions, simmer 2 minutes more and serve hot.

ORNAMENTAL GOURDS

Ornamental gourds are fun and easy to grow. They respond to the same warm temperatures, plentiful moisture and rich soil that squash, pumpkins and edible gourds welcome. They grow in the same way, too, gobbling up large chunks of real estate in their rambles. But since all come equipped with tendrils which enable them to climb, you might try training them up over porch, screen, trellis, fence, arbor or even a heavy shrub planting. With their heavy foliage, attractive white or yellow flowers and, ultimately, their confetti-colored fruits, they lend shade and a certain "zingy" charm to any southern exposure. Use strings or cord to guide them in the direction you want them to grow—and stand back!

Pick a sunny, southerly spot for your ornamental gourds, and be sure to wait until the ground is sufficiently warm before planting. These gourds do best if seeded directly where they are to remain, but they do need as much time to mature as winter squash and pumpkins. If your growing season is short, you can get them off to a head start indoors about six weeks before shifting them to the garden. Use the same indoor seeding techniques described for squash on pages 20–23.

Seeds may be planted in rows, or immediately below the structure you're training them to climb on, to a depth of ¼ to ½ inch, depending on seed size. Follow the instructions on the seed packet for distance between plants. If you're permitting the vines to sprawl, be sure to provide them with some kind of mulch once the seedlings are up and thinned. This will conserve moisture, hold down weeds and keep the fruits clean.

Ornamental gourds with their fanciful shapes and dazzling colors make splendid center-pieces and decorative arrangements, either alone or accompanied by evergreens or fall foliage. To prepare them for indoor display, cut the mature, completely ripe fruit from the vines with a sharp knife. Be sure to handle them carefully—injured or bruised specimens will not last long. Then, using a soft cloth saturated with strong disinfectant, carefully wipe each gourd to remove any lingering dirt or fungi (either is guaranteed to rot them).

Cure the gourds for three to four weeks in a dry, well-ventilated spot until the rinds are hard and dry. Be sure to arrange them so they do not touch, and turn them occasionally so that drying can take place evenly. Once they are completely dry, one or two applications of shellac or ordinary floor wax should preserve them and make their colors gleam.

Ornamental gourds are classed horticulturally along with squash and pumpkins. Turk's Turban Ornamental (see page 218) is a well-known decorative variety among the C. *maxima* squash. C. *pepo*, the same species that boasts summer squash and pumpkins, also includes the variety *ovifera*, home to a large and varied group of colorful, fantastically shaped ornamental gourds. There are dozens to choose from—too many, really, to detail here. Several of the most popular are listed on page 218. Research seed catalogs or scout garden center seed racks for new and exotic varieties. Most seed companies also offer packets of mixed ornamental gourds that include many choice decorative varieties.

SMALL ORNAMENTAL GOURDS

VARIETY	DESCRIPTION	VARIETY	DESCRIPTION
Aladdin's Turban	Similar in shape and size to orange Buttercup (see page 49), its turban is striped with green, yellow and red. (DeGiorgi, Gurney, Park, Stokes)	Miniature Bottle	Dark green with gold stripes. (Nichols, Park, Stokes)
Bicolor Pear	The top half of this pear-shaped gourd is yellow, the bottom green. (Gurney, Park, Stokes)	Miniature Ball	The smallest green and orange gourd. (Stokes)
Crown of Thorns	Cream and green in color, this variety comes in a number of strange shapes. (Glecklers, Gurney, Harris, Nichols, Park, Stokes)	Ornamental Pomegranate	Also called the Queen's Pocket Melon, this variety gives off a delightful perfume. (Nichols, Park)
Flat-Striped	A globe-shaped, flattened green and cream-colored gourd. (Stokes)	Spoon	Spoon-shaped, of course—a small ball with a long handle. Sometimes the latter is delicately curved. Golden yellow, or orange and green in color. (Gurney, Harris, Nichols, Park)

LARGE ORNAMENTAL GOURDS

VARIETY	DESCRIPTION	VARIETY	DESCRIPTION
Cave Man's Club	Knobby and long-handled, although sometimes smooth and flat. (Park, Stokes)	Large Turk's Turban	Large and green. (Park, Stokes)
Dipper or Birdhouse	Use as long-handled dipper or home for birds. (Gurney, Nichols, Shumway, Stokes)	Penguin	Shaped more like a powder horn. (DeGiorgi, Nichols, Park, Stokes)
Giant Bottle, or Chinese Water Jug	Self-descriptive. (DeGiorgi, Nichols, Park, Stokes)	Wild Cucumber	Fragrant and climbing, this variety is for covering arbors or unsightly areas. Often called Balsam Apple, there's also a variety of Balsam Pear. (Glecklers, Park, Stokes)
Hercules Club	Club-shaped and sometimes 6 feet long. (Nichols, Park, Shumway)		

GARDENING

RECITES

ABOUT THE AUTHOR

YVONNE YOUNG TARR is a veteran cookbook writer. Her books include *The Up-with-Wholesome, Down-with-Store-Bought Book of Recipes and Household Formulas, The Ten Minute Gourmet Cookbook, The Ten Minute Gourmet Diet Cookbook, 101 Desserts to Make You Famous, Love Portions, The New York Times Natural Foods Dieting Book, The Complete Outdoor Cookbook, The New York Times Bread and Soup Cookbook, The Farmhouse Cookbook, The Tomato Book, The Great Food Processor Cookbook, Super-Easy Step-by-Step Cheesemaking, Super-Easy Step-by-Step Winemaking, Super-Easy Step-by-Step Sausagemaking, Super-Easy Step-by-Step Book of Special Breads.* She is married to sculptor William Tarr. They have two children, Jonathon and Nicholas.

GRAPHIC CREDITS

The text of this book was set in Cheltenham, a typeface designed by Bertram Grosvenor Goodhue specifically for Ingalls Kimball, Cheltenham Press of New York. The Cheltenham face appeared in 1902; it owes little or nothing to historical inspiration, and in that sense it is truly a twentieth-century type design.

The text type was photo-composed by Superior Printing, Champaign, Illinois. The book was printed and bound by The Book Press, Brattleboro, Vermont.

Production and manufacturing were directed by Laurence Tucci.

The cover illustration and design, and the hand-lettered type on the part-title pages, are by Isadore Seltzer.

Zucchini engravings are by Hermann Griessle. All other art is from the Yvonne Young Tarr Turn of the Century Archives.

Book design and graphics are by Elissa Ichiyasu. Design and graphics were directed by R. D. Scudellari.